ABOUT THE AUTHOR

Jessica Jones grew up in Australia and New Guinea. After being 'asked to leave' high school she ran away to London to drown herself in music and fashion. Jessica's life has been a colourful tapestry of enriching experiences: paralysis; world travel; addiction; recovery and careers ranging from waitressing to writing. When she was diagnosed with breast cancer Jessica started the acclaimed blog *Chemo Chic: A Guide to Surviving Breast Cancer With Style*. *The Elegant Art of Falling Apart* is her moving and funny story of betrayal, break-up, breakdown and cancer.

THE ELEGANT ART OF FALLING APART

THE ELEGANT ART
OF FALLING APART

JESSICA JONES

unbound

First published by Hachette Australia in 2011
This revised edition first published by Unbound in 2013

Unbound
4–7 Manchester Street, Marylebone, London, W1U 2AE
www.unbound.co.uk

Note to readers: The medical treatments described in this memoir were
appropriate for the author; however, every treatment plan is different for every
individual. Always consult a qualified medical practitioner for medical advice.
Neither the author nor the publisher can be held responsible for any loss or
claim arising out of the use, or misuse, of the suggestions made in this book.

Text design and typesetting by Palindrome
Cover design by Mark Ecob
Author photograph courtesy of Ben Millar Cole

A CIP record for this book is available from the British Library

ISBN 978-1-908717-24-5

Printed in England by Clays Ltd, Bungay, Suffolk

Dedicated to Gabrielle Cole
07.03.1961 – 17.10.2008

INTRODUCTION

How does one judge one's life: success or failure?

I remember an old story . . .

Bad news: a man was trapped in a burning building. *Good news:* he jumped out the window. *Bad news:* the window was on the fourth floor. *Good news:* there was a haystack beneath him. *Bad news:* there was a pitchfork in the haystack. *Good news:* he missed the pitchfork. *Bad news:* he missed the haystack . . .

I never could get the point of that story when I was at school. Now I totally get it. Our perspective on life just depends on where we start and end the story. Pick a day. Pick a moment.

❖

My default position had always been: 'I can manage on my own. I don't need anybody.' It's not true. I am convinced that I would not have made it through the ordeals of the past two years without an enormous amount of support and help from family, friends and strangers. From the outset I had the advantage of a long history of attending self-help groups. My friends and my family supported me all the way through. But I still had to learn a lot about asking for and accepting help.

I have written this book in the hope that sharing my experience will go some way towards demystifying some of the horribly frightening and confusing moments that you may be experiencing if you or somebody you love is going through cancer or a similar traumatic event. And of course I wouldn't dream of suggesting for one minute that you have had any problems with romantic relationships but . . . if you have, you may relate to what happens in these pages.

It is not my intention to give medical advice or opinions. There are many excellent and informative books and websites, as well as numerous crazy ones, dedicated to saving your life. This book is about saving your sanity.

Some names have been changed.

MY LIFE IS ALMOST PERFECT...

DECEMBER

On a sultry Sydney evening I step hesitantly through a new doorway. My eyes scan a room filled with strangers as my heart does a quick calculation: Which vacant chair to occupy? Where will I feel involved yet not exposed? Safe but not isolated?

Sit in the middle of a block of empty seats? Too aloof. Sit next to the hard-faced blonde? Scary. The sweaty guy with darting eyes? Just no. The mousy girl nervously sipping tea? She may want to buddy up with me.

The cute guy contemplating his feet?

I sit down next to him.

The cute guy moves his chair back a few inches. I am acutely aware of his eyes scanning my profile. The air in the room is heavy; the backs of my legs begin to stick to my plastic seat. I compose myself and stare straight ahead for the next sixty minutes.

Proceedings concluded, I stand and half turn.

'Hi, I'm Nick,' the cute guy says, extending his hand. His eyes are hazel; his hair is dark, shiny and a bit Donny Osmond–flicky. So? He isn't a man obsessed with his coiffure. I like that. He favours me with a smile that is pure sunshine: joyful and kind. 'Would you like to join me and my friends for coffee?'

Outside on the footpath a group of people are chatting. Nick introduces me to Graham, Dave, Sue and Patricia.

'Jessica is visiting from London,' Nick says. I shake hands with each of them in turn. 'We're going for coffee,' he then announces, indicating himself and me. 'See you all later.'

❖

In March, nine months earlier, my beloved cousin Gaby had experienced some pains in her back. They had steadily grown worse. In July she had collapsed and been taken to hospital, where she was diagnosed with metastasised cancer everywhere, including in her spine. 'Unknown Primary Tumour' they called it. Prognosis: grim.

On October the 17th, Gaby died.

She was forty-seven years old and had been married only a year before. Gaby and her husband, Domenico, had lived in newly-wed bliss in a postcard Tuscan village. Those last few months were marked by a huge amount of love but also too much pain and confusion. None of the family knew anything about cancer, we clutched at straws trying to find cures and offering one another ill-informed opinions and advice. To everyone who loved her, Gaby's death was incomprehensible. Not fair.

After she died I only knew that I wanted to be with the rest of my family. Australia was calling me home.

At sixteen I had been 'asked to leave' my prestigious girls school. When I was seventeen I abandoned my nascent career as a purple-haired receptionist and ran away to London. At age eighteen I had felt it was time to get married. I chose Craig, a junkie and an all-round tortured soul.

Craig and I had tried to make our seedy tenement flat into a home – we really had. We plundered skips for broken rattan chairs and Dansette record players. We covered the stained couch with a bright tartan throw. Whenever Craig managed to steal some lamb chops and a packet of instant potato flakes from the supermarket, I would cook us a cosy meal and we would dine together at our foldaway melamine table.

When Ian Curtis hanged himself Craig wept with a wild emptiness. He played Joy Division records over and over again. He could no longer find any comfort in this world.

Craig diligently signed on for the dole every fortnight whilst I worked as a coat check girl at the Marquee club in Wardour Street. This was a dream job: I could see bands for free whilst I doubled my wages by pocketing half the pile of 10p pieces that constituted each night's cloakroom takings. Those old 10p pieces were the size of milk-bottle tops. I had to distribute them in different pockets so I wouldn't clank and jingle as I bid the manager goodnight.

After I was sacked from the Marquee I went down to Portobello Road market and bought myself an electric-blue 1950s sheer nylon dress with a black flock print and a pair of black stilettos with jet cabochons on the toes. That outfit was my only qualification for my new job as an usherette at the Scala Cinema. I definitely regarded this as a step up in the world. The job had three key aspects: tearing tickets; telling people off for smoking, and selling ice-cream in the interval. Well, four, if you count turning up for work before the movie commenced. I can tell you that I excelled at wearing the blue dress and tearing tickets. My other usherette-ing skills were a bit shaky. If I made it to work at all I would flick on my torch and shine it at the smokers.

'Stop smoking,' I would command.

'Fuck off,' they would reply.

I'd scuttle away and get the ice-cream tray with the little brass lamp above it and then sashay down to the front of the cinema and stand with my back to the screen dispensing Cornettos. Invariably I would fail to notice that the feature film had started until members of the audience began hurling popcorn and empty ice-cream wrappers at my head.

After that I decided to retire from work for a while.

Despite early success in my ambition to be a punk and take drugs in a squat, I continually felt like a failure. I fell in and out of relationships, friendships and careers. I travelled to America, France, Germany, Switzerland, Belgium, Italy, Spain, Morocco, Tunisia, Belarus, Russia, Chile, Hong Kong and Japan. All I could remember about some countries was the bar at the airport.

Decades whirled past in a blizzard of crises: I fell out of love with Craig; Craig fell in love with my best friend, Betty; Betty rejected Craig and he began to spiral into madness. I got a job working in a film production company. I was in love with an older man. He married someone else and was promptly killed in a booze-fuelled motorcycle accident.

At twenty-five I developed a neurological illness and became completely paralysed. I mean *completely*: I could not move or speak; I could not breathe. I spent two months in intensive care on a ventilator and another ten months building myself back up from the five-stone stick insect I had become. With the devoted guidance of a vast gang of National Health Service therapists I gradually learned to write, walk and then swim all over again.

Craig died from an overdose of heroin, that most seductive simulacrum of God. I only hope that Craig eventually found what he was seeking, in the arms of the ultimate Morpheus.

I met Brendan, a talented photographer. Brendan was married with two small children but 'his wife didn't understand him'. Brendan's marriage had broken down, Brendan assured me. They lived separate lives, he said. He wanted me to be his lover, his de facto wife, his assistant, his manager, his muse, his saviour – his everything. What young ego would not be flattered? Of course I obliged. He left his wife and kids and we moved in together.

Brendan was handsome and funny, a cocaine addict and an alcoholic. For nine years we travelled the world, living in luxury hotels and racking up our air miles. Brendan's camera captured the faces of the late twentieth century: the famous, the rich, the glamorous; prime ministers, astronomers, chefs and gardeners. I was constantly by his side, running the circus – sometimes cracking the whip, sometimes pulling the thorn from the lion's paw and soothing its coke-addled brow. For nine years Brendan's mood swings kept me at Defcon One. He spent all our money; I made deals with the taxman. He was too drunk to deliver an assignment; I told lies to his editors. He didn't show up on his son's birthday; I fielded the angry calls from his ex-wife. And I was happy to do it all for him. Brendan *needed* me.

I needed to be needed. Being paralysed had been an experience of losing all self-protection. I had lain in my hospital bed as exposed as a crab without its shell. My only means of communication was by blinking at an 'alphabet board'. I had been constantly alert to the fact that any small blunder by one of the medical staff (and there were many) or any malfunction in the life-supporting machinery (and there were a few of those too) could kill me. One point of the nurses' daily routine was to check the 'mattress straps'. I wondered what they were for. A nurse explained to me that if the hospital caught fire they would grab hold of these straps and drag me from the intensive care unit, down the stairs to safety. I didn't see how that would work, what with me being attached to about half a tonne of ventilators, drips, feeding tubes, heart monitors and whatnot. I am happy to say I still don't know.

Mum had flown from Australia to sit by my side every day. My friends had filled my room with flowers and cards. A nun had sprinkled me with Lourdes water and an Indian guru had blown on my chakras. The nurses had watched over me twenty-four hours a day. Teams of physiotherapists and nutritionists had cajoled me back to vitality. And then they had all gone away. I had been left to take care of myself and I was scared. I mean, clearly I was living in a world where such a terrifying event could just happen out of the blue. How could I face such daily uncertainty?

If Brendan needed me so much then clearly he would not leave me defenceless and alone. Thus I would devote my life to him. If he felt insecure about his work, I would encourage him. If he didn't like my friends, I would drop them. If he got drunk every day, I would get drunk too. If he wanted me to grow my hair long, I would grow it. If he wanted me to wear miniskirts all the time, I would wear them and oglers be damned. If he wanted to move to America, I would go with him.

Brendan and I were living in Los Angeles when a huge earthquake struck the city at night. In the morning the windows of our rented house in the Hollywood Hills were all broken; water was spurting out of the walls. There was no electricity or phone connection. Cellular networks were jammed. The freeway had collapsed.

We drove around the shattered streets inspecting the chaos and wondering what to do. We had made no earthquake preparations whatsoever. Shops were closed; ATMs were not working; National Guardsmen armed with automatic weapons patrolled outside the empty banks. Brendan and I pooled our resources: $25 in cash and half a tank of petrol. Eventually we found a grocery shop where the door was open. It was dark inside but the owners had swiftly cottoned on to the fact that their small stock of basic provisions like water, batteries and baked beans now had roughly the equivalent market value of gold bullion. To protect this treasure from crazed looters they were admitting two people only at a time. I joined a queue that stretched into the sunrise.

'There's no point us both standing here all morning, honey,' said Brendan. 'Why don't I go off and see what else I can find?'

Forty-five minutes later I had nearly reached the front of the queue. But – I now realised – Brendan had the money. With relief I saw our battered 1979 Cadillac pull into the parking lot. He strolled towards me. He had something in his hand: a brown paper bag.

'Here you go, doll,' he said to the asphalt, proffering a half bottle of whisky. The bottle was about one-third gone already.

'Brendan, how much did you spend on that?'

'Twenty-two dollars.'

I took our $3 emergency fund into the shop and bought two hot dogs. Under a searing azure sky we stood in the car park, ate the hot dogs and sipped the whisky.

A few weeks later we had a fight. Like all our recent disagreements it was blaming, spiteful and unresolved. Miserable and exhausted, I went to bed. The next morning Brendan was gone. I discovered that I had been sleeping all night in a house in Los Angeles with the front door standing wide open.

I packed my suitcase and drove up the canyon to the house of our only LA friend, Randall. Randall's front door was also agape. I stomped up the stairs and found Randall himself slumped sideways on the couch like a broken Action Man. He was unresponsive. Brendan stood on the verandah, staring blankly at the hazy horizon.

After dispensing a few sharp words I drove straight to the airport and left the car in the short-stay parking structure.

❖

London had never looked so beautiful to my eyes. Pompommed boughs of white cherry blossoms swayed outside the dazzling rows of white stucco houses. I walked in Kensington Gardens under a pale spring sky, as blue as the eyes of a Siamese cat. I read books. I started a journal but there was nothing to put in it.

I had called up all of my friends: 'Come over and hang out with me.' They had come. They had stayed. For days. We had drunk wine and laughed, and laughed, and gone out to a club and snorted cocaine, and come home and drunk the cooking sherry and grenadine from the back of the kitchen cupboard, and snorted more cocaine and told each other our grand schemes and the fascinating stories of our young lives, and cooked elaborate meals and left them uneaten in the kitchen, and passed out on all the beds and sofas, then woken up and started all over again.

I'd had no plan for my life. The absence of Brendan and all his chaotic addictions to drugs, booze and drama had exposed an unpalatable truth: *I* was chaotically addicted to drugs, booze and drama. Clearly this was intolerable. Something had to be done.

I moved in with our coke dealer. I started my own business as a freelance producer and got an office in Soho. I joined all the smart clubs. Since I was my own boss I could go to work at eleven, start drinking at lunchtime and spend the afternoons lying on a sheet of bubble wrap under my desk with the telephone parked on the floor, next to my head, in case it rang.

Now Gaby was dead and I was alive. I couldn't understand why that should be. For thirty years I had avoided going home. I felt I had so little to show for myself.

JANUARY

Tall gum trees crowd down to the edge of white sand. Their shadows stretch out across the beach, forming stripes of shade. I lie on my back and feel the warmth of the sand reaching into my body. Our legs touch lightly. I stare upwards into the stark blue depths. High above a sea eagle loops and soars, its magnificent form silhouetted against the sky. As I gaze the eagle seems to judder in its flight. It arches its great wings forward like powerful air brakes. *How odd.*

I continue to stare idly at the sky and then I notice a small dot spinning downwards. It twists and flutters like a leaf. It occurs to me that this leaf is far above the tree line. I puzzle about what this object might be as it slowly descends. And then I understand.

'Nick! It's a feather. There's an eagle's feather falling from the sky!'

Nick and I jump to our feet. We skitter across the sand towards the spinning feather. Nick scoops it up before it even lands and presents it to me.

❖

I'm supposed to be in London. I've got work to do. I'm meant to be ghost-writing a 'style' guide for a star of TV and gossip rags who is celebrated mainly for the size of her breast implants. Look, I'm not complaining – writing trashy books certainly beats the hell out of stacking shelves at Tesco. Although sometimes I do fantasise about becoming a street sweeper, pushing a little cart and broom around all day, lost inside the circles that I find in the windmills of my mind. But I yearn to live *my* life. Not spend it inventing the lives of others.

❖

On that first warm evening Nick and I chat outside a local coffee shop. For almost thirty years my body and my mind have been residing elsewhere, on another continent, on the other side of the world. In that far-away realm of London I have built the familiar walls of my existence. The encircling horizon of my life's possibilities begin and end there. I pay my bills in London. My car is in London. My dentist too. My loves and my heartbreaks, my triumphs and my humiliations, all have happened against the backdrop of those drizzly skies, beneath those majestic plane trees and in the backs of those black taxis. More than anything, my friends are in London.

Yet, as Nick and I stroll through the twilight of Potts Point I feel my body flush with a deep longing. These leafy streets with their steep steps, their packs of quarrelling crack-heads, their booksellers and cafés and their heart-stopping glimpses of white sails on Sydney Harbour, feel as familiar to me as the veins in my hand. And suddenly they seem as essential to my existence. For the first time in decades I experience an overwhelming sense of *belonging*.

Nick is easy to talk to and undoubtedly good looking. His attention is intoxicating but, more than that, I want the evening to go on and on so that I may extend the wonderful flirtation that I am secretly having with the city of my childhood.

Nick walks me back to my hotel. Charming? Handsome? I

make a point of not inviting him in. My friend Iris always says: 'It's easy to confuse alarm bells with wedding bells.'

I've done it in the past. My last boyfriend, Clive, was a small-time gangster. Our relationship marched from the Elysian fields of romance to the rat-infested trenches of mutually assured destruction in the space of about two months. Clive was as handsome as Satan and he came with an unlimited supply of cocaine. He was a pathological liar; it's part of the job description. I didn't know that back then. Nothing about Clive's life added up but I had simply never encountered such a level of deception. I'd concluded that I was going mad. Clive agreed. It was perfectly bloody obvious. After all, what kind of sane person would stick with a man who disappeared abroad for six weeks to pursue another woman and then returned to beg and plead through the letterbox for the sane person to take him back because it had all been a big mistake and he truly loved her? A man who then tried to kick her door in? Or with whom she found herself having conversations like this:

'Clive? My friend Petra has hanged herself. Her funeral is this morning. I've been trying to call you for five days.'

'Oh, baby. I'm so sorry. I've been busy.'

'Too busy to answer the phone?'

Silence.

'Clive, I don't think I can continue like this. You didn't pick me up from the hospital. You're never there for me when I need you.'

'Jessica, I love you. I'm there for you, baby. I promise I am.'

'Well, where are you now?'

'I'm at the airport. Gotta go.'

My friends sympathised. I spent hours and weeks crying on the phone. I lied about a black eye. One day I started up bemoaning my situation to cousin Ben.

Ben looked straight at me.

'Jessica, I am not going to talk to you about Clive. I don't ever want to hear his name again.'

'You don't understand him. Inside he's a decent, lovely guy.'

'If he's such a decent, lovely guy, why doesn't he ever do anything decent or lovely?'

Simple as that.

I began to seek new, unsuspecting acquaintances to help bear the burden of my love. And then others. Five years into our relationship Clive went missing on Christmas Day. I called his flat. A woman answered the phone.

'Who are you?' I asked.

'I'm Clive's wife,' she replied.

After that I started seeing a psychotherapist.

Less than two months later I woke up to find that my obsession with Clive had simply evaporated. He tried calling me late at night. He informed me that he had been in a ghastly pile-up on the motorway, five people had died, he had just got out of hospital and he realised how much he needed me. I didn't believe him so he threatened to post indecent photos of me on the internet. Eventually, he just gave it up.

I've been single since then.

❖

'Can I meet you for breakfast?' asks Nick.

For six years I haven't even been on a date. *Oh why not?* I am in Sydney for only another three weeks. Breakfast seems a pretty safe bet. What harm can come of it?

Nick pursues me every day. We go to the movies, the art gallery and the beach. We laugh and smile at one another. I find his constant attention flattering. I also find it a touch oily. I introduce him to my school friend Lulu. Nick cosies up to Lulu's grumpy old dad and offers to take him fishing.

'Lulu,' I confide, 'Nick is sweet but he's too keen. He's just a bit creepy.'

'What is wrong with you, Jess?' demands Lulu. 'Can't you just accept that this gorgeous man really likes you?'

We go swimming with my friends Deirdre and Ashley.

'He looks like Robert Downey, Junior,' sighs Deirdre.

'And he's a real man,' adds Ashley with a leer. 'Not like that last lizard you went out with.'

'Jessica,' says Deirdre in a stern tone, 'you can't stay on your own forever.'

'I just think he's a bit of a dick,' I reply.

A bit of a dick? Is that an eloquent or convincing reason for holding myself aloof and driving Nick crazy? Maybe I've occupied the throne of the ice queen for so long that my tush has frozen solid.

I'm taking the train to Queensland to spend a week at my Aunt Flora's place with my mum, who is flying up from Tasmania. Nick carries my suitcase and drives me to the train station. The train is delayed. Nick re-parks his car and waits with me on a wooden bench.

He waits for an hour, and then another hour. The silver train finally shimmers into sight. As I board I turn in the doorway, take a deep breath, cast aside my snowy crown and kiss him on the lips. With that kiss, six years of mistrust slip from my shoulders. Anxiety flutters in my stomach and is still. My body flows softly into Nick's arms. We kiss until the guard shoves past us, hustles me into my compartment and blows his whistle.

Now, a kiss like that would normally spin me into a delirium of fantasising, sighing and, within a few hours, sending coochy texts. But it doesn't happen. As the train pulls out of the station I get busy unfolding the bed, opening all the secret little compartments and choosing which revolting microwave meal to have for dinner. I gaze from my panoramic window as the serene loops and coils of the Hawkesbury River slide by – and I simply forget about Nick.

❖

During our week in Kin Kin, Mum, Aunty Flora and I plant

flowers. We harvest cucumbers and chop bamboo. We eat mangos and freshly laid eggs. We swim in the sea at Noosa, tour the markets and go to the theatre. Two or three times a day I am interrupted by lame text messages.

> Hi Jessica, it's Nick. Hope you're having a good time. How is your mum?

> Hi Jessica. Thinking of you. Hope you're having fun in the sun.

I feel for him, truly. But *what* do I feel? Admiration at his persistence mixed with a large dollop of pity. Eventually I reply:

> Nick. Sorry, I've been really busy. No phone signal at the house. Will be back on Thursday.

But here's an interesting thing: I ring the airline and delay my departure to London by a week.

Throughout the flight from Maroochydore back to Sydney I experience seeping dread. Nick has insisted on meeting me at the airport. How can I break the news that our kiss was a one-off? I don't want a boyfriend who lives in a different hemisphere. Nor am I interested in casual sex. Our flirtation is fun but going nowhere. I hang back as the plane empties. As I walk into the terminal Nick steps forward from the crowd. And in a split second I am blindsided. I beam inanely; I stride towards him. Despite my determination to maintain my position of haughty aloofness, I find myself inexplicably delighted to see his face again.

A few hours later we collect my suitcase from my hotel and move it to Nick's place. And now here I am, a week later, sitting on Nick's balcony wrapped in a sarong with twenty-five hours before my rescheduled flight to London is due to depart.

'Jessica, will you stay? Will you come down the coast with me?'

'No, Nick,' I say for the fourth time. 'I have to go to London. I live there.'

Nick looks downcast but finally resigned to the situation. He picks up the phone and calls his son.

'Hey mate, how about you and me going down the coast and

doing some surfing? I'll pick you up in the morning.'

As Nick hangs up I grab the receiver from his hand and dial.

'Hello, this is Ms Jessica Jones. I'd like to reschedule my flight.'

MAY

Hillsides of bright red poppies waver up toward ridges lined with dark silhouettes of flame-shaped cypresses and the rounded outlines of umbrella pines. The golden stone of a medieval hilltop town catches the sunlight, glowing against a deep azure lake of sky. For the past twenty years this is where I have come to visit my cousin Gaby. With every curve in the sweeping road I think of her, throwing back her blonde head in unsuppressed laughter. Beside each lavender bush I see her delicate face, bent close, minutely examining every leaf and bud. Amongst the boxes of vegetables at the greengrocer's I hear her throaty voice praising a tomato or a cabbage. But I won't meet Gaby on this trip. She died seven months ago.

On my return from Queensland I had moved straight from my hotel into Nick's flat. Wary of abandoning myself entirely in a pink fog of romance I made a point of arranging dinners and beach trips with Lulu, Deirdre and Ashley. I hadn't got to know any of Nick's friends but we bumped into people he said hello to here and there, once in the street and once at a restaurant. On each occasion Nick introduced me to the people we met and on each occasion they were surprisingly offhand. Almost rude.

Had we been in London I'd have thought nothing of it but I grew up in this town. If there's one thing that we Sydneysiders take pride in, it is friendliness. Had my compatriots lost their sense of grace in the decades I'd been away? Surely not. It had to be me. Did I have a 'keep off' sign taped to my face? Had I lived so long in London that I unconsciously gave off an air of European disdain? Maybe I had become the ice queen after all? This almost hostile response from several unrelated strangers bothered me.

But, then again, what did I care? I didn't know those people. If I ever got to spend time with them I'm sure they would soon learn to love me. I just wanted to be with Nick.

And I was. We ate in wonderful restaurants and relished the sensuality of one another's love of food. We swam in the sea and admired one another's oneness with the water. We talked for hours, each gaining confidence as the vulnerable underside of the other was gradually revealed. Whenever we were apart – for instance, when Nick occasionally went to work – we revelled in the finger-curling anticipation of seeing one another again.

We were walking hand in hand along the sweeping promenade of Bondi Beach when, for the third time, we bumped into some people whom Nick knew. Again he introduced me. Again they were less than friendly. Now I really began to wonder. I mean: these people didn't know me at all. I had met them with a smile, an extended hand and an open gaze. They had looked almost embarrassed. After exchanging a few uncomfortable pleasantries we walked on. Then I stopped. I turned to face Nick.

'Nick, do you have a girlfriend?'

He squeezed my hand, hard. 'Jessy! No! Well . . . maybe?' He looked at me with hopeful eyes. I squeezed his hand in return.

I flew back to London with Nick's question still hanging in the air. My heart and my head had set up their stalls on opposite sides of the street. In some ways I was relieved. I'd had a blissful month and now nothing could ever spoil it. I could keep the scenes of my holiday romance captured inside a mental cocoon of spun glass. I could come back to look at them whenever I pleased. Like one of those souvenir snow domes; I could give my memories a little shake and look back at my languid body draped in a chair on the verandah of our little beach shack. I could watch the pleasing curve of Nick's neck as he set down before me a plate of fresh fish that he had just cooked – fish that he had caught with his own hands earlier that day. I could again gaze up at his sparkling eyes and his heart-skipping smile. I could laugh as he dispatched the foraging possum that climbed down from the roof and tried to steal our dinner, by bonking it on the head with a frying pan. I could feel the thrill of perfect abandonment as we lay in each other's arms under the blazing stars of the Southern Cross. And then I could return to my kitchen, pull on my coat and boots and venture out into the snowy streets of Notting Hill to meet Flossie for coffee. I could lock Nick up in a jewelled box inside my heart, safe in the knowledge that he would always be there.

At Heathrow the first text I received was from Nick. The back of my neck tingled at the sight of his name.

Really, Jessica, my head told my heart, get a grip. You had a lovely time in the sun but Nick lives 11,000 miles away.

That's true now, said my heart, but you know it has been my dream to spend six months in Sydney and six months in London.

Oh, yes, the eternal summer. How are you going to manage that? You can't afford it.

But what if things work out between Nick and me? I might go to Sydney and be with him. Maybe he could come here and spend time in London too?

Don't be ridiculous, what man is going to go chasing all over the planet to be with you? Who do you think you are, Angelina Jolie?

And so the punishing ping-pong of my mind played on.

Nick continued to text, call and Skype me every day. Two weeks later he told me that he wanted to come to London. I caught my breath.

This is it, Jessica: your chance to prise the dead hand of mistrust from your heart. You have a choice: to allow the backwash of your relationship with Clive to ripple down through time and ruin any chance of getting close to this lovely man – or to have the courage to walk a different path. You've exorcised Clive. You've done therapy and twelve steps and all sorts of cringey personal development work. Nick is not Clive. You deserve a shot at happiness.

'Yes,' I said.

The next morning my eyes snapped open in horror. Nick was

coming here. *To my home.* He was going to put his toothbrush on the edge of my sink and leave his dirty underpants on my bedroom floor. He was going to listen to my music and look at photos of my family. Worse than that, he was coming to see me: not the sunkissed, carefree, postcard Jessica but the real item with all my work anxieties, bills, road rage issues, tidying up neuroses and snoring.

Nick was real. I would have to tell my friends about him. What if they didn't like him? What if *I* didn't like him?

I slipped a photo of Nick into my wallet and went out for a walk. My friend Sal was in the coffee shop.

'Wanna see my new boyfriend?' I said and flashed the photo. It felt like I was selling a dodgy porno.

'Good looking,' said Sal. After a few more tries I began to gain confidence and my introduction technique blossomed. Now I was proudly showing the photo to friends, shopkeepers and old ladies at the bus stop. I chirped on about Nick's handsomeness, his kindness and sunny personality, until they began shuffling their feet and murmuring about maybe having left the iron on at home.

Nick was Skypeing me three times a day. I work from home so I habitually spend my day clad in a pair of baggy old leggings with a hole in them, topped off with a decrepit cardigan. Sal and I went out and bought new Skypewear: a white t-shirt and a pair of cashmere trackie bottoms. Elegant, yet relaxed.

Every day my levels of anxiety and excitement rose in equal measure. At the dentist's I read a magazine and learned that I must 'make room for a new lover' in my home. Accordingly I started sleeping on one side of the bed only. I chucked out a couple of bin bags full of designer garments to create space in my wardrobe for Nick to hang his jeans. I bought an anti-allergenic pillow especially for him.

The night before Nick arrived I couldn't sleep. In the dark I arose and wiggled into my sexiest underwear, a tight skirt and heels. At Paddington station I was an hour early. I stood at the entrance to the Heathrow Express platform and watched train after train emptying the early-morning flotsam of dishevelled travellers. After forever my phone beeped.

Jessy where are you?

Nick had walked straight past me on the platform. With heels clicking on the flagstones I tore through the commuting crowd on the concourse and into his arms.

Nick's first priority was breakfast. To be honest, I was a little taken aback. *But that's good. We need to get to know one another again.*

❖

Gaby died only two months before I met Nick. At first I hesitated to invite him to her memorial service in Tuscany. Would it be appropriate to bring my new boyfriend to such an intimate and sad family event? Now I'm glad that I did. I would dearly love for Gaby to know Nick. I would want her to laugh at his capers, to flirt with him as she flirted with all the world. I'd love her to love him, as I am beginning to. Knowing Gaby's world – her family, her husband, her village and her garden – is as close as Nick will ever get to knowing her.

Nick and I check into a room in a seventeenth-century palazzo. As bed-and-breakfasts go it is on the salubrious side. The sitting room is furnished with books, chandeliers and a grand piano. Tapestries adorn the walls. There's a four-poster bed.

❖

On a hilltop at the end of a winding road stands Bagno Vignoni. This is a fairy princess of a village, possessing grandeur disproportionate to its tiny size. In its centre, where one might normally expect to find an open piazza, there is instead an expanse of gently steaming water: a sixteenth-century thermal bath known as a Vasca. Since the Middle Ages, popes, poets and painters alike have come here for their holidays. Around the Vasca stand imposing stone buildings. One of them, a palazzo dating from around 1400, was once the summer residence of Pope Pius II. It is now the hotel Le Terme. On the hotel's terrace, sad faces congregate in the sunshine. Friends and family have flown from the UK and America to gather together in a last farewell to our own sweet Gaby.

When you hugged Gaby you felt that you might crush her like a tiny bird. But her core was tempered steel. Nobody could crush Gabs. Nobody, that is, except Dave, her ex-husband.

They met when Gaby was seventeen. He was older, and secretive about his age. She tolerated his petulance, indulged his self-regard, bore his spiteful rage, excused his drinking, defended him against her family, worked to provide for him, cooked his faddish meals, drove him everywhere (he wouldn't learn to drive) and spoke for him (he refused to speak Italian). She endured him for twenty-five years. She even married him in the end. She did it all with tireless grace and humour. So he left her for another woman.

Best thing that ever happened to her, if you ask me. But Gaby didn't see it that way. Then, after years of sadness, she met a kinder man.

Gaby and her new husband, Domenico, came to Bagno Vignoni to live in a grace-and-favour apartment bestowed by a local countess who seems to pretty much own the whole place. In a corner of the Vasca was a small island of barren earth. Gaby asked the countess to give her the island. Gaby transformed this tiny corner into a vibrant garden, alive with scented plants, bees and dragonflies. It was her gift to the whole village. Gaby and Domenico had been married for less than a year when she began to have pains in her back.

By the time they found it, the cancer had colonised her liver, lungs and spine. It had eaten away part of her third vertebra. At the end it was ghastly to see her tiny body shrivelled almost to nothing, her neck supported in a plastic brace to prevent it from breaking, her pretty face swollen and lined with anguish. Her pain was immense, her fear greater and more terrible still. That hideous, unknown cancer simply ate her up in a summer season. She hardly cried. She hardly complained. I have come back to Tuscany to mourn and remember her.

❖

In the week that follows Gaby's farewell Nick and I roam the Tuscan countryside. We find our way to hilltop castles, churches, chestnut woods and, above all, restaurants.

Maybe the notion of a couple of starry-eyed lovers in their forties tripping through fields of golden wheat or gazing into each other's eyes over Florentine gelatos is just too gaggingly schmaltzy for you. But please try to show a little empathy: losing Gaby had ripped away a piece from my world; I couldn't conceive of all this beauty continuing without her. Then, I met Nick. His company has brought me sweetness alongside the mourning, like a daisy growing in the ashes of death. I revel in his sideways glances and the casual touching of our hands and arms. It seems so long since I have been celebrated for being me; so long since I have been romanced.

LONDON

Whilst Nick manhandles our suitcases from the taxi, I open the front door to my flat. There is an envelope on the mat. Inside it is an invitation to attend the breast care clinic at St Mary's Hospital.

Two weeks ago I went to see West London's loveliest GP, Dr Camilla Ducker. I'd been feeling a bit tired and, where most people would probably have a little lie-down, I opted for the full blood count. Whilst I was there I mentioned that my left breast had been feeling slightly hard lately. I wouldn't have called it a lump; it was just somewhat tender – the kind of thing that many of us females experience just before our period, only it didn't go once my period ended.

'Well, it may be a cyst. You'd better get it checked out,' she said, and wrote a referral letter.

I wasn't worried. There are two things that I know for sure about cancer:

1 It doesn't hurt.

2 It only happens to other people.

WHAT HAPPENED NEXT

I had an appointment at St Mary's this morning for an ultrasound scan. Nothing unusual about that. I'm not normally one to miss out on the chance of a morning hanging around in a hospital waiting room reading half a copy of *OK!* from September 2007 and stickybeaking at all the other patients, trying to figure out what their particular ghastly disease or disability might be. I'm always popping into St Mary's or Charing Cross or Hammersmith Hospital or the Cromwell for a scan or X-ray or something. Broken fingernail? Book an MRI!

This morning, however, cuddles with Nick held me to the bed like magnetic honey. Until, finally, guilt and a sense of civic duty prised me from our nest. All those posters admonishing the general public about the cost to the taxpayer (me!) of missed appointments have done their job. With many sighs and lingering backward glances I left Nick propped on the pillows reading the *International Herald Tribune* online and drinking a nice cup of tea.

'See ya,' he said lovingly.

An eager-looking registrar sought me out in the waiting room.

'Miss Jones' he asked, 'would you be willing to take part in the trial of a new diagnostic machine?' He described a device that claims to detect tumours by infrared or sonar or some such method.

How could I refuse? I'd get to have a scan and advance the

cause of medical science at the same time. I signed some papers and he ushered me into the presence of a white-coated consultant, Mr Dimitri Hadjiminas. Over the years I have learned that it is proper to call doctors 'Doctor' but surgeons are called 'Mister', don'tyaknow.

After a brief chitchat I half undressed behind the screen. Mr Hadjiminas applied the device. It made some thrumming sounds. Then he examined my breasts by hand. He filled out some forms.

'Okay, we'll just send you up for a mammogram and an ultrasound.'

'But I haven't come here for a mammogram,' I protested.

'Oh, it's routine, everybody has one.'

That statement felt unconvincing. Somehow I suspected that the National Health Service does not, as a matter of course, give out free mammograms to every hypochondriac malingerer who trips across their threshold.

I had always heard that a mammogram is a very painful procedure, especially for those with small-but-perfectly-formed breasts. Well, in my experience, it's not true. There's a certain amount of awkwardness involved in angling one's torso so that one's tit may be sandwiched flat between two sheets of clear plastic whilst one's jaw and cheekbone are crushed up against the back-plate of the machine and one's shoulder blade is wrenched backward to facilitate one's arm being twisted around behind one's waist. But that's all fairly routine stuff for a yoga bunny like me. And, of course, there is the sartorial pain of having to wander the public corridors robed in a hideously patterned hospital gown with half the tapes missing.

Next stop was the ultrasound. I lay still whilst some chilly goo was applied and then looked at the pulsating swirl on the screen wondering, as I often do, how anyone can make head or tail of it. The doctor doing the scan was French. And a woman. That's all I can tell you.

She looked at me and said, 'There is a tumour here and in my opinion it could be malignant. I'm sorry but I have to tell you this now, because I need to do a biopsy of your lymph node right away.'

Somewhere, far away, a mind that was not my own thought the following thought: *Who on earth is she talking to?*

The next thing I knew she inserted a long needle into my armpit. I don't think it hurt particularly, but I started to cry.

I dressed and returned to the breast clinic to wait whilst they emailed the findings to Mr Hadjiminas. The waiting room was now full. I looked around for a chair but somehow I couldn't really comprehend the information. My eyes relayed pictures of vacant seats to my brain but my brain couldn't figure out what to do with the images. I stood in the middle of the room staring helplessly this way and that. Finally I plumped down next to a striking black lady with an elaborate hairdo. I guess the autopilot said, 'Sit next to the most stylish-looking person in the room.'

It seemed that half the waiting room was for people having blood tests whilst the other half was for the breast clinic. Suddenly I felt too exposed. I wished all the blood test people would go away and leave us breast clinic people to ourselves. *We have serious things to worry about, like possible malignant tumours. Who cares if they're feeling a bit tired? Why don't they just go for a little lie-down?*

The elaborate hairdo lady put her hand on my arm.

'There's nothing that Jesus can't heal,' she said. 'It is God's will that you are to be well, healthy and whole.'

I gaped at her like a malignant carp. She handed me a photocopied sheet titled HEALING and JESUS LOVES YOU. She reached into her capacious handbag and pulled out a full-sized hardback Bible. She opened it at one of the many pages marked with fluttering Post-it notes. She began to read.

'He Shall Call Upon Me, and I Will Answer Thee, I Will be with Thee In Trouble, I Will Deliver Thee, and Honour Thee . . .'

I wanted to throw myself into her arms and weep. Of all the people in the waiting room, I had had the good fortune to sit next to someone who wasn't embarrassed to extend a hand of kindness; someone who had the courage to show empathy. Maybe it wasn't her hairstyle that my autopilot was attracted to after all.

'Miss Jones,' called a voice.

Back in the consulting room quite a crowd had gathered. Suddenly they were all being very nice to me. I took that as a bad sign. Mr Hadjiminas did another needle biopsy, this time from my breast.

'We'd like you to come back this afternoon for your biopsy results,' he said. And I thought to myself: *Surely you mean 'please come back in three weeks and hang around for two hours and then we might deign see you'?*

'What time?' I said.

'Oh, whenever is convenient for you.'

I took that as a very bad sign indeed.

I don't remember driving home. I don't remember parking the car. I do remember walking in the door and seeing Nick, still propped up in bed with the laptop and another nice cup of tea.

'Hey darling, how'd it go?' he asked brightly.

❖

This morning my life changed completely and forever.

Five-thirty p.m., I'm back at St Mary's in the waiting room. It's quite empty now. Nick is with me. We don't have to wait long. This time my name is called by a nurse who turns out to be lovely and named Suzy. She is the breast care nurse.

Mr Hadjiminas doesn't waste my time. He confirms the worst straightaway. I have a malignant tumour. It is 31 millimetres in diameter.

'Quite small,' says Mr Hadjiminas.

I hold up my fingers in an approximation of the size. It seems quite huge to me.

He leafs through a large desk diary: 'We can get you in for surgery in three weeks.'

I was seriously ill in my twenties and I am self-employed. Those two factors conspired to get me to do the one and only sensible thing I have done in my life – that is, to buy health insurance. I don't know how, but I managed to pay that subscription even when I was homeless and on the dole. I've paid it for twenty years. It's the power of fear, I guess.

'I have Bupa,' I hear a small voice say.

'In that case I can do you next Wednesday at Harley Street,' says Mr Hadjiminas.

Now he has to do a punch biopsy. Surprise is the tactic here. I probably shouldn't tell you how painful this procedure is in case you ever have to have one yourself. If I had known in advance I would have fled the scene and taken my 31-millimetre tumour with me.

After I've finished screaming and cursing we all crowd around on the chairs in the little consulting room and Mr Hadjiminas asks me if I have any questions. I can't think of a single one. Nurse Suzy hands me a bunch of leaflets. I feel sympathy for the medical professionals. Although they must break the bad news to patients on a regular basis, somehow I doubt that it ever gets any easier. Not if they are human, which these two definitely appear to be. In my experience, when people give one leaflets it's because they too are at a loss for words.

Fortunately, Nick knows no such reticence. He has gone into a sort of verbal panic, firing off questions in a scattergun kind of a way. 'Will she have to have a mastectomy?' No, it will be a lumpectomy. 'Will she have to have radiotherapy?' Yes. 'What about chemotherapy?' No, the biopsy didn't show cancer in the lymph node. 'What about diet?'

I hope that Nick will be able to cope with the reality of what may be ahead of us. Although I'm grateful to him for doing all the talking, I put my hand on his knee to quiet him. We all look at one other in silence. Then Nick pipes up with a final question.

'She will be okay, won't she?'

'Oh, yes, she'll be okay,' replies Mr Hadjiminas, as if he's only just thought of it.

WEDNESDAY 27 MAY

Nick has offered to stay on for another two weeks. He has already been in London, so far away from home, for three months. He has extended his stay twice. There is considerable pressure on him to go home. Obviously, he hasn't worked in all the time he's been here. Nick is a freelance TV cameraman so he doesn't have a job, as such, but I doubt he can afford to not work indefinitely. Added to that, his 21-year-old son has been running off the rails and getting into trouble with the police. Nick is terribly worried about him. Nick's ex-wife says that he should be there to support his son.

In principle I agree with her. I cast my mind back over my previous partners: Craig, the junkie; Brendan, the self-obsessed photographer; Clive, the sociopath criminal. Would any of them have stuck by me when faced with illness and fear? I already know the answer to that. Just this once I'm going to be selfish. I bite my tongue and accept Nick's offer to stay with me. It seems that I've found a good man at last.

From: Jessica
Subject: Nick's farewell dinner
To: Sheldon, Flossie, Seraphina, Ben, Antony, Doug, Jamie, Tess

---

Owing to unforeseen circumstances, Nick's farewell dinner is being postponed for a couple of weeks. Will advise new date shortly.
Love
Jess

From: Antony
Subject: Re: Nick's farewell dinner
To: Jessica, Sheldon, Flossie, Seraphina, Ben, Doug, Jamie, Tess

---

oh . . . ????

From: Flossie
Subject: Re: Nick's farewell dinner
To: Jessica, Sheldon, Seraphina, Ben, Antony, Doug, Jamie, Tess

Hurrah!

From: Sheldon
Subject: Re: Nick's farewell dinner
To: Jessica, Flossie, Seraphina, Ben, Antony, Doug, Jamie, Tess

I am retrieving my wedding suit from the pawn shop . . .

I don't know how to tell people what's going on. Do I pick up the phone and say, 'Hey, guess what . . .?' Do I send a round-robin email?

I don't want this cancer to be a big secret. Neither do I want it to start defining who I am.

Of course, I should tell my mum before the word gets out on the grapevine. But I can't bear to make that call. The thought of it brings me to tears.

Mum moved to Tasmania twenty-one years ago. I don't know how she will cope with the news, being so far away and helpless in the situation.

So I suppose whenever friends ask 'How are you?' I shall just have to tell them the truth.

Things I wish I'd known before #1
How to break bad news

I found that telling my friends and family, especially my mother, that I had cancer was way harder than receiving the news myself. I was so concerned about upsetting them – or crying – that I often ended up putting a jokey spin on things or being utterly deadpan.

There is no easy way to do this.

How not to break bad news: 'Guess what?' 'Ummm, you've won the lottery?' 'No! Guess again . . .'

> Don't beat around the bush: 'You know I had an appointment at the breast clinic?' 'Yeeees.' 'Well, I went there it was such a hassle to park and then I couldn't find the place and then I waited for ages and when I finally went in to see the doctor he sent me upstairs and I had to wear one of those hideous gowns – you would have laughed – then I had a mammogram – it's not nearly as painful as I thought it would be – then I went for an ultrasound scan and anyway it turns out I've got breast cancer. Tah-dah!'
>
> Give it to them straight: 'I'm afraid I have bad news to tell you. (Resist the temptation to pause dramatically here – just get on with it.) I've been diagnosed with breast cancer.'
>
> That's it. Now simply stop and listen, even if there is nothing to listen to. Don't bombard them with information just to fill in the silence.
>
> Do answer their questions as well as you can.
>
> If they choke or burst into tears, show empathy with their feelings: 'I know, it's a shock.'
>
> Don't try to shut them down: 'I don't know what you're crying about – I'm the one with cancer!'
>
> Don't feel that you have to support them: 'Oh, don't worry, I'll be fine.'
>
> Do communicate your own feelings: 'I'm very frightened. There's a long road ahead but I'm going to try to travel it one day at a time.'
>
> If they ask what they can do to help – tell them.

FRIDAY 29 MAY

This week has been a whirlwind. On Wednesday I phoned Bupa to get authorisation codes for a battery of tests and procedures. Then I cancelled all my appointments for the rest of the week. Yesterday I had an MRI scan of my breasts.

This morning I had a CT scan of my lungs. After that Nick and I went to meet Honoria, who is to be my breast care nurse at the Harley Street Clinic. She's small and blonde and wears lashings of eye make-up. I could tell straightaway that she's quite wonderfully batty.

Next up was a radioactive injection in preparation for the big one: a bone scan this afternoon. The technician warned me about radioactive contamination. No kissing. No fraternising with small children. Wash your hands twice after peeing and don't touch your clothes. And please use the special toilet reserved for radioactive people.

There's quite a bit of hanging around, waiting for the injection to do its work, before I have the bone scan. Eventually I felt the need to use the special toilet. I peed and then washed my hands twice. But then it occurred to me: *What if some of the other contaminated inmates failed to wash their hands? How do I get out of here without touching the radioactive door handle?*

Now Nick and I are in Mr Hadjiminas's consulting room. Mr Hadjiminas looks at me.

'Good news,' he says. There was no cancer on the CT scan of my lungs.

Then, 'Not such good news.' The MRI scan showed a second tumour in my left breast.

'Oh,' I say, 'and what does that . . .' My voice trails away.

'It means you'll have a mastectomy,' says Mr Hadjiminas helpfully.

I gawp at him for a bit. I look at my fingernails and then sit on my hands.

'But I don't want a mastectomy,' I say.

'It's for the best,' replies Mr Hadjiminas, and he's off: 'We save the nipple and the skin. And we can do reconstruction at the same time.' Then, warming to his subject, 'And it means you won't need to have radiotherapy. If there's no breast, there's no possibility of the cancer recurring.'

I realise that I am way out of my depth. What I really want to do is stick my fingers in my ears and sing 'la-la-la'. I don't know what I'm talking about but something almost subconscious prompts me further.

'Is there any alternative?' I ask. I sound desperate.

Mr Hadjiminas looks thoughtful. 'Well, yes, there is. We can do a quadrantectomy.'

'And what is that?'

'Well, we take away about a quarter of your breast and the sentinel lymph node, then we have to look at all that in the lab. If we've got all the cancer out and the margins are clear then we can do reconstruction surgery three days later. We use a muscle that we take from your back. If we find anything in the sentinel lymph node then we remove all the other lymph nodes from under your arm at the same time.' Suddenly, Mr Hadjiminas is just as fired up about *this* procedure.

'And does that mean I will still have feeling in my breast?'

'Yes, it does.'

'And will it look all right?'

Mr Hadjiminas reaches for his photo album. It is full of pictures of women's breasts. He opens it to a spread that obviously displays some of his best work. Before showing me the photo on the right-hand page he judiciously covers the left-hand page with a piece of paper; I guess it's the 'before' photo. Whatever lies beneath that piece of paper cannot possibly be as horrifying as what I'm now imagining.

The right-hand page shows a photograph of a woman's torso. She has the most beautiful pair of breasts.

'Those are fantastic tits!' blurts Nick.

'Not as fantastic as mine,' I say, a touch frostily.

'Oh, I don't know . . .'

'Anyway,' I say, slapping the desk decisively, 'that's what I'm having.'

Then I suddenly feel that maybe I'm being too forceful. I don't know what is the best treatment for me. Mr Hadjiminas does this every day. He's trained for decades. How can I tell him what to do?

'I mean, is it okay to do that?' I ask, sounding a bit sheepish.

'I wouldn't even offer it to you if it wasn't okay,' replies Mr Hadjiminas, 'but if the margins are not clear then we will have to do a mastectomy anyway. That's the risk.'

'It's a risk I'm prepared to take.'

We all look at one another. That, it seems, is a done deal. Honoria puts her coat on. Mr Hadjiminas looks at his watch. It's after six and it's Friday.

'What about the bone scan?' I ask.

'Oh, it's not ready. Probably fine. The full report hasn't come through. We'll let you know on Monday.'

I look at them both. I cannot possibly endure the anxiety of waiting two days to find out if there is cancer in my bones. I must insist. All in a rush I tell them the story of Gaby.

Honoria takes off her coat. Mr Hadjiminas sits down and picks up the phone.

'Please bring Miss Jones's scans and report across as soon as they are ready.'

We all settle down to wait.

After about twenty minutes a porter arrives with an A4 envelope. Mr Hadjiminas pulls out a piece of film. On it is a series of images of a teeny-tiny skeleton, about 5 centimetres long.

'These are all clear,' he says.

MONDAY 1 JUNE

In happier times, at my cousin Gaby's wedding, I sat next to a man named Hardress. (How could I forget a name like that?) As we all helped ourselves to *insalata tricolore*, various pastas, roast, stuffed *porchetta* and *pannacotta*, Hardress decanted brown rice, lentils and boiled leeks from a Tupperware lunchbox.

'What's that all about?' I asked him.

Hardress was not ashamed of his frugal fare. 'I've had cancer,' he replied. 'But I've cured it with a macrobiotic diet.'

He told me about his former life as an 18-stone bon vivant, entertaining friends with seven-course feasts and quaffing fine wines. He spoke enthusiastically about his macrobiotic practitioner, who prescribed a diet specifically for Hardress's body type. It was a diet that allows only local foods in season, high in grains, pulses and vegetables with absolutely no sugar, meat, wheat or dairy.

'Don't you get bored eating that?' I asked tactlessly.

'Not at all,' he replied with equanimity. 'I love it.'

Impressed, I began to experiment with my own DIY version of such a diet: you could call it 'macrobiotic lite'. I ate brown rice, amaranth or quinoa on a daily basis. I substituted almond milk for cow's milk on my muesli. I bought organic vegetables. I cut out sugar. But I'm also a great believer in the middle way, so I didn't become a prisoner of my eating plan. I would still go out for a curry with my friends.

Then we learned that Gaby had cancer. She went under the care of the same macrobiotic practitioner who'd had such success with Hardress. Because of the advanced nature of Gaby's illness he had put her on an extremely restricted diet that seemed to consist almost entirely of brown rice. A few vegetables were allowed but hardly any seasonings, no fruit and no salad.

Gaby dutifully ate up her brown rice, chewing each mouthful forty times. She sipped her twig tea. Gaby had always been such a good girl and never a complainer, but it became obvious after a while the whole thing was quite burdensome and, finally, it seemed to be a source of some misery. Gab soldiered on nonetheless. She really did her best but there simply was no remedy, conventional, alternative, physical or spiritual that was a match for that horrible unknown primary tumour.

I sometimes think that she would have been as well off to have had a few slices of chocolate cake and a glass of wine to cheer herself up. But that's all very easy to say with hindsight.

Ironically, whilst Gaby was dying I fell right off the wagon myself, noshing on pizza and pasta and guzzling buckets of caffe latte. Now I have resolved to resume my healthy path; henceforth only the purest of the pure shall pass my lips.

❖

I telephone Rowena, a friend-of-a-friend who is a naturopath. She encourages me in my resolve to abstain from sugar, meat, wheat and dairy.

Here is my basic understanding of the situation, possibly somewhat muddled . . . Sugar, it seems, is pure cancer food. Meat is slow to digest and so one's liver uses up all its resources in trying to deal with toxins released by the rotting meat, when it would be better deployed bolstering one's immune system. I'm not sure exactly what the problem is with wheat except that it is generally held to be a bad thing and all right-thinking alternative people are against it. And dairy always makes the black list too.

Rowena also suggests that I buy a juice extractor.

'That's exactly what I'm going to do,' I exclaim. 'Tomorrow, I'm going to Peter Jones.'

'What you need,' says Rowena, 'is a masticating juice extractor. It's the only way to really break down the fibre of the vegetables and release all the enzymes and nutrients.'

'Okay,' I reply, 'where do I get one and how much does it cost?'

Rowena explains that the best one is called The Champion. It is available on the internet for a mere £300.

'Surely a cheaper one will do the trick?' I protest.

Rowena adopts a stern tone. 'If there is one thing that you should buy, it is this. You will find the money somehow.'

Things I wish I'd known before #2
The basics of an anti-cancer diet

When it comes to cancer, there is a deluge of advice on what we should or should not eat. I was variously exhorted: 'Don't eat fruit'; 'Give up dairy'; 'Eat only foods that are native to the country of your birth'; 'Eat things that suit your blood type' (eh?); 'No sugar whatsoever'; 'Avoid tomatoes, eggplants and potatoes'; 'Eat cottage cheese and flax oil with every meal'; 'Drink Essiac tea'; 'Don't eat mushrooms'; 'Eat lots of mushrooms'.

These anti-cancer regimes can seem controlling and just plain loopy. I became very fearful at first, thinking that the next chocolate biscuit might seal my fate.

American food writer Michael Pollan has extracted the essence of healthy eating in seven simple words: 'Eat food, not too much, mostly plants.' Some diets advocate no dairy, others demand we go vegan, but it seems that almost all writers on the subject agree that we will benefit from eating plenty of vegetables, fruit, whole grains and pulses, and cutting out processed foods as much as possible.

According to Dr David Servan-Schreiber, author of *Anti-Cancer: A New Way of Life*, the anti-cancer plate should be filled with:

- about 50% vegetables (green, red, yellow, purple and white), fruit (berries, soft and hard fruits) and vegetable proteins (tofu, peas, beans, nuts)
- about 20% wholegrain cereals (brown rice, quinoa, buckwheat, wholegrain bread)
- about 20% animal protein (fish, organic meat, organic eggs)
- about 5% good fats (olive oil, coconut oil, flax oil)
- about 5% herbs (parsley, dill, chives, tarragon, coriander), spices (turmeric, cumin, coriander seed, black pepper, caraway, cardamom) and other stuff (dark chocolate, honey).

My heart sinks as I imagine chewing my way through a smorgasbord of raw cabbage, whole tomatoes, a banana, raspberries, a pile of boiled barley, a raw egg, a couple of sardines, a spoonful of olive oil, half a cup of dried lentils, an onion and a square of chocolate. But then I realise that I don't have to eat my food exactly as it is in this description. The anti-cancer plate gives me a guide to the kinds of food that will keep me in tip-top health and in what proportions to eat them. So, let us look at it another way.

Things I eat lots of and often (no, not all of them on the same day):
Berries (strawberries, blueberries, raspberries, mulberries, cranberries, blackberries, cherries); fruit (apples, pears, bananas, peaches, apricots, nectarines, mangos, pawpaws, melons); citrus fruit (oranges, grapefruits, lemons, limes); dried fruit; avocados; porridge; organic eggs; whole grains (brown rice, quinoa, buckwheat, barley); salad (lettuce, endive, watercress, rocket, tomatoes, carrots, spring onions, cucumbers, capsicums, radishes, fennel); green vegetables (cabbage, kale, spinach, pak choi, peas, celery, zucchinis); root vegetables (carrots, turnips, sweet potatoes, parsnips, swedes); allium vegetables (onions, garlic, leeks);

other vegetables (eggplants, okra, celeriac, corn, pumpkins, marrows); mushrooms; vegetable juice; buckwheat noodles; lentils; beans (broad beans, butter beans, kidney beans, chickpeas, pinto beans, mung beans, soya beans); nuts (Brazil nuts, almonds, walnuts, macadamia nuts, cashews); seeds (pumpkin, sunflower, sesame, flax, hemp); fresh herbs (parsley, coriander, thyme, dill, tarragon, chives, mint); spices (turmeric, dill seed, cumin, coriander seed, black pepper, cardamom, caraway); fresh ginger; garlic; seaweed; olive oil; coconut oil.

Things I probably shouldn't eat regularly but I do anyway:
Coffee; tea

Things I eat occasionally (3–4 times a week):
Organic lamb fillet; organic chicken; tofu; soya yoghurt; fish; wholemeal bread; rice noodles; sprouts (mung bean, chickpea, lentil, radish, alfalfa); dark chocolate (at least 70%); honey.

Things I eat rarely (once or twice a month):
Croissants; spaghetti; Chinese food; curry; organic fry-up (eggs, bacon, tomatoes and toast); jam or marmalade; almond and orange cake; potatoes; Vegemite; organic butter (well, you can't eat Vegemite with *no butter*).

Things I never eat:
Big Macs; Diet Coke; microwave dinners; Twisties; Mars Bars; Coco Pops; KFC; cheesecake; oil in plastic bottles; tinned peaches in syrup; any other tinned food; non-organic meat and chicken. (This list could circle the planet but you get the picture.)

Top cancer busters:
Turmeric (mixed with black pepper); brassicas (cabbage, broccoli, kale, Brussels sprouts, pak choi); carrots; alliums (onions and garlic); mushrooms (Shiitake and Maitake); berries; green tea; ginger; organic soya; whole grains (rice, barley, oats, quinoa).

Things to avoid like the plague:
Refined sugar; artificial sweeteners; artificial flavourings; highly processed food (white bread, tinned spaghetti, flavoured chips, instant desserts, etc.); hydrogenated or partially hydrogenated oils; processed meats; non-organic meat and chicken. Battery-farmed chickens (and their eggs) commonly contain antibiotics and 'growth promotants'.

- If in doubt, don't eat anything that contains a long list of ingredients or any ingredient that you can't pronounce. The closer food is to its natural state, the more wholesome it is likely to be.

- Avoid food that is packaged in soft plastic, especially if the food is fatty (like meat or oil). Never microwave or heat food or drinks in plastic containers. Unfortunately, food tins are routinely lined with plastic or lacquer that contains Bisphenol-A, a known hormone disruptor.
- Filter water with a charcoal filter or, better still, a reverse osmosis filter. Try not to drink out of plastic bottles.
- In general try to eat as much organic food as possible, particularly meat, chicken and eggs. Meat that is grass fed has a better balance of Omegas 3 and 6.
- Dairy products contain growth factors and hormones, not a good idea for those with cancer.
- Organic choices are often limited and/or expensive. Freeze organic stuff when it's in season, plentiful and cheap.

If you're reading this and you don't have cancer – why wait? The best treatment for cancer is to not get it in the first place. Dining the anti-cancer way will make you feel fit, fabulous and full. Trust me.

MONDAY 1 JUNE

Flossie calls.

'Can I take you out for dinner?' she says.

'Yes,' I reply graciously, 'but only to the Organic Kitchen.'

After we've ordered I tell Flossie the story of Rowena and the £300 juice extractor.

'But that's just what I've been looking for!' exclaims Flossie in delight.

The meal arrives. With steely determination she ignores it. As her fillet of organic salmon with shaved fennel and green lentils congeals on the plate, Flossie sits with head bent, a fork in her right hand and an iPhone in her left. She doggedly tracks down The Champion, reads the specifications, selects accessories, places an order and taps in her credit card details. Flossie is a psychotherapist so she is an expert in obsessive-compulsive behaviour.

'There,' she says at last, with the beatific smile of a junkie who has just had a hit, 'I've ordered two. One for you and one for me. They will be here on Wednesday.'

TUESDAY 2 JUNE

When I was a child, my mum's outlandish, gay, alcoholic friend Richard O'Sullivan came to stay with us for a couple of weeks. (I can use his real name because he is dead now.) We were living in Buderim, Queensland at the time. After a while we moved to Mooloolaba and Richard came with us, then we moved to Brisbane, then to Byron Bay and then to Sydney, and Richard came with us every time. Mum could not get rid of him no matter what she tried: changing the locks; calling the police; punching him; dumping him at her friends' houses . . . Richard got us into trouble wherever we went, drank us out of house and home, robbed our piggy banks, hogged our couch and farted when we were trying to watch TV.

Richard also brought untold riches. He introduced us to Stravinsky; antique silk kimonos; Italian cooking; Spanish language; Proust; the art of straining glass out of red wine through a silk scarf when you've smashed the top off the bottle in desperation because you've lost the corkscrew; and, not least, the very great skill of laughing in the face of adversity.

At heart, Mum and Richard were far too Bohemian to ever become proper hippies. But we did go through a health-food stage. That involved visiting vegan and macrobiotic cafés and being forced to eat boiled grains and vegetables with no butter or seasonings. Also to listen to the rather hypocritical self-righteous cant of alternative types who would spend their days telling others how best to live their lives, and then go home and hit their wives. Eventually I went on strike, refusing all health food. Richard used to make a repulsive brown rice, tuna, carrot and sultana salad. My mum still reminisces fondly about it.

All of this is a rather long-winded way of telling you why I have hated brown rice all my life. That is, until I learned that it may save my life.

Now I love brown rice. I eat it nearly every day.

How to cook brown rice:

Use everything organic, if possible.
Half a cup of short grain brown rice
One cup of water
A handful of sesame seeds
A sprinkling of Umeboshi plum vinegar (from Japanese shops or good health food shops)

Put the rice and the water in a small pan with the lid on. Bring it to the boil then turn the flame right down and leave it to simmer for 25 minutes. Do not take the lid off.

Meanwhile, dry roast the sesame seeds in a frying pan over a low flame. Stir or shake them constantly until they are golden brown because they can burn in a flash.

After 20 minutes or so, check the rice to see if it has absorbed all the water. The rice should be soft but a bit chewy, not mushy. If it is still wet, put the lid back on and leave it for another 5 minutes. Once all the water is absorbed, turn the flame off and let the rice sit with the lid on for another 5 minutes or so. Then stir in the sesame seeds and add a splash of the vinegar.

It is delicious with cucumber and seaweed salad.

WEDNESDAY 3 JUNE

At two thirty p.m. Nick and I arrive at the Harley Street Clinic. First, we go to see Mr Hadjiminas. Mr H injects me with some kind of tracer that will show him the way to the sentinel lymph node. I am learning lots of things in a very short time: we all have a series of lymph nodes in our armpits. One of their jobs is to catch and filter out nasties from the lymph. The very first one that drains from one's breast is called the sentinel node.

The latest fashion amongst breast surgeons is to remove the sentinel node and examine it to see if it contains any cancer cells. If the sentinel node is clear, the cancer is unlikely to have spread any further – hence it will not be necessary to remove all the other lymph nodes. And if the cancer has not spread, there is no need for chemotherapy.

Next, we go down into the labyrinthine basement for an ultrasound scan. I change into the standard-issue blue patterned back-fastening robe and gown monogrammed with 'HSC'. I guess they monogram the gowns so that if one absent-mindedly wanders off into the West End, the staff at Selfridges will know where to return one to.

As we sit in the tiny waiting area we hear a most distressing wailing and crying coming from the ultrasound room. Nick and I look at each other in alarm. Then a young woman and her husband appear. She is clearly about eight months pregnant and her eyes are wet with tears. She sits down and stares at the floor whilst her husband holds her hand. I am horrified to even imagine what terrible news they have just received. I want to say something or to give her a hug but it feels too intrusive. I try some empathetic glances but cannot catch her eye. We all sit silently in the tiny waiting area together; then my name is called.

Another jolly female doctor applies the goo and then the scanner head, searching for my tumours. We pointedly avoid mentioning the previous occupant of the couch. By way of making conversation the doctor asks me who my surgeon is, although the answer is right there in my notes.

'Mr Hadjiminas,' I reply.

'You're lucky,' she says. 'If I had to have breast surgery I would definitely want him to do it.' I can't tell you how comforted I am by that remark.

Scan done, I dress and we are shown through the subterranean corridors to a lift. It brings us out into the main hospital reception area. I book in and we sit down to await a porter. My mind returns to the pregnant lady: no matter what one is facing, there is always somebody worse off.

'Did you happen to find out what was the matter with that poor lady?' I ask Nick.

'Oh, yes,' he replies in a cheerful tone. 'She just found out she is having a baby. She had thought that she had a growth in her stomach. She was crying and wailing with joy.'

The porter escorts us upstairs to a room. This is unlike any hospital room I have ever previously experienced. It is sunny and light with big windows. On the bed are slippers, a pair of paper knickers, a robe and a pair of pressure stockings. There are menu cards to be filled in. The bathroom is stocked with white towels and mini toiletries. It is like a very sanitary hotel room. And there is only one occupant – me!

Before we know it, Mr Hadjiminas has arrived. I strip to the waist. Mr H produces a big black felt-tip pen and marks a circle on my left breast, around the area where the MRI scan has shown the tumours to be. Then he draws a huge black arrow from my shoulder pointing to my breast. I look at him quizzically.

'They won't let you into theatre without that,' he says. I may look comical but I am greatly reassured by the thoroughness of the procedures here.

Soon, a businesslike theatre nurse comes to take me 'downstairs'. We wave goodbye to Nick as the lift doors close. I am trying to be all light-hearted and cheerful but I feel sick. Then we are back in the underground corridors. As I walk with the nurse in my gown and slippers, scenes of final walks in those death-row movies come to mind. Except, I remind myself, this is a walk to save my life.

❖

Some time later my eyes flutter open. A face swims into view. Voices burble somewhere far away. Strip lights slide by above me. The air temperature changes. More faces; more voices. One of them is Nick's. I'm being lifted. Then my body sinks into cool, starchy sheets.

THURSDAY 4 JUNE

I wake up early this morning, ravenous. I look down at my breast. It is covered with a big absorbent bandage but, from my perspective, it looks the same size as it was before. I ask Nurse Tiziana how that can be.

'That is swelling,' she tells me.

Mr Hadjiminas shimmies onto the scene. 'We've removed the tumours and your sentinel node and we've sent it all off to the lab. By tomorrow we will know if the margins are clear and the result on your lymph node. How are you feeling?'

'Great.' I really am.

'Good, you can go home after you've had breakfast.'

FRIDAY 5 JUNE

Back at home Nick gives me a cuddle. I turn over to snuggle up to him and I hear it: a kind of sloshing, like water inside a bucket, but muted.

'Sshhh,' I say. 'Can you hear that?'

'Hear what?'

'It's a slooshing sound. It's coming from inside me,' I whisper.

'I think you're imagining that, darling,' says Nick.

He brings me a cup of tea. If there is one thing in the world that is guaranteed to make me feel loved, it is being brought tea in bed. I sit up to accept the cup.

'There it is again,' I say.

'I can't hear anything,' says Nick.

'It's coming from my breast,' I say. I'm quite alarmed now. Nick looks at me, clearly wondering how far to indulge this anxiety. 'It must be your stomach,' he says. 'I'll get you some breakfast.'

After breakfast in bed I finally haul myself up and into the bathroom. As I walk down the hallway the sound is more pronounced.

'There!' I gasp in horror.

'You know, maybe there is something,' says Nick.

I phone the hospital immediately and get through to Honoria, the breast care nurse.

'I was just about to call you,' she says. 'How are you getting along?'

'It slooshes when I walk!' I squeak, realising how mad that sounds.

'Oh, that's quite normal,' she replies. 'It's fluid build-up in your breast.'

❖

We're in the car on the way to the hospital to see Mr Hadjiminas for my pathology results.

'I just thought of something, honey,' Nick pipes up. 'You should make a will.'

I chew on my nails with renewed vigour. But he is right. I don't have anything like that: a will; a pension; an ISA; sickness cover; life insurance; stocks and shares. *What are you on about?*

'I will put that on the list of things to do,' I mutter, perhaps with a slightly curt tone of voice.

'Well, the good news,' says Mr Hadjiminas, looking at a computer print-out, 'is the margins are clear.' That is good news indeed. I already know what it means: Mr H can now go ahead and perform reconstructive surgery. I won't be requiring a mastectomy!

However, I've also grown wise to his good news/bad news routine. There is something more to come. I can tell.

Mr H looks at his fingers and then at me.

'I'm afraid we found cancer in the sentinel node,' he says.

My mouth opens and closes. I'm not sure that I actually say anything.

'It's only in one node,' he continues. 'Two others have what we call micrometastases, just a few cells, and the other one was clear. It's unlikely to have spread any further. But we'll have to take out all the other lymph nodes under your arm just to be sure. And it will mean you'll have to have chemotherapy.'

Mr H gives me a look as if to say, *And please don't argue with me on this one.*

SATURDAY 6 JUNE

Today I will be having the axillary clearance and latissimus dorsi flap reconstruction. What that means is that they will take out all the lymph nodes from under my arm and then rebuild my breast using a muscle from my back.

You probably don't want to know that much. I know I don't.

Nick and I check into the Harley Street Clinic at two p.m. I feel familiar with the drill by now: don the gown and paper pants; roll up the pressure stockings; fill in the menu cards; on with the telly; order tea for Nick.

Nurse Anne comes to take my obs and swabs. Nick's tea arrives and I hand the menu cards to the housekeeping lady.

'I don't think you'll be needing those,' says Nurse Anne, 'you'll be spending the night on ITU.' That is, in intensive care.

Mr Hadjiminas arrives with his black felt-tip pen. After he has drawn the big arrow and X marks the spot I say, casually, 'The nurse said I'm going to ITU – that's not right, is it?'

'Oh, yes,' he replies. 'It's quite a big procedure. You'll be in theatre for about five hours.'

That shakes me up. I look him in the eye. 'Mr Hadjiminas,' I say, 'I know that you're going to do your finest work. I just want you to know that I intend to be the next cover girl on that photo album of yours.'

❖

When I come round in the Intensive Treatment Unit Nick is smiling at me.

'Hey, honey,' he says.

'Hey, honey,' say I. Sometimes that is enough.

❖

I gaze around me. The unit has a slightly menacing aspect: it is filled with machinery; there are no windows. But as long as Nick is by my side I am not afraid. His presence calms me. After a couple of hours Nick leaves to collect my sister, Miranda, and my six-year-old niece, Eloise, from the Heathrow Express at Paddington. Miranda is flying in from Moscow, where she works as a diplomat. A kind and funny nurse, Caroline, takes care of me whilst he is gone.

'You have a good attitude,' she says. 'You should recover well.'

'Do some people have a bad attitude?' I say.

'You bet they do,' she replies. 'Some people just moan and complain and feel sorry for themselves.'

I wonder about that. I am so happy simply to be alive. What with that and the free morphine, moaning seems a bit surplus to requirements.

It must be late, maybe near midnight, when the gang arrives. I am overjoyed to see Miranda and Eloise's faces. If they find the situation upsetting they don't show it. Miranda positively beams at me. Eloise climbs up onto my bed, ignoring the mass of tubes and wires.

'I made you a card, Aunty Jessy,' she says.

On the front of the card is a pink garden full of hearts and flowers. Diamonds glitter in the sky. Inside is an inscription: *Dere Jesica I hope that you are not filing to sick. I woil be siying you agen. we wel visit you. and you get to play A game of Spot the difrins.* On the facing page is a drawing of two cats wearing pink dresses. One cat has a bow in its hair; the other does not. One cat is wearing pink slippers whilst the other cat's slippers are red. There are several other observable variations. So at one a.m. Eloise and I sit up in bed in the intensive care unit playing 'Spot the difrins'. It is one of the high points of my life so far.

SUNDAY 7 JUNE

The door to my room opens and my eyes are filled with a vision of sunshine and flowers. There's a gorgeous bunch of pink peonies and roses with a card from Nick; an extremely elegant arrangement of white peonies, roses and cow parsley from Cindy; a huge explosion of deep crimson long-stemmed roses from Flossie.

Miranda, Eloise, Nick and Flossie are also in the room.

The nurses slide me onto the bed, plump up my pillows and hook my jugular vein up to the morphine dispenser.

'Just press the button whenever you need it,' says one. I press it immediately.

Nick sits on my bed, kisses my forehead and strokes my hair. Iris and Jamie arrive with more flowers. There is a carnival atmosphere in the room. Everyone is chatting and ordering up cups of tea from the catering lady. Miranda and Nick have stocked the fridge with fresh fennel and grape juice and my favourite healthy sprout salad. Eloise pumps fistfuls of alcohol sanitising gel from the bottle at the foot of my bed and smears it all over the floor. She then begins scrubbing it all around with paper towels. Once the floor is awash with the stuff she pumps out several more big gloops and starts in on sanitising the doors.

'Eloise,' says Miranda sharply, 'enough of that alcohol gel.'

'But, Mummy,' replies Eloise plaintively, 'I love the smell.'

Flossie shoots me a knowing and slightly worried glance.

Jamie fetches some Blu-Tack and sticks all my cards up on the wall. Eloise falls asleep, so Miranda obtains pillows and blankets from the nurses and puts her to bed in the bath. Iris and Flossie buzz down to Marylebone High Street and return with a clock shaped like a gigantic pocket watch. They hang the clock on the wall. It wouldn't look out of place at the Mad Hatter's tea party. In fact, the whole event could be the most surreal and best party I've ever hosted. Beneath this avalanche of love and flowers and drugs, I feel as though I've won the lottery.

Things I wish I'd known before #3
How to prepare for a week in hospital

Dr Allan Hamilton, neurosurgeon and author of *The Scalpel and the Soul*, asserts that patients who maintain a sense of who they are fare better in hospital than those who do not. Making your hospital room into a piece of your own world helps to promote feelings of security and well-being. More importantly it helps the medical staff to connect with you as an individual rather than as just another inmate in a blue patterned surgical gown.

Here are some suggestions.

What to pack:
- Any medicines you are currently taking (show these to the admitting nurse when you arrive)
- Glasses or contact lenses

- Blu-Tack (to stick up all your cards)
- Organic room spray (to counter the smell of sanitising gel)
- Moisturiser, lip balm, body lotion, hand cream and rose water in a spray bottle (you will need a lot of moisturising and hydration. The rooms tend to be artificially heated or air conditioned and full of machinery, making the atmosphere very arid. A tip – put a saucer of water on the radiator to stop your skin drying out too much.)
- Lipstick (to cheer your face up)
- Toothpaste and toothbrush
- A hairbrush
- Cashmere bed socks (to keep your feet warm)
- Mobile phone & charger (hospitals generally charge rip-off prices for phone calls)
- Eye mask
- Earplugs (it is always noisy and the nurses come in and out all night and all day)
- A light robe
- A cotton nightie cut up the back (this will save you the horror of having to wear a hideous hospital gown. Buy a large size cotton nightie, cut it up the back and attach some long ribbons that tie at the front to draw the open flaps together so that your bum doesn't hang out.)
- A t-shirt and a pair of shorts
- Slippers
- A pashmina
- A snuggly pillow (the hospital pillows are lined with plastic)
- A photo of the people you love
- iPod loaded with happy music, relaxing music, guided meditations and audio books
- A portable computer (check if the hospital charge for internet access – this can also be a bit of a racket. If they do, it might be worth investing in a dongle from your mobile phone provider.)
- Notebook and pen
- Camera (you may think that this is one nightmare that you just want to forget but, some time in the future, you may be glad that you kept a record of this time.)
- Nice teabags, soya milk or a pint of organic milk
- A clock
- A small amount of cash to buy newspapers and sweets
- Your health insurance details
- A pair of ridiculously high-heeled shoes (put them by the bed to remind you that it won't always be like this)

What to ask your friends and family to do:
- Everyone will bring flowers – there will never be enough vases, so ask them to bring vases too.
- You will be bombarded with chocolate and will soon feel sick; ask friends to bring organic grapes and berries.
- Make you fresh juices and salads
- Bring mineral water in glass bottles
- Coordinate a visiting roster
- Read aloud to you
- Stick your cards up on the walls
- Rub your feet
- Be available to take you home when you are discharged

What not to take to the hospital:
- Tight, revealing or synthetic nightwear
- Jewellery
- Credit cards
- Cigarettes

MONDAY 8 JUNE

Mr Hadjiminas arrives bright and early, Nurse Honoria trailing in his wake. He gives my torso the expert once-over and mumbles to Honoria, 'Thirty-six C.' Honoria buzzes out of the room. Mr H changes all my bandages, and by the time he's done that Honoria is back with a device that looks like a cross between a sports bra and a straitjacket.

'This,' says Mr Hadjiminas, 'is a compression bra.'

When my friend Iris heard that I had been diagnosed with breast cancer, she reportedly said, 'What do you mean Jessica has breast cancer? She doesn't even have breasts.' I inform Mr Hadjiminas that I am actually a size 36A.

'Oh, this will fit,' he says. 'The surgery will have caused a lot of swelling.'

He and Honoria carefully manoeuvre the contraption around my ribcage. They engage the huge zipper in the front and then fasten the thick Velcro shoulder straps securely in place. The compression bra is completely smooth and made out of a thick but soft stretchy fabric. It hugs me firmly right down to the bottom of my rib cage. For something that looks so formidable it is remarkably comfortable. And it fits like a glove. Mr H is right again.

When Flossie arrives I'm sitting up in bed proudly showing off my new, very white, compression bra.

'Oh,' gasps Flossie, 'I want one of those!'

'Think about it, Flossie,' I say. 'You really don't.'

❖

Now that I'm all spruced up in my new compression bra and all juiced up on morphine, I'm ready to entertain. And it's just as well.

Flossie is already on the scene. Next through the door are Miranda, Nick and Eloise. Miranda and Nick have been buying up West London's organic vegetable stockpile and juicing for Britain. It seems that they each have firm, yet distinct ideas about how juicing should be done. I take delivery of two separate and distinct flasks of juice.

Eloise is excited to the point of collywobbles because today she is going to meet her cousin Phoenix for the first time. They are both from one-child families. Eloise lives in Moscow and Australia, and Phoenix lives in Goa and the UK. I've been trying to engineer their meeting for a very long time. I'm truly delighted that it's going to happen at last, even if it's taken me getting breast cancer to bring it about.

Cousin Ben arrives with Phoenix. She and Eloise take one look at each other and fall instantly in love.

'Being cousins isn't funny,' announces Eloise, 'so why are we laughing?' Collapsing in giggles, they skip into the bathroom, where Eloise shows Phoenix how to put dolls to bed in the bath.

Jamie and Iris arrive. They have agreed to take the little girls to Regent's Park to play with Chilli and Hugo, the chihuahuas. Off they all go.

Next in is Jean-Claude, Miranda's husband. He has just flown from Barcelona, where he lives and works.

I can tell that you're beginning to suspect that my family and friends have some pretty complicated living arrangements. Let me take a moment to fill you in. I am Australian but I live in London. My boyfriend, Nick, lives in Sydney. At the moment Miranda and Eloise live in Moscow. Miranda's husband, Jean-Claude, is French. He is an advertising man and he lives and works in Barcelona. Jean-Claude is not Eloise's father. Eloise spends her holidays in Adelaide with her father, his partner and his two older daughters. When she's not in Adelaide, Eloise visits our mother in Tasmania. Our mother moved from Sydney to Tasmania a couple of decades ago. My cousin Ben is a film producer. When Ben and his wife, Sayeeda, separated, Sayeeda moved to Goa in India. When Ben is not working he spends his time in Goa with his daughter Phoenix. Jamie and Iris are not a couple. Jamie lives in the penthouse flat: Mayhem Mansions, Marylebone, in a homosexual ménage à trois with Ted and Muttiah. Iris spends a lot of time at Mayhem Mansions for two reasons: 1) she and Jamie are both chihuahua owners, and 2) Ted cooks a lot of pies.

You get the picture?

Antony arrives, with more flowers. Flossie pops out to the shops and returns with yet another gift for me – an Aveda face spray. I thank her and, to show just how useful this gift is, spritz my face.

On the wall by the door is a Perspex leaflet holder containing an A4 laminated card with graphic illustrations of the surgical procedure that I have recently undergone: the latissimus dorsi flap. If there is ever a lull in the conversation, Nick takes the opportunity to pass around the card, saying, 'Look, this is what Jessy had done.' Most people, like me, cannot bear to look.

The park gang returns. Eloise has fallen over and grazed her knee, and by all accounts created so much hullabaloo that Jamie and Iris felt obliged to return her to her mother. The girls switch on the TV and settle down to watch *Kung-Fu Panda*, my new favourite movie. Miranda and Antony try giving me amateur reflexology. They work on one foot apiece, 'to help you relax'.

It's standing room only when the door opens and Mr Hadjiminas enters the scene. The look on his face turns from stunned to confused but Nurse Anne quickly bustles in behind him.

'Right-o,' she says, 'everybody out.'

The visitors traipse off to continue their party on the staircase or in the lift or somewhere. Mr H regains his composure and takes a seat.

'We've got the lab report on the remainder of your lymph nodes,' he says. 'They were all clear.'

Suddenly I relax and it feels as if I've been clenching my teeth for a week.

'That's great news, thank you.' I sigh. 'So I won't need chemotherapy?'

'I'm afraid I will still be recommending chemotherapy,' replies Mr H.

'But you got all the cancer out.'

'Well,' says Mr Hadjiminas, 'if there is any spread to the lymph system at all, then there is always a possibility, however slight, that it may have spread elsewhere in your body. We simply have no way to know. So the chemotherapy is precautionary. It's sort of a belt-and-braces approach.'

'I see,' say I. 'Well, I'll have to think about it. I'll let you know when I've made a decision.'

Mr H gives me an ever-so-slightly exasperated glance.

TUESDAY 9 JUNE

Miranda and Eloise are going home to Moscow. After dropping them at the Heathrow Express, Nick returns. He has made a big hit with Eloise. That pleases me no end.

There's a mid-morning lull in hospitals. Mr Hadjiminas has made his early morning visit. The nurses have finished making my bed, taking my temperature, checking my chest drains and all that well-meaning prodding and poking that they do. The breakfast-shift visitors have departed for work or the airport. The lunch-shift visitors are still at home brushing their teeth.

Nick and I settle down together for a nice cup of tea. We chat about the lovely times we've shared. We chat about the craziness of the past ten days. About how wonderful it is that we have had so much fun because, hey, one's life can change completely in any moment. Then, at last, we can no longer avoid the subject that is pulling on our coat sleeves, nagging at our consciousness like a nascent toothache: Nick is returning to Australia in a week's time. We don't know when we will see one another again. I had planned to go to Sydney this autumn. That won't be possible now, if I'm to have a course of chemotherapy.

'How do you feel about that, baby?' I ask.

Nick looks at me and his face goes all weird, like he's trying on different expressions, unsure of which one will be suitable for the occasion. He takes my hand in his.

Then Nick looks me in the face and says, 'I think we should agree to see other people.'

I stare at him. For a long time.

'So are you saying that you'd like me to go out with someone else?' I finally ask. 'Because I can do that if you like. But just to be clear: if I do go out with someone else then I will be going out with him – not with you.'

Nick shakes his head and looks at the floor. Then he says: 'I don't think I can be faithful, Jessica.'

WEDNESDAY 10 JUNE

After Nick announced that our relationship had ended my mind went blank. Eventually I said the only thing that occurred to me:

'Nick, you're an idiot.' All day, tears have been sliding silently down my face. But I guess the nurses are used to women who have just had breast surgery crying; they don't ask what's up and I don't offer an explanation.

'We should think about taking you off that morphine,' says Nurse Sarah this evening. 'Would you prefer to do it now or in the morning?'

I mull it over. I have already come to terms with separation from a large part of my left breast. I have resigned myself to being abandoned by my boyfriend. I suppose I can take breaking up with morphine in my stride.

'Do it now,' I say with bravado.

Then I back-pedal like mad. 'But what will we do if I have pain in the night?' I whimper.

'Oh, we can leave it until the morning if you like,' replies Sarah. I feel like a malingering dope fiend. 'No,' I say with finality, 'do it now.'

Sarah scoots out of the room and then returns with a giant horse syringe. She holds it up.

'This,' she says, 'is morphine.' She lays it in a little cardboard tray on my bedside cabinet. 'It will be right here if you need it.'

THURSDAY 11 JUNE

The last couple of days have become a bit confused in my mind, what with the emotional distress, the comings and goings of my friends, the late-night phone calls and the morphine.

I tried not to be upset but I did cry a lot on Wednesday. I've had to deal with the difficult business of telling friends and family the news about Nick and me breaking up whenever they called or visited. I've kept it in perspective, though. Compared with the magnitude of bad news that Mr Hadjiminas could have given me, and didn't, Nick's pronouncement seemed less like a bombshell and more like an exploding paper bag.

At the same time – and this may sound odd – I didn't fully believe Nick. Not in the sense of 'I don't belieeeeeve it!' but that what he said seemed inauthentic. His words and his actions did not match up. First of all, Nick has been genuinely committed to sticking with me as much as he possibly can. He had a cast-iron excuse to leave the country when I was diagnosed with cancer: his son was in trouble and his ex-wife was pressuring him to go home. His mother has been ill for some time. He needed to get back to work. Instead, he extended his stay in London by another two weeks. He came to all the appointments with me, sat with me in the very distressing ITU and has been on call day and night, making me salads and driving my sister around. Nothing has been too much trouble. Second of all, he did not give me the old 'it's not you, it's me' speech and then skedaddle to a safe distance. Rather, he hung around in the hospital all day, looking like a kicked dog and enduring the frosty reactions of several of my friends. It became quite painful to watch. I felt relieved when he finally decided to go home (to my home).

Flossie and Iris arrived first thing on Wednesday morning; I checked their handbags for guns and ropes. Flossie sat down looking grim. Iris stalked about the room, picking up heavy, blunt items and testing them out on the palm of her hand. Flossie, in her psychotherapist persona, explained to one and all the concepts of Love Addiction and Love Avoidance expounded by Pia Mellody, and the origins of those compulsive behaviours in childhood trauma. As far as I understood it, in my drug-addled state, these are the basics:

- Some original childhood trauma (taking care of an alcoholic, pill-popping mother; being fiddled with by Uncle Freddy; trying to be the peacemaker between warring parents; finding Daddy with his head in the oven, and so forth) causes us to have an incomplete understanding of close, mutually supportive intimate relationships. This leads us in adult life to behave either as Love Addicts or Love Avoidants (or commonly, both).

• The Love Addict is drawn to people who are emotionally or otherwise unavailable. They create a fantasy about the other person and fall in love with the fantasy, rather than the real person.

• The Love Avoidant enters a relationship behind a wall of seduction but they soon become overwhelmed by the intimacy of the relationship. They ascribe their panic as being caused by the other person's neediness (I imagine that having cancer could be classed as neediness) and engineer a situation that allows them to escape.

• A person can display traits of both the Love Addict and the Love Avoidant or switch between the two.

'Hmmph,' I muttered, 'so what does that say about me?'

When Nick walked through the door (yes, he came back, *again*) I swear I could see white-hot sizzles of static electricity arcing across the room. Flossie took Nick out for a little walk. I imagine she wanted to set him straight on a few things. Flossie returned.

'Well?' I said.

'Hmmm,' she replied, tight lipped, 'I don't think I've ever met anyone with such an overdeveloped sense of entitlement.'

What on earth does that mean? Is a sense of entitlement a good thing or a bad thing? But I dropped the topic. I sensed that Flossie felt she'd said too much already. Getting details of personal conversations out of Flossie is somewhat like trying to open an oyster with a plastic fork. And quite right, too, seeing as how she makes her living listening to other people's darkest secrets.

Some other events happened yesterday. It's all a bit of a jumble in my mind.

The nurses removed the compression bra and changed my

dressings. I took the opportunity to have a proper look at the site of the surgery (that's possibly an avoidant way of saying 'my breast'). Then I passed out cold.

Cindy visited and made a very good job of being all matter-of-fact and pleasant to Nick. Pete visited with more flowers. He was less able to keep up a jolly front. He looked at his shoes a lot. Royston swooped by and bundled Nick off to a steak house for dinner, no doubt to set him straight on a few more things, but from a manly perspective. Nick came back to the hospital late at night and begged me to give him another chance. I said something along the lines of 'let's see how it goes'.

❖

Nick bounces in as if nothing had ever happened. He sits on the bed and holds my hand.

Nurse Tiziana enters and says, 'Now you're off the pump we can take out that central line.'

The central line is a catheter that has been inserted into my jugular vein. It has three or four different tubes and valves attached to it, all rattling and clunking against my throat.

Tiziana busies herself at the side of my neck, removing bandages, cutting a stitch. Finally, with a swift movement, she pulls out the central line and drops it in the yellow bin. Nick's eyes seem to bulge and then his face goes a kind of grey–white colour.

'All done' says Tiziana, applying a fresh dressing.

After she has left the room, Nick remains quiet and still for a few minutes.

'Get us a cup of tea, then,' I say.

He looks at me, uncomprehending. 'Did you see what she pulled out?' he asks.

I shake my head.

'It was this long,' he says, holding his hands about a foot apart.

Now that I'm no longer physically plugged in to life-preserving machinery I can actually get out of bed. I swing my legs over the side and then remember the two long tubes that are draining fluid from my back, where Mr H removed the muscle. Attached to the end of these tubes are two glass bottles. I press the call button and Nurse Tiziana pops in.

'I want to go to the bathroom. What should I do about these bottles?' I ask. Nurse T pops out again. She comes back with a paper carrier bag from Pret A Manger.

I make a couple of practice runs around the perimeter of my room and a foray into the bathroom, with rests in between. Now I feel ready to up the ante. With my right hand I take Nick's arm. In my left hand I take the Pret bag with drainage bottles. We open the bedroom door.

A fellow patient has collapsed immediately outside. Nurses and doctors are rushing about with oxygen and needles. We step right over her and, waveringly, we walk the entire length of the corridor.

FRIDAY 12 JUNE

Mr Hadjiminas visits every morning, always wearing a tailored suit. This morning he expresses great satisfaction with my progress, going so far as to call me his 'star patient'. I think that great doctors are defined not just by their brains and technical skill but also by their ability to enlist patients in their own recovery. Mr H certainly fits my great doctor criteria. His enthusiasm in turn encourages me to make every possible effort to get back to vibrant health.

After the success of my corridor walk yesterday afternoon, Nick too is keen to egg me on to higher achievements. He suggests that we aim to go out of the hospital today. I am excited by the idea. 'We could walk down to the Providores and have tea,' I exclaim. 'Only, what am I going to wear?' For the past few days I've been dressed only in my compression bra and a pair of stretch jersey shorts.

A physiotherapist came to see me a couple of days ago. She gave me a leaflet entitled *Exercises After Breast Surgery*. Since then I've been assiduously doing my exercises so that I don't end up with restricted shoulder movement. They're quite simple, for example: brushing my hair, drying my back with a towel or raising and lowering my elbows to shoulder height. But I don't think I could put anything on over my head just yet. I will need an outfit that is comfortable and easy to don, that covers up the bandages and the compression bra.

Flossie arrives. It's more of an early morning fly-past than a visit. She lingers just long enough to knock back a caffe latte and drop off her latest gift to me – a sparkly silver bat-winged top with a V-neck. Now I can guess what you're thinking: 'That Flossie has finally lost the plot. Tipped right over the edge, so to speak. You're in the hospital, not auditioning for *Saturday Night Fever*.' I hear you. When I open the bag I have to look, long and hard, at the sparkly silver top and then remember to close my mouth. But wait a minute. The top is loose enough to wiggle into without too much trouble, the bat-wing sleeves are not restricting, the V-neck exactly covers the neckline of my compression bra. Flossie is a genius. She has discovered the perfect post-breast surgery attire.

Nick helps me into the silver top and leggings. It's really a smart look. Then I regard the two tubes protruding from my waistband with drainage bottles attached: 'The whole outfit will really be let down by that Pret A Manger sandwich bag.' Nick shoots me a look of excited triumph and then produces a black crocodile Bruno Magli handbag. He has rifled through my wardrobe and picked it out himself. The two bottles fit perfectly inside.

❖

If you ask me, there's a lot to be said for morphine. Of course there is the very real risk that one may become addicted, lose one's job, sell all one's furniture, take up shoplifting, go to gaol and end up living in the subway at Kings Cross station.

The immediate downside is constipation.

I just went to the loo for the first time this week. *Oh dear.* I press the nurse call button. Nurse Sarah comes in. 'I'm sorry,' I say, 'I seem to have blocked up the toilet.' Nurse Sarah marches into the bathroom. I hear the sound of flushing and then a shriek. She comes reeling out the door, shaking with laughter. 'The pan has filled up to the brim with water.' I'm glad she thinks it's funny.

Nurse Sarah exits and then returns a few minutes later wearing a plastic apron, gloves and goggles and armed with a stick. 'Plumbing is one of my many skills,' she says, with pride.

SATURDAY 13 JUNE

Mr Hadjiminas doesn't have any days off. He's in the hospital every morning. But on the weekends he visits wearing casual consultant attire: an open-necked shirt; chinos and – you guessed it – boating shoes.

Today I am going home. It is disconcerting. After a week, the hospital feels like home. And home feels like a scary place where I will have to cope with doing the laundry, cooking, cleaning, shopping and bathing. To be honest, I only just about manage those chores at the best of times.

Nick is still here, so I'm going home with him. And that seems disconcerting too. Only four days ago Nick dumped me out of the blue for no good reason whatsoever. I accept that it was some kind of emotional short circuit that caused him to freak out. But I don't know that he won't do it again. I don't feel that I can completely rely on him the way I did a week ago. So I'm feeling somewhat ambivalent about going home.

Nevertheless, I've been in hospital long enough. There comes a point when one begins to pace one's room like a caged tiger – or, in my case, giraffe. I've reached that point.

Mr H removes the chest drains with the assistance of Nurse

Tiziana. I keep my eyes firmly averted. We don't want any more fainting.

'The wound will fill up with fluid now,' Mr Hadjiminas tells me. 'You will have to come in to have it drained once a week.' Nurse Tiziana gives me a strong painkiller. I gratefully accept it. Every day brings its own opportunity to try some small thing that takes me forward in my recovery. This morning I will have a proper bath, rather than a sponge wash, for the first time. I turn on the taps and lay out my clothes.

Nick won't be here to collect me until lunchtime, so I slowly begin to pack up the room. I'm astonished at what an accumulation of stuff one can acquire in just a few days. There are cards; an assortment of vases; the crazy clock; an array of Tupperware containers; my laptop; clothes; boxes of teabags, snacks, biscuits and so on. The painkiller has done its work. I happily fold things into perfect squares, making neat little piles whilst I hum away to myself. Some time later I remember to check on the bath. The bathroom is ankle deep in water.

I press the nurse call buzzer and Nurse Sarah comes in. Nursing can sometimes be a thankless profession, so I hope that it makes Sarah feel good to know just how much I, for one, appreciate her plumbing skills.

MONDAY 15 JUNE

Everything is strange. I'm in my own home but it all seems different. As if the spectrum has shifted. Colours that were warm and bright now appear bluish and muted to my eyes. My body feels brittle; my hair and skin seem to have lost their glow. The phone has gone quiet. I guess that my friends are leaving Nick and me alone to work things out.

Nick has been solicitous. Nothing is too much trouble: he plumps my pillows and brings me tea. We go for slow walks. But I am distant. It is not my intention to punish Nick; I am just finding it hard to look at him. The sight of that profile of his that used to bring out in me an instant smile now burns my heart.

Nick and I have talked about his crisis. He has cried. He has revealed how he regrets all the relationships that he has messed up in his life. And he seems so truly sorry to have harmed me. He says that he has taken on board what Flossie said to him about love avoidance.

'I realise it's a problem for me, Jessy, and I want it to stop,' he tells me. 'I love you and I want to be with you. I am going to go to a self-help group and work on my unconscious fears. I promise you.'

I need Nick so much now. Yet I doubt him. Is it fair to keep him at arm's length like this when he is trying so hard? Is it fair to myself to throw away a wonderful relationship because I'm too afraid to trust my lover? Being strong and alone is familiar to me. I feel safer that way. But what use is being strong and alone when I have cancer?

❖

Nick is leaving tomorrow. It really is make-up-my-mind time. But I don't know what to do. It won't be any good to just say, 'Okay, Nick, I trust you. I love you. You're wonderful . . .' and all that bollocks. We are about to be on opposite sides of the world and there are dark days ahead. Sweet sentiments will not hold us together. Nick is offering his hand to me. I have to find a way to reach out and take hold of it across time and distance and never let go. I must find out if I am able to really commit myself to him – to us – with every fibre of my body and spirit. In other words, I have to take a risk. A big risk. The biggest risk I may ever take.

For the first time, I remove the compression bra and show Nick my wounds. He takes me gently in his arms. As we make love I find the courage to look at him. Really look at him. Nick is looking right back at me. And I see it all: his fear; his fragility; his determination and his love. There is nothing to say. We're going to be all right.

TUESDAY 16 JUNE

At Paddington station I watch the Heathrow Express recede into the distance. I stand on the platform until the train is no longer visible. I continue to stare westward along empty tracks.

Nick has started on his journey home to Sydney. I turn and take my first steps alone on a very different journey that lies ahead of me.

CHEMO CHIC

JUNE

I'm not sure how I'm going to do this. I gaze around my flat.
Nick isn't in it. Not anywhere. Everything *looks* the same: the
couch is still there with its cushions neatly arranged in ranks; the
orchids nod gracefully on their corner shelf. Will I continue to
water and trim them or just let their flowers drop off and their
leaves wither?

Nick has actually gone and got on the train to the airport, to
the aeroplane to fly across France, Switzerland, Greece, Turkey,
Iran, India and Thailand to Sydney, Australia.

I could just forget about him. That might be the sensible thing
to do. 'It's been lovely, Nick, but I have cancer now. I don't think
I can give you the time and attention that you need from me.' No
harm done. It could be that simple.

I examine my motives. I don't really fear being alone – after all,
I'm not. I have so many friends. And now I have a team of highly
trained medical consultants and nurses on my side. If Nick and I
go our separate ways now there will be no possibility of my being
hurt by him in the future; or of my hurting him. I will be safe. Or
am I simply being a coward?

There are some rather patronising assumptions buried in my
thinking: that Nick is so infantile that without a constant supply
of my attention and adoration he will start to look elsewhere;

that he won't be able to cope with his girlfriend having cancer. Yes, he freaked out in the hospital, but he's facing up to that. He has made a commitment to me – and to himself. Shouldn't I believe in him enough to respect that he will step up and show his qualities of strength, compassion, tolerance and love? Isn't that what I want more that anything? And isn't it my greatest fear that I will somehow be unworthy of receiving such unconditional support from a man?

My shoes lie askew on the carpet where I kicked them off. Will I put them on again or just leave them where they've come to rest? Will I empty the dustbin or let it overflow with soggy teabags and egg cartons? There are calls to make: appointments with Mr Hadjiminas, Dr Suzy Cleator – who is to be my oncologist – and Dr Ducker, my GP; more authorisations from Bupa. An induction at the Breast Cancer Haven has to be arranged. I need to find out about benefits. What am I going to do for money?

I stand on my balcony for a while. There are people walking around in the street below. They seem to know what they are doing and where they are going. They don't appear to be having any difficulty understanding whether or not they should step into the corner shop, park their car, make a phone call, turn left or right. They are unaware that there is a woman looking down at them from above whose very next moment of existence is a complete puzzle to her; a woman whose whole life from now on has lost all of its known parameters.

I don't have any reference material for this. The nurses at the hospital have loaded me up with more information pamphlets: *Diet and Cancer*; *Coping With Fatigue*; *Breast Reconstruction*; *Chemotherapy and Hair Loss*. Not one of the pamphlets is entitled *How to Understand That Your Life is Now Not Going to Be Anything Like it Was a Few Weeks Ago or How You Expected it Would Always Continue to Be*.

As the early sunshine warms my shoulders I am aware that I have made a conscious decision: to trust Nick.

But what am I going to have for dinner?

Before long, Sheldon and Flossie are at the door laden down with boxes of snowpea and sesame salad; grilled cod with salsa verde; chocolate pie and other bounteous offerings from Ottolenghi.

Things I wish I'd known before #4
What your friends can do for you

Before breast cancer it had never occurred to me that I didn't have to do absolutely everything myself. Much is written about giving and getting 'emotional support' in times of trouble. But what exactly is that? I have heard it said that 'if it's not practical, it's not spiritual'. Think about it. Do I want someone to ring me up on the telephone to commiserate with my woes? Maybe – but not for long. On the other hand, a phone call from a friend who is in the supermarket asking, 'Is there anything I can bring you?' is truly an act of kindness. Nothing says 'I love you' like taking the trouble to travel halfway across town in order to take out the rubbish.

Many people were quick to say, 'Let me know if there's anything I can do for you.' At the time that they said it I couldn't think of anything. More accurately, *everything* needed doing. And what if I asked them to do something and they said 'no'? For me the problem was not 'What are my friends prepared to do for me?' but 'What am I prepared to ask my friends to do for me?'

May I suggest that you write two lists: one of friends and family; the other of things that need doing. Now, match up who you think will be up to what job. The first job on the list should be 'administering the rota'. Choose someone who is bossy, capable and well liked to be in charge. This lets you off the hook from making lots of emotionally draining phone calls and trying to juggle everybody else's schedules. You will have enough to do with organising all your hospital appointments.

Suggest that the newly appointed rota chief sets up a Facebook page called something like *What Can You Do For Jessy?*

Some jobs to find volunteers for:

- *Transport*: driving you to and from the hospital.
- *Household*: cooking; shopping; gardening; laundry and cleaning; making the beds; taking out the rubbish.
- *Family*: collecting the kids from school and babysitting.

- *Financial and administrative*: filling in benefits claim forms; arranging hospital appointments; writing letters; filing; lending you money.
- *Emotional*: accompanying you to medical appointments and chemotherapy sessions; going for walks; watching TV; someone to phone in the middle of the night.
- *Well-being*: giving you a massage; teaching you gentle yoga; taking you out to lunch; helping you to go through your wardrobe and devise new 'Chemo Chic' outfits.

Life has become quite fast-paced lately.

I feel like I've been preparing for some sort of military campaign or safari. In a way, that is exactly what lies ahead: an extended holiday in the heart of darkness. I want to make sure that I'm well provisioned for the journey, physically and emotionally. So I'm marshalling my resources – but in a way that, I think, would not receive the official seal of approval from one of those *Who Dares Wins* commando blokes.

For a start, I don't know what I may need and, for a second thing, I don't have a map of where I'm going. So it's a bit like gathering up a hairbrush, a tin of pineapple rings, some dry biscuits and a beach towel, chucking it all into a big black bin liner and saying 'Bon voyage' before jumping off the side of a cliff.

Checklist:

Money – no

Health insurance – tick

Medical advisers – tick, tick, tick, tick

Boyfriend – yes but 11,000 miles away

Friends – yes indeed

Physical fitness – pretty good

Inner resources – we shall see

It seems wise to reduce my outgoings as much as possible. That, in itself, is an onerous process. I've spent many hours in the past week holding on the phone, cajoling and reasoning with phone companies, broadband providers, utility companies and various other mean-spirited mothers.

Financial anxiety has dogged me all my life. My parents separated when I was very young and Mum had to bring up Miranda and me on her own. This meant that we always rubbed up against a degree of poverty. We lived in rundown houses. Mum stripped the woodwork, painted, polished and gardened until the houses resembled movie sets. She cleaned and restored furniture that she found at the tip and remodelled op-shop clothes into the latest European fashions.

Our father contributed zero to our upkeep so Mum worked hard in all sorts of jobs, from teaching to antique-buying. As a family we ran a tea stall at a local market. I made the sandwiches and Miranda baked the biscuits. Mum managed to keep us in stylish, home-sewn clothes and send us to the best schools. Nevertheless, sometimes we only had chokoes for dinner: choko soup; chokoes stewed in butter and sweet choko pie (like apple pie but made with chokoes). Now, in Europe the choko – or chayote – is an exotic vegetable held in high esteem because it is low in calories and high in amino acids, fibre and vitamin C. However, in Sydney in the seventies, eating choko was strictly the preserve of the penniless. We had about a million of them growing on our roof. I picked baskets full and tried to sell them to the neighbours. But they all had choko infestations of their own.

I grew up completely clueless about the mechanics of money: where it comes from and, more to the point, where it goes. That's not to say I haven't tried. I've run my own businesses – from a market stall to a production company – with varying degrees of success. In between times I've worked at jobs from waitressing to life modelling to creative consultancy. But no matter how well things were going, I managed to maintain a hand-to-mouth lifestyle. Every time a crisis struck I found myself completely unprepared and lacking the financial cushion to see me through. The last time things went awry, about ten years ago, I lost not only my business but my home as well. That was tough. *But it's not my fault*, I cried in anguish, *when it comes to money I just don't get it.*

In my experience, it is wise to keep finance and romance quite separate. Nick has money. But I am determined not to ask him for any.

As a veteran of twelve-step programmes I have learned this much: no, it's not my fault – but it is my responsibility. For the past few years I have been attending a group that focuses on issues of money, or the lack of it. Actually, 'lack' is the key word here. I have done a lot of personal development work and discovered that I am hampered by low self-esteem and an expectation that I don't deserve anything. As a result of addressing those negative attitudes I have recently lived comfortably – some would say in style. But I suspect that at heart I still believe that poverty is my destiny.

So here I am, standing on the brink again. Ahead of me I can envisage only hardship, a path of deprivation beginning with a red electricity bill and ending with Jessy alone in a flat piled high with old newspapers, eating cat food.

❖

The first step on the road into the unknown is a meeting with the woman who is to be my pilot from here on in, oncologist Dr Suzy Cleator. 'Please call me Suzy,' she says shaking my hand and then waving me to a chair. I sit down. Honoria, the breast care nurse, sits down next to me. The breast care nurse is the patient's advocate, so she always sits on the patient side of the desk. Honoria gives me an indulgent smile. I've seen this smile stretched across quite a few faces already, sometimes accompanied by a little sideways tilt of the head. I suppose I will have to get used to it.

Suzy Cleator gets straight down to business. She refers to my notes.

'Your tumour was grade three. The histopathology showed that one of your lymph nodes had metastatic cancer and three others contained micrometastases. So now I am recommending that you have a course of chemotherapy. That should be followed by radiotherapy and then hormonal treatment. The chemotherapy I will be recommending will be Adriamycin and Cyclophosphamide. We call it AC. That will be every two weeks for four cycles. In between we will give you an injection to boost your white blood cells. Then you will have Taxol. We may give you that weekly. There have been some new studies showing that the Taxol is better tolerated if you have it in smaller doses but more frequently.'

Just to be sure I'm keeping up, Suzy sketches out her fiendish plan on a piece of paper:

```
AC 1      2 weeks
AC 2      2 weeks
AC 3      2 weeks
AC 4      2 weeks

T
T
T
T
T 8 weeks – weekly
T
T
T

1 month gap

Radiotherapy: 50 Gy / 25# – 5 weeks, Monday to Friday

Hormonal tablets
```

She goes on: 'Your tumour was positive for both oestrogen and progesterone receptors. That indicates a course of hormonal treatment. Because you haven't yet reached the menopause I will suggest that you take Tamoxifen. Tamoxifen works by blocking your body's uptake of oestrogen. Aromatase inhibitors, on the other hand, limit your production of oestrogen. We usually give those to women who are past the menopause.'

'Do you have any questions?'

I shake my head. Then, 'Actually, yes I do.' I fish in my handbag for a piece of paper that I prepared earlier. I begin to read it out aloud: 'What are the statistical outcomes for people with the same grade, type and size of tumour as mine: one, with no treatment but radiotherapy; two, with only chemotherapy; three, with chemotherapy and Tamoxifen? What do you think about genomic assays such as Oncotype or MammaPrint? When do we start? When does it end? Can I get vitamin C infusions? Should I have more physiotherapy? Do you think I should have counselling? What happens at Christmas? What about the swine flu?'

Suzy looks down at her notes. I can see that she is fighting the urge to clutch her head in her hands. 'I think I should see you again next week. Phone my secretary. Ask her for an extra-long appointment.'

You may have guessed that I've been busy on the internet, genning up on things like genomic assays (these are really expensive genetic tests that claim to predict the likelihood of recurrence of breast cancer) and vitamin C infusions (one of the more prominent alternative cancer treatments, advocated by Linus Pauling). I promised myself that I wouldn't go there. For several days I resisted the itch to click. Then I just looked up one little thing. And then I followed a link. Before I knew it I had forty or fifty web pages open on my laptop: Breast Cancer Care (useful); Wikipedia (information overload); DoctorYourself.com (DIY oncology); cancer chat rooms full of desperate cases (distressing and depressing); OncologyStat.com (incomprehensible). I read and read until my head began to throb. Every answer begat another two questions.

I'm in a life-threatening situation, though. What would you do? And that, really, is the nub of the problem. Because I fear that my life is at stake, I feel duty bound to follow every breadcrumb trail of information, to investigate every suggestion, no matter how loopy.

So I've been getting costly vitamin injections, re-stocking my pantry with mountains of organic brown rice and quinoa, juicing for Britain, and then this:

Jamie dropped me off for an appointment with Ingaborg Thoresen, a highly regarded biopath to the stars (no, I don't know what that is either).

There is a note stuck to the door 'Do not ring the bell. Wait in the shop next door'. It's a sunny morning so I take a seat on a wooden bench outside the shop and wait.

And wait.

Twenty minutes go by. I'm beginning to wonder if this is normal procedure for Ingaborg. I head into the shop and ask the lady behind the counter, 'Do you know Ingaborg Thoresen? I've been waiting outside for an appointment with her.'

'Did you ring the bell?' asks the shop lady.

'No, there's a note on the door saying not to ring the bell.'

'That's strange.' She looks blank.

'Well, I will just go outside and wait a bit more. If she happens to call you could you let her know I'm here?'

I sit on the bench for another five minutes. A strangling feeling of anxiety is rising in my throat. Jamie is coming to pick me up in just over half an hour and my consultation with Ingaborg hasn't even begun. I realise that I'm attaching great importance to seeing her. I'm desperate to find out if there are any alternatives to chemotherapy. I've read so much scary stuff on the internet about how chemo may blight my life for evermore. I really want to understand all my options.

Another five minutes passes. I get up with the intention of re-interrogating the shop lady. As I do so, Ingaborg's door bursts open and a rather cross-looking woman bustles out.

'You're very late,' she says to me and the whole street.

'I'm not,' I answer in confusion, 'there's a note on your door...'

'What note?' she looks at her own front door. 'That means don't ring the bell if you're early.' I bite my tongue and follow Ingaborg into her consultation room.

'So, what can I do for you?' She knows full well why I am here. I told her when I made the appointment.

'I've got breast cancer and I want to know what I can do,' I burst into tears. To be honest I think that I may have almost ascribed some kind of magical powers to Ingaborg, alternative high priestess of West London ladies who lunch.

Ingaborg looks taken aback. 'Well, clearly the first thing is to get you calm. Your stress levels are too high.' She shows me to a big reclining armchair. I sit back with my feet up. Ingaborg rotates a piece of machinery on an extending arm, positioning it in front of my head. Suddenly I feel as though I'm at the dentist's. She switches it on and a bluish light shines into my face. 'This is negative ionising light. You need to sit there until you calm down,' she commands and goes away.

Ten minutes later she's back. 'Are you calm yet?'

'I think so.'

'No, you're not.'

I sip water and stare into the light. My shoulders drop a little more but I can't help reflecting that I would feel a lot more relaxed were I at home on the couch watching repeats of *The Wire* on the iPlayer.

'We won't have time for a consultation today,' says Ingaborg. 'You have to come back another time.'

I try to mask my disappointment. 'Oh, well, shall we make an appointment now?'

'No. I will call you.'

The doorbell rings. It's Jamie. He was never one for reading signs. Ingaborg makes it plain that she is too busy to show me out.

And that was the last I ever heard from Ingaborg Thoresen.

❖

'Please come in, Jessica.'

Suzy Cleator looks me in the eye and gives me a warm smile. She is boyishly slim and dressed in a stylish blue jersey dress with a long drapey pleat down the front. I'm pleased that Suzy doesn't favour suits. It makes her seem more human and approachable. Nurse Honoria takes a seat next to me. 'Now, I know we have a lot to get through today,' says Suzy. Thus begins Jessy's education in the dark arts of oncology.

She explains again that I will be having two types of chemotherapy: Adriamycin and Cyclophosphamide (AC) followed by Taxol, the first being fortnightly and the second being weekly. She gets out a calendar so that we can have a look at the schedule.

'Do you have any major commitments coming up?' she says. 'Any weddings or anything like that?'

'Well, I have booked to go to a convention in Barcelona in August for a week with my friends.' My mum will also be over from Australia, visiting my sister in Moscow. Mum, Miranda and Eloise had planned to meet me in Barcelona so we could all have a few days together before my convention begins.

Suzy consults the calendar. 'If we start your chemo next Friday, then you will have finished the AC phase and had a few days to recover before you go. You can go to Barcelona for a week then come back and start the Taxol.'

So that's not a problem. But hang on. I've got so many unanswered questions. The main ones being: *Do I really need to have chemotherapy and if I do decide to have it, will it work?*

Suzy produces a print-out. 'We just can't tell you what your personal outcome will be. But we can look at the overall picture of outcomes for people with similar circumstances to yours. This is a print-out from a big American database of breast cancer statistics.'

We look at the papers together. Suzy interprets the graphs and figures. I can see that these are the statistics for patients who are forty-seven years old, in perfect health, with a grade three oestrogen-positive tumour between 1.1 and 2.0 centimetres in size (as my tumour turned out to be, not 31 millimetres after all) and with one to three lymph nodes found to be positive for cancer. So in other words, patients just like me. There are two sheets; the first shows the statistics for relapse, the second for mortality.

With no treatment whatsoever, after ten years the picture looks like this:

46.6 per cent of people are alive and free of cancer.

51.6 per cent have relapsed.

29.8 per cent have died of cancer.

1.8 per cent have died of other causes.

With chemotherapy and hormonal therapy, this is the picture after ten years:

81.6 per cent are alive and free of cancer.

16.6 per cent have relapsed.

11.6 per cent have died of cancer.

1.8 per cent have died of other causes.

There are variations in between – outcomes for those who have had only one or other of the treatments. But the headline figure that I am interested in is 'alive and free of cancer after ten years'. That's the gang I intend to be in.

'So you see,' says Suzy, 'the likelihood of your being alive and free of cancer after ten years is 34.8 per cent higher if you have the combined therapy.'

I have to say, it is pretty compelling.

'So . . .?'

I chew my lip. My friend Christobel's mum was diagnosed with cancer last year. The hospital gave her chemotherapy but she died anyway. In Christobel's opinion the chemo only served to make her mother's last weeks of life a misery. My cousin Gaby declined chemotherapy but the cancer she had was advanced and very widespread; even her doctors didn't really think chemo would help.

Many of my friends are pressuring me to have the chemo. Foremost amongst them is Nick. But they're not the ones who will be having it. The final say has to be mine alone.

If you'd asked me a year ago if I would have chemotherapy, my answer would have been a definite 'no'. But that would have been before I was actually diagnosed with cancer.

I've always been open to alternative therapies. The internet abounds with stories of people who have demurred chemo and healed themselves with diet, exercise, Gerson therapy and suchlike. On the other hand, I have also benefited hugely in the past from the wisdom and expertise of conventional doctors and hospitals. Quite simply, I was paralysed and they saved my life. I'm not really swayed by theories that the medical profession is intolerant of any treatment that does not exist primarily for the enrichment of drug companies. And yet. And yet . . .

There is so much conflicting information, all of it thoroughly convincing. It doesn't help that the conventional and alternative camps are so mutually antagonistic. Who does one trust? Will the chemo work? *There are no guarantees, only statistics.* Do I even need it? We can't tell you that. I don't see how I am meant to make a logical decision based on facts when even those who have studied the matter for years seem to have no definitive answers. To sum up: I'm facing the most difficult decision of my life.

I look at the statistics charts again, trying to digest the information. What it really comes down to is this: if I decline the chemo and then in ten years' time I find myself dying of cancer, will I feel comfortable that I made the right choice?

'Yes. I'll go ahead with it.'

'I think that's wise.'

Suzy fills in a form. 'AC chemotherapy can damage the heart. Before you come on Friday you need to go for an echocardiograph so that we can see how healthy your heart is.'

Already I'm reconsidering my decision. 'And what about other side effects?' I've been wandering around on the internet so now my head is full of all the terrifying worst-case scenarios.

'The side effects really vary from person to person. It helps that you're strong and healthy to start off with. We will give you drugs to help reduce the nausea. Chemotherapy lowers your immune function, so you'll also have an injection to boost your white blood cell count. How the chemo works is it destroys fast-dividing cells. Cancer cells are fast dividing but so are the cells that make up the mucosal membranes: the linings of your mouth, throat and nose. So you may develop ulcers in those areas. We will be monitoring you all the time, taking your blood counts and so on.'

'But can I do anything to boost my immune system? Can I take supplements? Should I go on a macrobiotic diet?'

'Please don't take any supplements without clearing it with me. Some of them can interfere with the effectiveness of the chemotherapy. As for food, there's no scientific evidence base to prove the efficacy of macrobiotics, but if you want to do it then that's up to you. My advice would be to eat healthily.'

Suzy regards me for a moment. 'I can see that you take a lot of pride in your hair.'

'Yes,' I agree, nodding so that long, luxurious waves of auburn bob all around my head.

'We can give you the cool cap.'

'What's that?'

'It's a device that chills your head whilst you're having the chemo. The idea is that the cooling restricts blood flow, thereby reducing the amount of chemicals that reach your scalp.'

'Does it work?'

'Sometimes.' She pauses. 'But I suggest that you get your hair cut. The weight of your long hair can be enough to pull it out by the roots.'

Honoria detects my panic and confusion. 'Don't worry too much about anything,' she says. 'And you don't have to stress yourself out with macrobiotic food. Eat your veggies but have a cream cake and a glass of wine if you want to.'

I gaze at Honoria. I can't help thinking that maybe she's been enjoying a few cream cakes and glasses of wine herself. Her jacket is positively straining at the buttons. I look back at Suzy. And then it hits me: Suzy's drapey smock dress; Honoria's rotund figure – they're both pregnant! And I haven't had the courage to ask the question that has been waking me up at nights with a feeling that I'm being suffocated: will chemotherapy trigger the menopause?

❖

I'm back on the internet. Possible side effects of chemotherapy: tiredness; nausea; mouth, throat and vaginal ulcers . . . ulcers! In my vagina! I'm too horrified to even read about that so I swiftly scroll on . . . numbness; constipation; diarrhoea; infections; liver failure; heart damage; hair loss . . .

Full of fear, I relay the gloomy outlook to my cousin Ben.

Ben tries to reassure me: 'It's probably no worse than going on a three-day bender,' he says.

❖

I'm always happy to hear the soft burring call of Skype. It signifies that I'm about to see one of the faces I love.

It's Nick, with his mile-wide smile.

'Hey darlin', how did it go with Doctor Cleator?'

Nick has been incredibly tolerant in the face of my indecision about treatment. From his point of view, contemplating alternative therapies is dangerous lunacy. A couple of weeks ago I started having vitamin C infusions administered by a Dr

Schumacher. Nick's opinion is that Dr Schumacher is a nut job. And he may be right: she is certainly not an oncologist. But what harm can it do, apart from driving me into debt? He has cajoled and argued; I have stood firm in my determination to evaluate every alternative. I understand Nick's frustration. It's a frustration born of love: he's only just got me – he doesn't want to lose me. In Nick's mind there is no question. *Have the chemo!*

If our positions were reversed I know I would feel the same way that he does. And I'm certain that I would be far more relentless in making my case.

'I'm going to have the chemo,' I tell him now. Nick's smile widens just a tiny bit more.

❖

Brrrr – brrrr – brrrr – : This time it's Mum. I tell her of my decision. Mum has kept her own counsel throughout. She has helped me to comb and gather my thoughts on a dump truck full of conflicting information about short- and long-term side effects of chemo versus the efficacy of selenium, apricot kernels and mistletoe. She has listened to the saga of Ingaborg Thoresen and the negative ionising light machine. Mum has been a solid sounding-board and has not felt it necessary to tell me what she thinks I should do. I explain the statistics for survival and relapse.

'The thing is, Mum, I'd still like to consider complementary therapies. I imagine that the healthier I am, the better my chances will be of becoming one of the alive and cancer free statistics.'

'Okay, my darling. Why don't you have a consultation with Michael Thomsen?'

Michael Thomsen is a naturopath and medical herbalist. Mum has known him for decades and holds him in high regard. Originally from Denmark, Michael now practises in Hobart, Tasmania.

'Mum, I know you mean well but it's not very practical is it?'

Wily old Mum has thought about that. Before long I'm having a face-to-face consultation with Michael on Skype. I tell him about the treatment that Suzy Cleator is recommending and read him my histopathology report. To my surprise, Michael knows a great deal about breast cancer and the particular chemo regime that I am about to undergo. First of all he talks me through my diet. I tell him all about my brown rice and vegetables kick.

'That all sounds positive but do make sure that you get enough protein.' Michael also suggests that I avoid processed food as much as possible. Next he explains the potential damaging side effects of the chemo. I'm becoming all too familiar with these.

'But there are a lot of things we can give you to support you through it.' He draws up a long list of supplements designed to strengthen my liver, heart and general immune function. One of them is a Japanese mushroom extract, something that I have never heard of.

'Will all this really work? My oncologist has told me not to take any supplements. And, more to the point, how much will it cost?'

I am not anti complementary therapies. Not at all. I'm just skeptical about everything. Michael isn't fazed by what could be interpreted as my questioning of his knowledge and motives.

'I will email you peer-reviewed studies about everything that I'm recommending. I suggest that you show them to your oncologist. And don't worry about the cost. Your mum has agreed to pay for everything.'

Soon my email pings. Michael has sent me a stack of scientific papers. I've been up all night reading them. It's pretty impressive stuff.

Things I wish I'd known before #5
How to evaluate complementary therapies

When serious illness strikes, we search for cures. It's a perfectly sane reaction to a life-threatening situation. In fact, it may feel almost irresponsible not to do so. Unfortunately there are some people ready and willing to exploit our fear and desperation, whether it be for profit or personal aggrandisement. Others have more philanthropic motives but may be strongly influenced by their own personal belief system.

Then we must contend with our friends – and their friends. Everybody knows somebody whose aunty's husband's cousin was 'cured' by eating apricot pips or drinking twig tea. Try not to get irritable with them. It's their way of letting you know that they don't want you to die.

The problem is that there is just *so much* information and advice swirling around on the internet. There are websites devoted to promoting the healing properties of flax oil, herbal extracts, mistletoe and bicarbonate of soda. And there are websites that are vehement in their damnation of all complementary therapies without exception.

For the patient, this situation is not helped by the fact that the conventional and complementary professions can be quite mutually antagonistic. Some medical doctors regard all complementary therapists as loony crackpots whilst many in the alternative camp look upon conventional doctors as no better than lazy dupes of the venal drug companies.

There is a problem at the heart of this debate: allopathic (conventional) medicine tends to focus on treating a specific illness and curing its symptoms. Holistic medicine, as the name suggests, tends to focus on the whole organism (that's you) and preventing illness.

To me it seems axiomatic that anything that contributes to our health and well-being, for example, eating nourishing food, learning relaxation techniques, gentle exercise and hands-on treatments like massage and shiatsu, can only be positive. Even if the benefits have not been scientifically proven (and in many instances they have) these practices feel empowering and they certainly will do no harm.

There are a growing number of doctors who are beginning to practise what is known as 'integrative medicine' where the best aspects of conventional and complementary approaches are combined, for the ultimate benefit of the patient. Unfortunately, their numbers are growing far too slowly.

There is a difference between 'complementary' and 'alternative' therapies. Complementary therapies are used alongside conventional medicine to help us to remain as fit and healthy as possible whilst we are undergoing what can be extremely violent and damaging treatment (for example, surgery or chemotherapy). Alternative therapies are given *instead of* conventional treatment.

If you are considering complementary or alternative treatment, ask yourself these questions:

- Have there been any peer-reviewed studies that demonstrate the efficacy of the therapy being recommended? If so, discuss these with your oncologist.
- Is the practitioner able to answer detailed questions about the therapy in an informative manner? How, exactly does it work? What are the mechanisms? Can you analyse the evidence? Do they have case studies? What are the potential dangers and side effects?
- Is the therapy being presented to you as a 'miracle cure'? This may be hard to accept but, when it comes to cancer, there are no magic bullets.
- Is the therapy being presented as an alternative to chemotherapy and radiotherapy or as a helpful adjunct to conventional therapies?
- Is the therapy being sold to you in a manner that seems vaguely bullying or blackmailing? For example: the practitioner tells you about patients who have died after stopping the recommended therapy.
- Is the therapy vastly expensive?
- Will you find following the regime punitive and stressful?
- Does the practitioner belong to a recognised professional body?
- Does the practitioner have a hostile attitude towards the medical profession?
- Has the practitioner been disbarred from the medical profession?

Use your common sense. If the practitioner seems mental give them a wide berth.

And one last thing: just because a substance is herbal in origin doesn't necessarily mean that it is benign. Vitamins, minerals and herbs may interact adversely with other drugs. Please don't take any kind of supplement without discussing it with your oncologist.

JULY

As I opened my front door this morning the key sheared off in the lock. Just tore away as if it were made of paper. Luckily the snib had released before the key snapped so at least I could get into my flat. But what a strange occurrence. Is the universe trying to tell me something?

I still haven't had my hair cut, as Suzy Cleator advised. I can't put it off any longer. Chemotherapy starts tomorrow.

'Hello, Kell Skott Salon, this is Jacqueline.'

'Oh, um, hi, Jacquie. This is Jessica Jones.'

'Hi, Jess, how are you?'

'I'm fine. Well, um, I've got breast cancer and I'm starting chemotherapy tomorrow and I have to have my hair cut. Can Kell do it today?'

There's a silence whilst the information percolates.

'Can you hold on a minute?' Then, a minute later: 'Kell is booked up all day but he will stay late for you. Can you come at eight p.m.?'

I call Pete, who offers to come over and replace the front door lock. Next I call Cindy and ask her to come to the salon with me. I don't think I have ever before felt in need of a friend to hold my hand at the hairdresser's.

Oh! I get it. Today is my day for losing locks.

❖

This morning I had an echo scan to look at my heart. 'Strong as an ox' was the doctor's verdict. 'Full of love' was mine.

Now I climb the sweeping staircase of the Harley Street Clinic and open the door to the chemotherapy unit. Sunshine floods through tall sash windows. The high white ceiling is decorated with elegant mouldings. A dozen or so wine-red lazy-boy recliners are spaced around the room. Nurses sit behind a high desk on one side.

I approach and give my name. A dark-haired nurse looks up. I guess she's the ward sister. Her uniform is a deeper shade of blue than all the other nurses.

'Hi, I'm Lottie,' she says in an Australian accent. Immediately I feel confidence in her. 'I'm going to make up your prescription then I'm going to explain everything to you. Just go and sit in one of the armchairs.'

A blonde nurse sits down by my chair. 'Hello, I'm Bess. I'm just going to take a blood test. Which side did you have the surgery?'

'The left.'

'Okay, so from now on whenever you have a needle of any kind it will be in your right arm. That's to avoid lymphedoema.' Lymphedoema, in case you're wondering, is a fat, puffy arm. It is not a life-threatening condition but I would imagine it might rather bugger up one's hopes of ever wearing strapless dresses again. I certainly do not want it. 'We're going to test your blood before each session to make sure that your white cell count is high enough for you to have the chemo.'

I turn my head away. A moment later Bess is taping down the cannula that she's inserted into a vein in my forearm. I haven't felt a thing.

'Get yourself a cup of tea while we wait for the results,' she says.

'Where are you from, Bess?'

'Brisbane.'

Twenty minutes later Lottie comes over carrying a tray full of drip bags and a sheaf of papers. She hangs up all the bags on one of those T-stand things on wheels, then pulls up a stool and the explaining commences. She tells me that the bags contain different drugs: one is an anti-sickness drug and one is an antihistamine in case I have an allergic reaction.

'The antihistamine will make you drowsy,' she says. 'You might fall asleep.'

The other bags contain various flushes. I nod and pretend that I'm taking it all in, just like the first day of school.

'Then which one is the chemo?' I say.

'You're having AC. That will be administered separately.' Lottie consults her notes. 'I see that Dr Cleator had also asked that you have the cool cap.'

'Cool cap', I shortly discover, is a highly misleading euphemism. This device, Lottie explains, is designed to freeze one's head to minus 6 degrees Celsius. It's a kind of a helmet with tubes growing out of it. The tubes are attached to a refrigeration unit. Lottie hands me a bottle of hair conditioner.

'Go into the bathroom and put this on all over your head,' she instructs. 'Use lots.'

I come back with my hair all gooey and reeking of synthetic strawberries.

'The conditioner will protect your scalp from being burned by the cold,' Lottie says before placing the helmet on my oleaginous bonce and securing the chin strap. Next she connects the tubes to the main frame. The machine hums softly as it gets into gear and then *wham!* It's as though I have suddenly been smacked around the head with a baseball bat. And again. And again. Ten thousand ice-cream headaches all come at once. I wince. Lottie hands me a couple of paracetamols.

'How long do I have to keep this on?'

'Four hours – the pain may ease off a little.'

Lottie consults the ID tag on my wrist: 'Name, date of birth.' I reel off the info. Lottie nods approvingly as though I've done exceptionally well in a maths test. She hooks up the first drip to the cannula. My chemotherapy has begun.

The ice hat continues to beat at my brain, making reading impossible. In any case, it is quite difficult to put one's spectacles on when wearing a tight-fitting helmet full of slimy pink hair conditioner.

My teeth begin to chatter. Lottie fetches me a hospital blanket and an electric heat pad to keep me warm. I snuggle up and try to doze but soon an alarm is going off. The first bag of medication has finished. Lottie hooks up the next one. Then a lady with a menu appears: 'Would you like some lunch?' I order soup, an omelette, fruit salad and a pot of peppermint tea. If I can't read or sleep, I may as well get busy eating.

A white-coated therapist arrives.

'Hello, Jessica, I'm Sandra. Would you like to have reflexology treatments during your chemo?' *Yes please.*

The next alarm goes off. Now it's time for the antihistamine. As it drips into my vein I yawn and my eyelids begin to flutter.

Raucous laughter shreds my veil of drowsiness. I crank open an eye to find Antony and Iris standing over my armchair. Iris regards my lounging form, wrapped in a blanket with socks protruding and this mad contraption on my head.

'Hmm, very *Grey Gardens*,' is her verdict.

My friends pull up chairs, help themselves to cups of tea from the hot drinks machine and get busy befriending all the nurses and generally getting in everybody's hair. Lunch arrives. The catering lady strives valiantly to pile it all onto the tiny side table along with the magazines, the iPhone and the box of tissues. The alarm goes off and Lottie changes the drips again.

Relaxing, chemotherapy is not.

After the next drip has run through Lottie returns. But this time she is wearing a plastic apron, gloves, face mask and goggles.

'Now we're going to start your AC,' she says, before pulling the mask up. She sets down a slim plastic tray in which lies a large syringe of glowing ruby-red liquid. That plastic tray, the syringe and the red chemical combine to create a small tableau, a still-life snapshot that, to me, conveys a shuddering sense of quiet menace.

❖

My cousin Gaby had/has (I'm not sure of the correct tense in this case) a good friend, Marianne. Marianne's mother and sister both died from cancer. Marianne nursed each of them in turn. When Gaby fell ill, Marianne flew from America to nurse her too. Marianne was with Gaby on the day she died.

I saw Marianne again at Gaby's memorial service only six weeks ago. I was wearing a vintage 1970s pendant in the shape of an owl. Marianne admired the pendant: 'That's great. My grandmother used to wear jewellery like that. She left me some pieces in her will.'

This morning a package arrived from the USA. Inside were two of Marianne's grandmother's pendants, one in the shape of an owl and the other in the shape of a tortoise.

After opening the door to the postman, then trying on my new jewellery, I climbed back into bed. As I did so I noticed that my white pillowcase was shimmering. The shimmering was caused by a fine gauze of red hairs spread across the indentation where my head had been, all catching the morning light.

❖

Every day I'm finding more and more strands of hair in my bed. I'm trying to avoid hair combing or washing, as advised by Honoria. She suggested that I buy one of those very soft baby's brushes but I haven't got around to it yet. What I have ordered is a soft, stretchy cotton cap to sleep in. The idea behind it is that the cap will prevent my hair from pulling out as I toss and turn in my sleep. I wish it would hurry up and arrive. Waking up every morning with a giant hairball nesting on my pillow is quite distressing.

On the plus side, I don't look bald, or even thinning. Apparently we have at least 100,000 hairs on our heads and an awful lot of them have to fall out before anyone notices.

Already two weeks have gone by. It's time for my second chemotherapy. Jamie rolls up in his car at twelve-thirty on the dot. At the age of forty – or is it thirty-two, who can tell? – Jamie has recently passed his driving test. He has generously offered to drive me to and from all my chemo appointments. Jamie's driving skills are still developing. I don't mind. Given the choice, I would choose death in a dramatic pile-up on the Westway over being slowly eaten by a malignant tumour any day of the week. I'm just grateful that I don't have to drive myself. The fewer things I have to think about, the better. If I simply keep my eyes tightly closed I can relax and enjoy the ride.

Lottie is not attending to me today. I surmise that she's the boss, so she does the induction day and then palms you off onto one of the other nurses. A Canadian nurse by the name of Eleanor is taking care of me. After I've slathered my hair with strawberry conditioner she straps on the ice hat. I grip the arms of my chair as the head pounding begins. As the session progresses I begin to develop the distinct impression that Eleanor understands the term 'taking care of' more in the Tony Soprano sense than the Florence Nightingale sense. She is less than enthusiastic about bringing me paracetamols and heat pads and generally waiting on me hand and foot.

Honoria and Suzy Cleator come to visit. 'How are you feeling?' they ask.

'Okay. Scared. I don't know. The nights are difficult. I've been crying a lot.'

'Maybe some Valium would help?' suggests Honoria.

'Maybe not,' interjects Suzy with ever-so-slightly pursed lips. 'But I would suggest that you try some anti-anxiety medication.' She writes the name of a drug on a piece of paper and hands it to me. 'Some medications are contraindicated with breast cancer, but this one should be fine. Maybe you could ask your GP for a prescription.'

Another drug? Instinctively I rebel.

'Thanks,' I say, 'I will think about it.'

When it comes time for the AC chemo to be injected Eleanor turns up wearing almost a full tox suit: gloves; mask; goggles; hat; apron and arm covers. At least she has to sit down for this bit so I get a chance to chat to her.

'Why the body armour?' I ask.

'It's for my protection. I want to have a baby one day, you know.'

Now I feel not simply like a pesky patient but that somehow my illness, my treatment and my very presence are repellent to her. I remember how very s-l-o-w-l-y Lottie administered the raspberry-red AC. It seems to me that Eleanor is pushing it through rather more quickly. Maybe it's just her impatient demeanour that is giving me that impression. Nevertheless, it is the impression that I am getting and it makes me feel uneasy.

❖

My head was so itchy this morning I decided to wash my hair. I lathered it up, and as I rinsed it through, it started to come away in big clumps. So there I was, sitting naked in the bath with half my hair in my hands, like a mop.

Nothing anyone said could have prepared me for that.

I'm meeting Iris at the Electric Cinema on Portobello Road. I arrive a bit early and notice that Appletree is open. This shop is a treasure trove of quirky and inexpensive dresses, bags, belts, brollies and hats. I slip in to see if they have any affordably fabulous headgear. They do – lovely crocheted cotton cloches for £12 each. I take three: one in olive green, one in cornflower blue and one in sunflower yellow.

Iris catches me coming out of the shop. In my mind it's as though I've been spotted sneaking out of the back entrance of the clap clinic. I confess to her about this morning's big hair fall-out. For some reason it feels like a horrible secret. But why? I mean I've already received the shocking news that I have cancer. I've undergone major surgery. I'm managing to present myself at the hospital and allow the nurses to pump heinous poisons into my veins. I'm coping with taking handfuls of pills three times a day. I'm putting up with the nausea and feeling as if someone has just poured a pint of kerosene down my throat. But losing my hair seems to be the most traumatic experience of them all. Am I really so shallow?

Iris looks at me with genuine sympathy. 'That's just crap,' she says.

The next day I dare to have a proper look in the mirror. My hair is awful. I look like I've just escaped from Abu Ghraib prison. It will all have to go now. I call my hairdresser.

'This is Kell Skott Salon. We are closed for essential maintenance work today. The salon will re-open tomorrow. Please leave a message.'

The one day of my life that I have a genuine hairdressing emergency turns out to be the one day of the year that my hairdresser's has a refit. Still, I leave a message.

If you don't have a good relationship with your hairdresser my advice to you is: develop one – fast. Otherwise one day your hair may fall out and you'll find yourself crying in Sainsbury's car park and you'll be on your own, baby. Thank God that didn't happen to me.

As I'm brushing away the tears and stowing the groceries in the boot of my car, the phone rings. It's Kell.

'I got your message on the answerphone. Can you come in right away?'

I fire up the car and zip straight round to Golborne Road at top speed. Kell gets me a cup of mint tea and one of Jacquie's world-famous home-made chocolate brownies to soothe my nerves.

'Just shave it all off', I instruct him. But Kell has other ideas. Using only scissors and a comb he begins to sculpt this monstrous mess. He clips it all to about 2 centimetres long. It's more baldy on the left-hand side than it is on the right. He manipulates the hair so that it is all lying flat and forward and sideways. Sort of a high-art comb-over. He feathers the front into a little fringe. Watching him work is like watching a magician intently conjuring a silk purse from a sow's ear. When he's finished it looks sort of like Audrey Tautou 2001 meets Mary Quant 1966. Only shorter than either of them. It's just so cute.

I want to take a moment here to praise my hairdresser. Today has been, without doubt, the low point of my life as far as how unattractive I feel. Despite that, Kell made me look great. He opened up his salon especially to come to my aid. He didn't charge me a penny for doing it. In my career I've had the displeasure of the acquaintance of prima-donna hairdressers who wouldn't deign to pass one a hairpin, let alone deal with one when half one's hair has fallen out. I mean it can't be good for business can it? Having a bald woman walk out of your salon?

❖

As I wait for Nick to answer the Skype my heart is turning over. *Brr – brr – brr.* For the first time he is going to be confronted with the graphic reality of chemotherapy.

'Hello honey,' I rush in with a false brightness, 'I've had my hair cut. What do you think?'

Then I fall quiet and turn my head this way and that so Nick can inspect it from all angles.

'Oh, baby,' says Nick; his voice catches, 'you look so beautiful.'

❖

Today I have an appointment with Dr Ducker, my GP. I want to talk to her about Suzy Cleator's suggestion of anti-anxiety medication, which I'd felt hesitant about. I wondered about side effects. I was concerned about how I would come off the pills when this would all be over. And wasn't I taking enough drugs and pills already? Following the big hair fall-out I began to revise my position. I explain myself to Dr Ducker now: 'Well, you see, I'm having the chemo and I don't know what I'm going to do about money and I feel sick, I can't sleep, and Dr Cleator suggested anti-depressants but I don't know if I should take them, but most of my hair fell out on Sunday and it was such a shock, what do you think I should do?'

'Yeeees,' she says. 'Why don't you try some anti-anxiety medication? I'll give you the lowest dose.'

My shoulders relax. 'And you're going to need a wig,' she adds.

My shoulders shoot up towards my ears again. 'But how do I get one?' I plead.

'I don't know but I will find out,' she says in a soothing tone. Now that's the kind of practical help I need.

❖

In past times of trouble I have found it a useful strategy to write a gratitude list. Just five things but they must be a different five things each morning. It's amazing what a turnaround in one's perspective this simple strategy can effect in just seven days. Only it doesn't seem to be working at the moment. 'I'm grateful for the sky', and 'I'm grateful that I don't have cancer in the other breast'; 'I'm grateful that we live in a land where there is social security, even if they make it so bizarrely complicated that one might think that they're hoping that one might die before they send one any money.' Oh do bugger off.

But I've come up with a more pragmatic approach that may help; 'Things I Got for Free Today':

A free haircut

Free consultation with my GP

Free prescriptions

A free jar of body lotion

Free shiatsu treatment

A free lift to the doctor's

2 free iPhone apps

still to come . . .

free dinner at Jamie's place

What an abundant world!

It's Jamie's birthday. It's my first time going out with almost no hair. The trick to working the Chemo Chic look is to wear the hugest, most glittering earrings and the reddest lipstick one can get hold of.

I don't mind showing my friends my new coiffure but I'm hesitant to let the neighbours see me like this. What's that all about? Well may you ask. I'm not sure I know. Am I ashamed? Or do I not want my neighbours to pity me? Am I afraid of appearing weak? I can't put my finger on it but I think you might feel the same way in this situation. As I walk out the door I grab one of the new crocheted cloches.

Jamie comes to pick me up. He's been so generous with all the lifts to and fro. Back round at Mayhem Mansions in Marylebone the customary bedlam is in progress. The two chihuahuas – Iris's Chilli and Jamie's Hugo – refuse me entry with frenzied yapping. Valentina the Russian neighbour wiggles about in tight Lycra, batting her eyelids and calling everybody 'Dahlink'. Muttiah, recently sprung from the nut house, swans in and out of the kitchen dressed in a sari. Sheldon arrives looking very Gonzo in his sports shirt and flat cap.

I remove my hat and sit back to gauge the effect. 'Oh, it looks really cute,' they say, and 'Lovely' and so on.

About ten minutes later I join Iris on the balcony. 'I think I'm pleased with it,' I say, 'only I'm worried that it's quite bald on the crown.'

'It doesn't matter,' she replies, 'you're so tall nobody can see it.'

That's it! I jam the hat back on.

AUGUST

I love food. I don't drink. I don't take drugs. I don't smoke. Can't you just leave me alone and let me enjoy a kebab?

Hell, no. Even if the anti-cancer diet permitted such déclassé fare as kebabs, there's no point. Everything tastes revolting: metallic yet cotton-woolly at the same time. Possibly like steel wool? Yes, that would be it. Everything tastes like a rusty old bit of steel wool that has been sitting in the bottom of a greasy saucepan for a day or two.

❖

Lately I've been staying in too much. Not just in my flat but in my bathroom. I sit on the edge of the bath amidst a phalanx of mirrors. I inspect my head from every angle. I ponder my forehead. Is it possible to arrange the few short hairs into a Joan-of-Arc-style fringe? I examine the back. Is my crown one giant bald spot or is it just the angle of the light? Would it be less apparent if my hair were a different colour?

Mostly, though, I just stare at myself in much the same way that a cat regards its own reflection. That is to say, with an attitude of wary puzzlement. I look away and then back, trying to catch myself unawares. My mind won't seem to come to terms with my new appearance. That thing looks strangely familiar but what is it? Do I look like a baby? An old man? David Bowie? ET?

I consider the notion of getting dressed and going out into the street just as I am. But the thought of it makes me feel like I've just woken up from one of those dreams where I'm naked on a crowded tube train. It's too confronting.

❖

The phone is ringing. Shivers of nausea course through my stomach. My brain pulsates with a force 10 Texas-chainsaw-massacre headache; my chest and shoulders heave. Every muscle groans as my eyes adjust to the light.

I'm experiencing this extra-sized misery because I caught a cold. On Sunday afternoon my glands came up. By Monday morning I knew things were going to get rough. I went to see the available GP du jour. She issued me with prescriptions for penicillin and Tamiflu then sent me packing with instructions to consult my oncologists before taking either of them and, 'Probably best to stay indoors for the next five days, just in case it is swine flu.'

Suzy Cleator is on holiday. Several hours later I spoke to a very jovial Doctor Leslie who is covering for Suzy. He advised me not to take either drug.

Then in the night a battalion of trolls visited with jackhammers to pound my head, hot coals to wrack my shoulders, and a bucket of green-grey phlegmy oysters to coat my lungs.

The next morning Dr Leslie suggested that I start in on the penicillin. 'If you're no better tomorrow we'll get you into hospital,' he said. So here I am in bed, nearly unconscious and on the verge of being admitted to hospital with a cold. This is my first experience of what a compromised immune system really means. And the phone is still ringing . . .

'Hello, this is Janine from the surgical appliance department at St Mary's. I have a letter from your GP requesting a wig for you.' Somehow I can tell that Janine is not pleased to have received this letter. 'You are not a patient at this hospital.'

'No,' I agree.

'Where are you having your chemotherapy?' demands Janine.

'At the Harley Street Clinic,' I reply warily.

'Well, we won't be able to deal with them,' states Janine flatly.

'Well, that's okay, I don't want you to deal with them, I want you to deal with me. I'm the one who needs a wig,' I say, trying to sound brightly optimistic.

'But you're not a patient at this hospital.'

'No.'

'Then you should ask the Harley Street Clinic for a wig.' *Case closed*, she implies, but quick as a flash I rejoin.

'I did – and they suggested that I contact you.'

She parries: 'Won't your private health insurers give you a wig?'

'No.'

'Oh, so they don't provide total care?' crows Janine in triumph. I crumple. 'I suppose not, but I'm still entitled to a wig.'

'But you're not a patient at this hospital.'

'But St Mary's is my local hospital and I am entitled to a wig – and, what's more, I need a wig because I hardly have any hair.' I add this just to give her the full picture, in case she thinks that I am some random transvestite chancer trying to build a free wig collection courtesy of the NHS.

Janine pauses, no doubt considering the futility of the situation. 'I'm going on holiday for two weeks,' she says finally. 'I'll do my best but I don't see how this can possibly be sorted out before then.'

❖

Time passes in a delirious, underwater-movie kind of way. It's day three in the bed. The phone is ringing . . .

'Hello, this is Janine from the surgical appliances department at St Mary's.'

I detect a change in Janine's demeanour. Not exactly kindly, but 'conciliatory' may be the word to sum it up.

'I've sorted everything out. I'm going to send you a voucher for a wig. Take it to the wig shop in Craven Street. You can have whatever colour you like. It won't be human hair because your hair is going to grow back. I'm sending the voucher by first-class post. You might not get it today but you should get it tomorrow.'

I'm speechless with gratitude. Thank you, thank you, Janine, or Janine's twin sister, or whoever you are.

I call Iris pronto. She is overjoyed at the prospect. 'Get out of bed and get a cab and let's get down there NOW,' she cries. I hang up and sink back into delirium.

❖

It's been four days since Janine promised to send the wig voucher.

From: Iris
Subject: Wigless

I take it the voucher never came today?

From: Jessica
Subject: Re: Wigless

No. But no post at all so I'm still hopeful. There have been some postal strikes around London.

From: Iris
Subject: Re: Wigless

I got a stack of mail actually. But some parts of outer London have been affected by the strike.

From: Jessica
Subject: Re: Wigless

Portobello Road is NOT outer London.

From: Iris
Subject: Re: Wigless

It'll come tomorrow or Monday it probably has to sit in a post room for a day or two before it even leaves the hospital.

From: Jessica
Subject: Re: Wigless

Yes there's probably a troll who collects it from surgical supplies in cupboard-under-the-stairs and trudges it through the Gothic labyrinth to some post room in the bowels of St Mary's where they wait for a flight of owls to deliver the magic envelopes.

❖

During the last week, in which I've been confined to my flat, Skype has been my lifeline. I still can't believe that somebody invented a way for me to talk face to face with people on another continent, show them things and see what they're up to. And then they gave it to the world for free. Nick and I Skype one another every day; often twice a day. When I wake up at four a.m. feeling tearful and afraid, it's one in the afternoon in Sydney. I Skype my honey and he gives me a healing dose of love and laughter. What I like best is simply having him there on the screen. Oftentimes we're on Skype and just going about our business. I take the laptop into the kitchen and we chat away whilst I prepare my breakfast. Nick comes with me into the bathroom whilst I put my make-up on. Then we settle down on our respective couches in front of our respective television sets and watch the cricket together.

❖

I've completed chemotherapy number four – the last of the AC phase. Afterwards Jamie picked me up from Harley Street with instructions to drive at top speed to Ottolenghi for rose and vanilla cupcake supplies. Then we drove straight home and ate them all before I started gagging.

The nausea began mildly in the car but now it is becoming gross. I've already taken three different anti-sickness medications.

I'm hungry but I can't bear to eat anything more substantial than a grape. I feel dizzy. I have a headache.

I made a radical decision earlier today – to not wear the ice hat. My appointment with Dr Cleator wasn't until after the chemo session so I couldn't discuss it with her beforehand. I talked it over with the nurses, weighing up the pros and cons: It is so painful. It makes the chemotherapy session two hours longer than it might otherwise be. It looks ridiculous. And two-thirds of my hair has fallen out anyway.

On the other hand, there is *some* hair clinging to my cranium. Maybe that is worth trying to save? And I still have most of my eyebrows and eyelashes; I definitely want to keep those.

The nurses told me that, in order to administer the ice hat, they would have to apply barriers of wadding to the most moth-eaten-baldy patches on my head. That is done to avoid scalp burns. They also explained that the ice hat would do nothing to save my brows and lashes. Well, that was the clincher. Feeling comfortable with my decision, I settled hatless into my lazy-boy recliner for a cosy session of hideously toxic but life-saving chemicals and chats with the nurses.

I'm most cheered by the way that, every time I go into the chemotherapy unit, one or other of the nurses compliments me on my appearance.

'You're looking grrreat today, Jess,' says Lottie.

Then Nurse Bess usually shouts out, 'She always looks great.' It is simply the ultimate cherry of flattery on my cake of vanity.

You occasionally read about psychotic-serial-killer nurses but I've yet to come across one who was not some sort of reincarnated angel. No matter how grim the personal circumstances of their day may be, they invariably manage to put on a smile and find the generosity to put me first. They seldom bitch about rude and demanding patients who don't even bother to remember their names. You hardly ever hear them moan about the shift work; having lunch breaks at four o'clock in the afternoon; dealing with hazardous, toxic and just plain disgusting substances; commuting vast distances, or working obscenely long hours for scant cash. The first inkling anyone gets that the situation is intolerable is when the nurses suddenly leave the profession that they've spent years training for.

Later that afternoon Suzy Cleator looked at me across her high-end specialist's desk in a kind yet pained sort of a way. She is, after all, my consultant. And I was aware that I had just changed my treatment plan without consulting her.

'Oh, well, I can always start the ice hat again next time,' I blurted.

'You will probably lose your remaining hair this week,' Suzy replied.

I do admire her matter-of-factness. This is not a situation where soft-soaping is required.

❖

From: Jessica
To: Iris
Subject: Wigs, at last!

The wig voucher has arrived!
It has been to three different postcodes. Someone kindly opened it and sent it on to me. Shall we try to go today or on Monday?

From: Iris
To: Jessica
Subject: Re: Wigs, at last!

We can go this afternoon if you'd like call and see if they are open and I'll meet you in a few hours.

From: Jessica
To: Iris
Subject: Re: Wigs, at last!

Oh damn. The wig makers are only in on Monday so I have to call then to make an appointment.

Before I can press send on this last one the phone rings . . . 'Well? Are we going to get the wig?'

❖

May comes to visit with her friend Renée. They're here to practise their shamanic healing. It's very much the latest thing in West London. They haven't really come to see me but, rather, are drawn here by the fact that I am the custodian of a rare and coveted eagle's feather that just dropped on me out of the sky in Australia. It seems so long ago and so far away now, but I took the feather as an auspicious omen at the time.

I lie on the floor whilst May and Renée shake maracas and pepper pots over me, clear my energy blockages with a pendulum and comb my aura with the eagle's feather.

For comfort I've removed my bright yellow crocheted snood and replaced it with my white terry-towelling sleeping beanie. Suddenly I have gone from vibrant eye-catcher to looking, and feeling, like a giant baby. But it is lovely to have people taking care of me.

My philosophy is this: everything is beautiful, in its own way. Having been seriously ill in my youth, I'm aware that miracles happen that defy medical explanation.

I was twenty-five years old. I'd been at yet another party in some draughty old English country house. I awoke with a thumping hangover and flopped into a hot bath, trying to soak away the stale cigarette smoke and red wine vapours that clung about my body. My toes were cold and numb. I scrubbed and scrubbed with a bristle brush to restore the blood circulation. My toes did not respond. *Must have crashed out with my feet sticking out of the covers.*

Within a few days the numbness had reached my arms and chest. I could hardly walk or put on a jumper. Food tasted peculiar. My vision went blurry. *Maybe I should go to the doctor.*

The doctor put me into a taxi and sent me straight to St Mary's Hospital. Other doctors were waiting on standby for my arrival. They rushed me in and did a lumbar puncture. *You have Guillain-Barré Syndrome.*

Guillain-Barré Syndrome attacks the myelin sheath that transmits messages along your peripheral nerves. Bad news:

there is no cure. Good news: it is what is known as a self-limiting illness – at some point it goes away on its own. Bad news: nobody knows when it will go away, nor how bad it will get before it does so. Good news: modern medicine has the means to keep one alive in the interim.

Within another two weeks I found myself in a bed in the intensive care unit of the National Neurological Hospital, unable to move, breathe or speak. An unscratchable itch on my leg could drive me to the brink of insanity. Dust fell into my eyes and I couldn't blink or wipe it away. Being speechless, I could not cry out for assistance.

Upon learning of my perilous condition, Mum had dropped everything at home, packed a suitcase and flown to London. Now she spent twelve hours a day sitting by my bedside in the intensive care unit. Mum stuck all my cards up and the walls of the room became like a colourful patchwork quilt. There were poems, paintings and photographs, dried flowers, drawings and prayers. At night mum slept at the house of her friends Chrissy and Ralph. Chrissy and Ralph were devotees of an Indian guru by the name of Swamiji.

Thus, Swamiji learned of my situation and offered spiritual support. First off, he began to call my mother and tell her of his visions for me. 'I see yellow,' spake the swami. The next day Mum arrived at the hospital bearing armfuls of daffodils and yellow tulips. She filled all the vases in the room with them. Two days later, Swamiji called again: 'I see purple.' Out went the daffodils and in came swathes of irises. Mum wore a purple silk kimono that she'd borrowed from Chrissy.

Next, Swamiji came to the hospital, without shoes, and through his flowing grey beard blew into my chakras. The matron tried to hustle him from the room but Swamiji resisted. At that point Sister Mary entered the scene.

Sister Mary had been hospitalised for an acute attack of multiple sclerosis but was now on the bounce back. She busied herself by ambling about the hospital with her walking stick, rescuing the souls of her fellow patients. Some of those ingrates did not want to be saved but in me she found a compliant mark. I didn't have much choice in the matter, being fully paralysed.

Sister Mary visited most days and sprinkled my motionless body with Lourdes water that she kept in a plastic bottle. She left a specimen jar by my bed containing some small pieces of black stuff. 'Relics of Padre Pio,' Sister Mary said. Not being much of a Christian I didn't cotton on to the significance of these. I was rather taken aback when I later learned that they were bits of the charred remains of a revered Catholic priest.

Swamiji blew and Sister Mary sprinkled and as they did so the two of them fell into deep philosophical and theological discussions. They did not see eye-to-eye about how best to save me but each of them gave as good as they got. Their conversations continued; Swamiji began calling Sister Mary on the payphone on her hospital ward. She would then appear at my bedside in high dudgeon, 'I had your friend Swamiji on the phone last night. He's a very irritating man.'

'He's not *my* friend,' I wanted to say, but I couldn't speak.

Each morning Nurse Ermine would unhook me from the ventilator and ask me to blow into a spirometer – a device that measures the volume of air expired from one's lungs. A person needs to be measuring a minimum of one litre to safely be allowed to breathe unaided. It is expected that one's lung capacity will show a slow but steady increase, a gentle upward curve on the chart, until it reaches a litre. Mine was measured in millilitres. Day after day I would blow into the spirometer. Day after day Nurse Ermine would enter another dot on the flat line along the bottom of my chart. One morning she unplugged me from the ventilator as usual. I screwed up every fibre of energy that my immobile body had to offer and *blew* into that baby until I saw spots. Ermine looked at the spirometer and then at my chart. 'It says a litre,' she shook her head, 'there must be something wrong with it. Have a little rest and I'll go and get another one.' She plugged me back into the ventilator. Five minutes later she was back. We started the procedure from the top. I truly was flaked out after my first effort. Nevertheless, I wound myself up to a crescendo once more and let rip. One litre! This time Ermine wrote it down on my chart. I'd gone from zero to hero in a single day. As Ermine left the room she turned in the doorway. 'I've never seen that before. Somebody's prayin' for you, girl.'

So bring on the prayers and the chanting and the chakra clearing, the crystals, reflexology, shiatsu and laying-on of hands. All well-intentioned, freely given spiritual aid is gratefully accepted by me. Just don't bring me anything that tries to play on my fear. I've no tolerance for that kind of manipulative Svengali-ism and if you care to try it on with me you'll soon find yourself out the metaphorical door with a real live flea in your ear.

❖

I'm up early in great excitement. Today is wig day. I miss the bus.
Text to Iris:

> Just missed bus. Phone about to die. Please go in and tell them if you get there before me.

Text from Iris:

> The Bakerloo line is down and the traffic is gridlocked I have been trying to get bus for 30 min.

After the delay in receiving the voucher, I feel there is a wig curse upon me. But that's just unnecessary pessimism. As I've learned, it's likely to give one cancer or shorten one's life in a dozen of other ways so I shrug off the curse and, sure enough, another bus comes along.

Raoul's turns out to be a fusty, old-fashioned place with hairdressing stations in the front and a wig-fitting establishment in the back. They do all the wigs for patients at St Mary's. I'm ushered into a curtained cubicle decorated with textured wallpaper and a blue-painted dado rail.

A nice enough but not very interested blonde lady comes in. She does not ask me my name nor bother to introduce herself. I guess she fits wigs on cancer patients all day every day and has heard all the stories. I imagine it could be quite a depressing job if you let it get to you. She asks me what my hair used to be like.

'Rita Hayworth in *Gilda*,' I reply hopefully.

'I don't think we have any wigs like that,' she states.

'Well, what have you got?'

The look on her face says *This is going to be a long session . . .*

First up is a short, spiky number. It is brown with reddish highlights. I have never imagined myself as the head of the Human Resources Department but now I see that, with the right hairstyle, anything is possible. I hand it back with a shudder.

I realise that wig choosing might be more tricky that I'd thought, especially since I have no idea what I want. Luckily for me, at this point Iris arrives.

The next wig is a winner. It's a dark brunette – 'cappuccino' – with no highlights, cut in a stylish bob with a blunt fringe, shorter at the back and then angled down to curl into the jawline. It's by René of Paris, Van Nuys, California – made in Thailand. I study the care instructions. How to wash it (cold water only, use wig shampoo and conditioner). How to dry it (shake and hang upside down overnight). And then WARNING: Avoid exposure to heat such as; blow dryers, curling irons, hot rollers, ovens, barbecue grills . . . Well, I understand that heated styling tools may cause the nylon hair to frizz in an undesirable manner and I am often in need of a reminder not to stick my head in the oven but under what dreadful circumstances, I wonder, would I be desperate enough to barbecue my wig?

Next is a long black coif – too Morticia Addams. Then a layered, short ash-blonde look – too Lady Di. Then a long, yellow-blonde style – Iris suggests adding a pair of sunglasses and a kaftan and going out disguised as Cousin Itt. Finally a copper-red wig with highlights in about ten different shades. It's very long and multi-layered with a flicky fringe. To me it looks like a cross between Suzi Quatro and Farrah Fawcett. Iris insists it's got potential.

I try the dark bob again. It's very French and sexy. Then the red mop. 'I don't think so,' I tell Iris.

'Wait,' says Iris, 'look at it from the back.'

'Hmmm,' say I.

Iris enlists the support of the wig lady, who holds up the mirror so that I can see it from every angle.

'It looks lovely,' says the wig lady.

'It's better than your own hair ever was,' says Iris.

'Hmmm,' I say again, but not in nearly such a definite way. 'I'll take them both.'

❖

Wigs on board, it's time to head for Harley Street. Today is the first day of my new chemo regime. From now on I will be having Taxol every week for the next eight weeks. *Taxol* – sounds like a weed killer, doesn't it?

Iris and I decide to get the bus to the hospital. In Oxford Street the traffic is properly gridlocked. After a long time of being stuck we go downstairs and ask the driver if he will let us off. I explain that I have a hospital appointment and that I am not feeling very well.

'I'm not allowed to open the doors,' is his flat reply. He doesn't look at us.

Another fifteen minutes pass, only now we're standing up. It's hot. I start to feel faint. What has been an inconvenience is spiralling into a crisis. I'm about to push the emergency door-opening button when the traffic breaks and we chug into the bus stop. I'm still not convinced that the driver wants to let us off, but by now he is on the receiving end of so much customer-generated flak that he reluctantly releases his hostages.

At the hospital I collapse into one of the recliners. Nurse Karen begins to insert the needle into my arm. Suddenly I begin to sob.

'Hey, darling, what's the matter?' asks Karen.

'I've had enough of this.'

After my mini-breakdown blows over I cheer myself up by eating a block of Green & Black's Organic Dark Mint Chocolate and modelling my new wigs for the nurses on the chemo unit. Then it's downstairs for an appointment with Dr Cleator.

She outlines the possible side effects of the Taxol: aches and pains; fatigue; nausea; mouth ulcers; anaemia; loss of eyebrows and lashes; diarrhoea; liver damage; numb hands and feet . . . But there's good news too: she explains that the weekly regime that she is recommending for me is a new method from America, whereby one receives a lower dose, but more frequently. Apparently it means that the chemo is 'better tolerated'. Hallelujah to that!

Then Suzy explains that she will not be overseeing my radio-therapy: her baby is due in November. But she will refer me to another consultant.

'Someone very good,' she says, reassuringly.

I've no doubt about that but I'm sorry to hear it all the same. I feel safe with the understanding that develops with continuity in a relationship. I've started to feel at ease with Suzy and I trust her.

Then, as I get up to leave, she shoots me a parting morsel of bad news: another side effect of the Taxol is that it can make one's nails go 'manky'. Oh hell.

At seven p.m. I'm back at Kell Skott's salon on Golborne Road. His wife, Jacqueline, is there. They both give me a welcoming hug. I'm in and out of the salon so often lately; they're starting to feel like family.

I don't think Kell is aware that he's running a special 'three for the price of one' promotion this evening. First, I ask him to give me a number one crop. There really isn't all that much else to be done now. I could shave my head completely yet I still hang back from that.

Next, I don the dark bob. Kell chops into the fringe and thins out the sides, giving it a delightfully messy-chic look. Then comes the red mop. I'm still dubious but Kell thinks it perfect just as it is. He thins some of the front sections, just for the hell of it, and then runs some hair wax through it. Who would ever have thought of waxing a wig? Suddenly it looks rock and roll. Suddenly I like it.

Wearing the cappuccino wig I Skype Nick. 'Wow' is his verdict. I rip it off and don the red one. 'Baby, you are ravishing. You *have* to wear that one when I get back to London.' Talking to Nick is a tonic for my self-esteem. I'm so glad that he doesn't give me the furrowed brow and sad-eye treatment. His enthusiasm makes me feel sexy for the first time in months.

❖

So far, so good with the new chemo regime. I don't feel sick at all. Just rather tired.

As a precaution I've removed all the fluorescent pink varnish from my fingers and toes. A minute examination reveals lots of tiny ridges running the length of my fingernails. Could this be the beginning of manky nail syndrome?

I've been on the internet, of course, and read up on all the horror stories: nails turning black; spooning; cracking; peeling; falling off and just plain disappearing. I've also read up on prevention. One suggestion is to ice one's hands and feet whilst having the chemo. That makes sense. I guess it works in the same way as the ice hat was supposed to – that is to say, by restricting blood circulation to the extremities, thereby reducing the amount of chemicals to reach those parts.

Except the ice hat didn't work – but maybe that's because I'm such a natural hothead. I will go out tomorrow and get some of those insulated freezer bags and several packets of frozen peas with which to build my DIY nail preserver. My next question is – should the peas be organic?

SEPTEMBER

Today is chemo day. It's very windy. I'm worried that my wig is going to blow off. I console myself with the thought that if such a hideously embarrassing thing were to happen, there is sure to be some thoughtful member of the public standing by with a mobile phone to video the whole event and put it on YouTube. Luckily, I've worn a hat over the wig so I can clamp my hand onto the top of the hat and nobody will guess that I'm actually holding my hair on.

Nurse Bess looks at today's blood test results. 'Your haemoglobin is quite low,' she says.

'What does that mean?' I ask.

'It means you'd better eat a lot of red meat and green leafy vegetables, things with iron in them to get your levels up. It might work.'

'And what if it doesn't?'

'If your haemoglobin gets any lower you will have to have a blood transfusion.'

'Oh.'

That shut me up. The possibility of serious chemo side effects suddenly seems real. I tell her that the vein in my forearm, where they regularly put the cannulas, has gone hard and is hurting.

'That's called sclerosis,' she says. 'It will get better eventually. Meanwhile, we'll have to find another vein.'

I've come to Harley Street alone this week. Jamie is on holiday and I feel that Iris and Antony have done their fair share of chemo-sitting. The trouble is that I'm not very good at asking people to accompany me. Fear of rejection makes it difficult for me even to invite friends to dinner or the movies. I can't imagine anyone gladly volunteering to sit around all afternoon reading *OK!* and watching Taxol drip into my arm.

Just then, May calls on the phone. I ask her if she would come with me to chemo next week.

'Oh, that will be fun,' exclaims May.

'That depends on your idea of fun,' I reply.

I've had the anti-sickness drugs and the anti-allergy drugs and the various flushes. It's time for the main event: the Taxol. Nurse Karen returns with the frozen peas that I'd brought to the hospital in an insulated picnic bag. She ingeniously devises an impromptu pea-administering system by binding the bags of peas to my feet with surgical tape.

'Did you used to be a model?' asks Karen.

'Ah, erm, no,' I reply.

Karen shouts across to Bess: 'She said no but she hesitated.'

I tell them the truth: that I did give it a go in my youth but I was hopeless, both at modelling and at being treated like a farm animal by vile hairdressers and narcissistic fashion designers. Once, in the past, I expressed regret to my cousin Ben: 'If only I'd done modelling, I'd be rich,' I'd sighed. 'Jess, you'd be dead,' said Ben. I love the people who know me better than I know myself.

'I want to get a wig like yours,' Karen enthuses. 'I'll wear it on Hallowe'en with my catsuit, whip and gloves.' Now there's a back-handed compliment if ever I heard one, but Karen doesn't mean it that way at all. She chats blithely on: 'I tried one on the other day. It is such a sexy look . . .'

'I'm proud to be such a fashion icon for you,' I reply, glancing down at my pea-clad toes.

❖

I know that I probably come across as all confident and full of myself but that is sometimes far from the truth.

Over the last few days I've been spending more and more time in bed. I know from experience that too much time alone can lure me into some very weird and warped ways of thinking. Add a few reversals of fortune and situations where things don't go my way and suddenly I'm spiralling into negativity, self-pity and anxiety.

The hair loss seemed to have slowed down in the last couple of weeks but it's back up to full speed today. My eyelashes have seriously started coming out too.

It's very upsetting.

When Nick went home to Sydney it was with the hope that he would come back to London in the autumn. The weather has turned, yet Nick and I have not spoken about it recently. I haven't wanted to put pressure on him. I'd rather leave him to make his own decisions about his life. But I'm longing to see him again; I mean I am longing to touch him and hold him and make love with him and have time with him. As technologically advanced as Skype is, it is not a substitute for my real live boyfriend.

The fact is, Nick's mother is ill with Alzheimer's disease. Nick went to visit her last week and was shocked at how much she had deteriorated in the few weeks since he had last seen her. Now he's made his decision: he needs to spend as much time with his mother as he can, while he still can. So he won't be returning to see me. It's the right decision. It's the only decision he could make and I know it. Or, at least, the adult part of me knows it. There's another part of me, though, that wants to stamp her foot, throw her wig on the floor and scream, 'IT'S NOT FAIR.'

On Sunday morning I went to one of my self-help groups. I arrived late, wearing my 'cappuccino' bob and dark glasses, Anna Wintour style. As I walked in and groped for a seat, I felt painfully aware that everyone was looking at me. And why wouldn't they? When they saw me last week I was a redhead. After the meeting ended I slunk off, wrapped in a suffocating blanket of self-consciousness. I felt like an object of pity. I felt that some would be making fun of me as soon as I was out of earshot. To be honest, I felt ashamed to be me.

The phone has not rung today. I imagine that all my friends have stopped calling me.

I Skype Nick.

'Hey, darlin'. How are you?' he says.

I do not count to ten. I just let him have it: 'I'm tired, I'm so tired, you have no idea how tired I am, I'm all on my own, I've got no one to help me, I look awful, my hair has fallen out, I'm having panic attacks and all I do is worry about money. I'm tired all the time and I have to cook and shop and do the laundry and go to the hospital, and I just can't do it all, and then when I ask people for help they just let me down like they've let me down all my life, and I always have to look after myself and earn money and make sure the bills are paid because if I don't do it no one will. You don't know what it's like and now I'm sick and I'm too tired and everyone's abandoned me just like my father did, and I always end up on my own and now I've gone and got a boyfriend who lives on the OTHER SIDE OF THE WORLD and can't be there for me when I need him, why does this always happen to ME?'

By this time tears and snot are pouring out of my face. I don't dare look at Nick because then I will have to see myself on the little screen in the corner. So I bury my face in my hands and avoid his eye.

Nick does not terminate the call in disgust. Instead he says, 'Can I ask you a question?'

'Okay,' I snuffle.

'How old are you right now?'

'Oh, don't start!'

Nick tries a different tack. 'Darling, I think you're beautiful and sexy. You're doing so well. You have so many friends and people who love you.' Now that's more like it. 'I'm so proud of you. You're an inspiration to all of us,' he adds, trowelling it on.

I lift my head and give Nick a tearful blink.

'Now, sweetheart,' he says soothingly, 'you know what they say?'

'What?'

'You mustn't get too Hungry, Angry, Lonely or Tired.' I nod.

'So why don't you get something to eat and then have a little lie-down, hmmm? Then when you wake up you can phone Iris and have a chat with her.'

'Mmmm, I do feel quite sleepy now . . .'

'Shhh, that's it, darling, you get some rest.'

I awake three hours later and look at my phone. Five missed calls, two texts. It seems that my friends have not abandoned me after all.

❖

One of the great benefits of having breast cancer (yes, there are some) is that I have an iron-clad excuse to get back into contact with friends that I've mislaid along life's highway.

The reasons that I've lost these friends are varied and usually trivial. The consequence of that is that the damage cannot easily be repaired because it is too embarrassing for either party to mention the cause.

A good case in point is my friend Wanda. We got on so well and had lots of fun and then we fell out and didn't speak to one another for several years. A couple of weeks ago we had lunch. In the years since I've seen her Wanda has got married. I missed that. It was such a gas to spend hours stuffing our faces and taking the piss out of one another and everyone we know. I couldn't even think of what had happened to cause the rift.

I've had calls and emails from friends in Australia and the USA who I usually only speak to once a year. I've received messages from all my far-flung family around the world. I am convinced that love and prayers really do work in the process of healing.

As if in answer to my reflections on friends, love and healing, Nick Skypes. I'm sitting in bed in my nightie and terry-towelling sleeping cap. Nick is sitting in his parents' stylish beach house in Noosa. I apologise for my meltdown.

'It's okay, darling, that's what I'm here for,' says Nick. I adore him more than ever.

Behind Nick's shoulder a figure moves past the door. 'Hey Dad,' shouts Nick, 'come and meet Jessy.' It's too late, there is nowhere to hide. Seconds later a handsome, silver-haired man is smiling at me.

'Dad, this is Jessy. Jessy, this is Dad.'

I pull the duvet up around my neck, wishing that I could pull it right over my head. Of course I have looked forward to meeting Nick's family but somehow this was never how I pictured it would be.

❖

I meet May for lunch. Apart from being a budding shaman, May is a talented artist as well as incredibly stylish and loads of fun. We dine on exotic tapas then stroll on down to Harley Street for a spot of post-prandial Taxol (me) and reading of *Harper's Bazaar* (May).

'I love, love, love that wig,' says Nurse Lottie. I'm wearing the red one today. I love, love, love the nurses' ability to live life to the full. They are a terrific counterpoint to some of the uptight skeletons I see wandering about this locality, their plumped-up lips walking three paces ahead of them, looking so angry and miserable you'd think they'd just had a Louis Vuitton poker rammed up their fundaments. Harley Street is home to numerous aesthetic surgeons. Not that I'd say no to a little 'anti-ageing therapy' myself if it was offered, but I just think if you're going to spend all that money on making yourself look good, you may as well use the new visage to crack open a smile. What's the point of going about with an expression that suggests you've just found dog excrement in your wheat-free-organic rocket and carrot sandwich?

Chemotherapy today is uneventful. That's a good thing. It seems that Suzy Cleator's new, weekly regime is working a treat. I mean working not in the sense of killing the cancer that I don't have. I hope it is doing that. I mean working in the sense of having fewer and less severe side effects. As I've said, I don't feel sick. My sense of taste has returned to normal. I'm very tired but so what? I sleep a lot.

What's cheering me up is that it's another one off the list. Yay!

Only five more to go. The future seems all sunshine and rosy.

❖

It will be Nick's birthday in ten days. I miss Nick every day but missing his birthday seems singularly unkind.

Only four days ago he decided to have a party. Since then he's been buzzing about, organising a venue and catering, booking a band and fretting that he doesn't have enough friends to invite. I am delighted that he is going ahead with it. I had feared that Nick's birthday would slip by unmarked amidst all the dramas of his ill mother, his problematic son and his Chemo Chic girlfriend.

This morning he sent me an email invitation. It shows a busy beach scene filled with frolicking 1960s ladies in bikinis. Atop a VW Kombi bus stands a champagne-toting muscle-bound physique with Nick's head superimposed onto it. When I saw the picture I laughed out loud. The whole thing was so frivolous and silly. The next minute I was overwhelmed with sadness. It seems so long ago that I last felt frivolous and silly. I'm sad that I won't be with Nick on his birthday. I'm sad that Nick has to take care of everybody and organise his own party.

But, really, we are all okay. It just is how it is.

❖

Only four more chemos to go now.

When this all started I was consumed with free-floating anxiety: *What is going to happen to me? How will I cope on my own? What will I do for money?*

Will Nick leave me if my hair all falls out?

And there lies my deepest, darkest fear.

My past relationships have been with men who were somewhat narcissistic in nature. I'm not saying that they didn't love me, in their way; it's just that their idea of love was very self-involved. Both Brendan and Clive saw their partner primarily as someone who existed to enrich their own lives: to give them what they lacked in terms of self-esteem. They saw love as something that you get rather than something that you live. What I provided them with was a good-looking piece of arm candy who would also cook delicious meals, tell them how handsome and clever they were, fight their battles for them, sort out the paperwork and give them unlimited great sex. They were grateful for that and told me that they loved me. They weren't lying – they were just clueless about what love is. And, to be fair, so was I.

I may have longed for emotional reciprocity but I never asked for it. Inside I felt worthless, just as they did. We clung together like beggars at a banquet, emotionally starving each other and ourselves in the midst of a universe whose very substance is love.

So, up to now, my experience of love in a romantic context has been pretty threadbare. Despite all the therapy and personal development work I've done, I have to be aware of my underlying tendency to see myself as lovable only if I'm bolstering my man's ego: being beautiful; being sexy; being fun.

And now all the decorations in my shop window have been stripped away. My hair is gone. Mr Hadjiminas has done a spectacular job but in reality I have had part of my breast removed. I'm afraid that Nick might regard that as a physical disfigurement. I worry that the drugs will put me into menopause. I fear that Nick will think of me as 'past it'. Worse, I'm afraid that if I discuss my fears with anyone, especially Nick, I will only cause them to manifest.

I run the imaginary tape in my head:

JESSICA: 'Nick, I'm afraid that you'll leave me because I'm not the Jessy you fell for.'

NICK: *Hmm, she's right, you know. Jessy was a fabulous girlfriend for a while but now she's sick and old and ugly – and bald!*

JESSICA: [looks at Nick with beseeching eyes, silently begging for reassurance]

NICK: *And now she's getting all needy.* 'Jessy, it's not you, it's me . . .'

I bury this fear daily and every night it resurrects itself to stalk around my bed as I'm trying to get to sleep. I remind myself that I am not the Jessica of ten years ago and Nick is not Brendan or Clive. And, as you have read, what has happened has happened. There have been good days and dark days but I'm still here, my family and friends are still with me, Nick is still hanging in there and the world keeps on turning.

Over the years I have learned that all resentment is in the past and all fear is in the future. Right now everything is just fine.

Well, that's the theory. It takes me a great deal of introspection and using techniques like meditation, gratitude lists, yoga and positive thinking to keep myself cognisant of right now and not spending all my time dwelling on what was and what might be.

Like I said, I now have four more weeks of chemotherapy, then a month break, and then five weeks of radiotherapy. In other words, I'm halfway through my treatment. So now I've started tormenting myself with a new set of anxieties: *How am I going to get my life back together? Will I ever work again? How will I repay all the money I've borrowed? What if the cancer comes back? Will Nick and I have grown too far apart after not having seen one another for seven months?*

I take some deep breaths. The crazy person in my head insists that, because I don't know what is going to happen in the future, it will inevitably be the worst possible scenario. I think it through.

So I want to know what is going to happen tomorrow. And I want to know what is going to happen next month. And I want to know what is going to happen in three months' time. If I follow that through to its logical conclusion then I will need to know what is going to happen every day for the rest of my life in order to feel secure.

That's just nuts.

❖

When I get home there's an email in my inbox from Nick.

From: Nick
Subject: Surprise

Attached is a flight itinerary from Sydney to London in Nick's name, arriving on the 22nd of October.

As Iris always says: 'It's turned out nice again.'

❖

This chemo is a bit of an up-and-down business. They told me at the beginning that the effect is cumulative. I think I've been getting away with it so far. I've kept myself fit, eaten well and had relatively few and minor side effects, compared with what some people go through. But I'm starting to feel bone tired. I've spent many hours in bed or on the couch in the last couple of days and it just seems very difficult to do anything. Nonetheless, things must be done. And one of them is dealing with the Department of Work and Pensions.

There is no short or simple way to write this . . .

In order to qualify for a free wig I need a letter from the Department of Work and Pensions (DWP) confirming that I am in receipt of *income-related* benefit (whatever that may mean). After many phone calls – being put on hold, being told different things by different people, and waiting days for somebody to call me back – I turned to the Macmillan charity benefits helpline for help. I spoke to Jo, a benefits advisor. Jo spoke to the DWP. A young man at the DWP promised Jo that he would send me a letter confirming that I am receiving income-related benefit. I, in turn, promised to present that letter to the surgical supplies department at St Mary's Hospital to prove to them my entitlement to the wig that I already have.

That last bit was about two weeks ago.

For those of you who have never made a claim – don't ask. You'll never understand the benefits system in a million years. I don't understand it. The advisors at the Macmillan benefits helpline don't understand it. Even the people at the DWP don't understand their own rules and cannot give one a straight answer about anything.

I call the Macmillan benefits helpline again. This time I speak to Min. She listens to my long tale.

'What does it say in the original letter that they sent you?' she asks. I riffle through a very long letter. On page 4 it says: '. . . We call your benefit *contributions-based and income-related Employment and Support allowance*.'

'I think that means you are on *contributions-based* benefit,' says Min.

'How d'you figure that out?' I ask, perplexed. 'It says "contributions-based *and* income related . . ." Does that mean I'm getting both?'

'No,' says Min, 'it probably means you are getting contributions-based allowance.'

'*You* might think that's what it means, Min,' I reply. 'It is not clear to me, neither is it clear to the chap at the DWP to whom your colleague Jo spoke a couple of weeks ago. He promised to send a letter confirming that I am in receipt of *income-related* benefits. I have been waiting for that letter because I need to take it to St Mary's to prove to them that I am entitled to a free wig.'

'If you've paid your National Insurance contributions then you would be receiving the *contributions-based* benefit,' Min opines.

'Does that mean I can get a free wig?'

'No. You have to be on *income-related* benefit for that.'

'So, because I have paid my NI contributions I am not entitled to a wig?'

'Yes.'

'Whereas if I had *not* paid my contributions I *would* be entitled to one?'

'That's right.'

I can tell that both Min and I are doing our best not to sob out loud at this point.

'Well,' says Min, 'I will send you some HC1 forms to fill in so that you can claim a wig on the basis of low income in case you are, in fact, receiving contributions-based benefits.'

'But I don't want to fill in any more forms, Min,' I say in a hopeless tone.

'Are you receiving any help with your housing costs?'

'No. I haven't filled in the forms for mortgage relief because I fear that the bank will penalise me for claiming benefits by offering me less favourable mortgage terms in the future. The repayments are very low at the moment so I thought I would borrow some money from my sister and just tough it out.'

'But you have to be receiving help with your housing costs in order to establish that you are on a low income.'

'But I have already established that I am on a low income. The DWP asked me to send them six months' worth of bank statements and financial records. They know I've got no money,' I wail.

'Yes, but getting help with your housing costs is the trigger.'

'Min,' I plead, 'do we have to go through all this hoopla again? They already admitted to your colleague Jo that I am receiving *income-related* benefit. Now we just need to get them to do what they promised and put it in writing.'

'I will call them,' offers Min.

'Thank you, Min.' I sigh, untying the rope from the shower rail.

Later . . . The telephone rings: 'Hello, Miss Jones, this is Min.' I'm holding my breath.

'The DWP are going to send you a letter confirming that you are receiving *income-related* benefit.'

I exhale.

'And they are already paying your mortgage,' adds Min.

'No they're not, Min,' say I, 'I haven't filled out the forms.'

'Well they are paying £18.29 per week towards your mortgage interest.'

'But, Min,' I protest, 'my mortgage interest is way more than £18.29 per week.'

'I will call them,' says Min.

Later . . . Min calls: 'Hello, Miss Jones. The DWP confirm that they are paying £18.29 towards your housing costs. I can't tell you exactly what it's for. Best you fill out those forms. You need to claim all your benefits when you've got cancer.'

Min is right. I have a deep fear of filling in forms. My loathing for bureaucracy and my shame at having to claim at all conspire to keep me half out of the system. I'm not claiming what I am entitled to.

'I will, Min,' I say, contrite.

'They also confirm that you are receiving £25.50 a week because you are in the *Work Related Activity Group*.'

'And what does that mean?'

'It means that they expect you to get a job.'

'But, Min,' I reason, 'I'm sick. They know that. My doctor has written to them and told them that I am undergoing chemo-therapy for breast cancer.'

'Did your doctor state that the chemotherapy was intravenous?'

'I don't know if she specified that it is intravenous. But, as far as I'm aware, all chemotherapy for breast cancer is intravenous.'

'Nonetheless, you'll have to get a letter stating that your chemotherapy is intravenous, then write in and make an appeal.'

I don't even know what to say any more.

Things I wish I'd known before #6
Living within your means
There is no getting away from this. If you're seriously ill your income will go down and your expenses will go up. Taking steps to streamline your finances will go a long way towards reducing stress in your life.

Reduce all your credit card payments to the minimum for the time being. You can increase them again when you're back at work.

Look at all your utility bills. Are you paying too much? Could you negotiate a better deal? I found that I was paying way over the odds for my phone and broadband and I found a package deal that was a third of the price. You may be tied into a contract but usually the mention of the 'C' word will prompt your suppliers to find you some wriggle room.

Apply for benefits. You have paid for these in your taxes. Now you're sick. You are entitled.

Go through your bank and credit card statements. Are there any subscriptions that you can live without? Payments to charities that don't need your help right now?

Do you have any insurance policies that will pay your mortgage or credit cards in case of illness? If so, claim!

Check out the charities. There are many that provide cash grants, help with transport or medical expenses, home help and so on.

Write a list of things you need. When friends ask what you'd like for Christmas or your birthday ask them to choose something from the list. Here are some of the useful things that I was given: a juice extractor; super-market vouchers; vitamins and supplements; a travelcard; an aeroplane ticket; beauty products; singing lessons; some payments for a cleaner; an Hermès scarf; light bulbs and home-made meals to put in the freezer.

If your friends and family offer to lend you money, say yes. Allow them to take you out for lunch and dinner too.

Go through your cupboards and see what you have to sell on eBay.

Cash in your loyalty points. I found that I had enough supermarket loyalty points to buy several books that I needed. Every little bit helps.

Get healthy and save money – eat loads of vegetables, brown rice and lentils.

Suspend your gym subscription. It's too strenuous for now. Go for a walk and do gentle yoga at home instead.

Develop financial awareness. Carry a small notebook and write down every penny that you spend. Better still use a smartphone app. You'll be surprised what a difference this habit makes to your financial manageability.

Anxiety can only make a drama out of a crisis. Ask yourself: have I got enough today? Have I got food? Have I got warmth? Have I got a home? Have I got clothing? Have I got transport? If the answer is 'yes' today then it is likely to be so tomorrow.

My fatigue is now so pervasive that it's quite hard to do everyday things. With that comes a sense of helplessness and defeat that leads to the kind of petulant outburst that I had a few days ago on Skype to Nick.

But I hate asking friends for help. I don't like to think that I will put them on the spot and then they will have to say 'yes' out of a sense of guilt. I like even less to think that they may say 'no' and then I will feel crushed and rejected. So I've come up with a cunning plan that I think gives everyone a get-out:

From: Jessica
Subject: Help needed
To: Flossie, Iris, Sheldon, Seraphina, Justin, Tessa, Jamie, Pete

Dear friends,
I have reached a stage in the treatment where the chemo is starting to make me extremely fatigued so I'm spending a lot of time on the couch. You know how much I hate to ask but I could really do with some help doing a few things. I need to fill in a form for the benefits people. That involves going through my files and finding information. Also need to do some filing and general plant watering, laundry and shopping.
   If you have any time this week, your help will be gratefully appreciated.
Love
Jess

I don't expect to receive a reply before this evening so fall back into bed. On arising from an hour-long doze I find the following in my inbox:

From: Iris
Subject: Re: Help needed

Chilli and I will be over when I have had a bath x

The next thing I know there's a welcome rap and a *yap yap yap* at the door.

❖

At seven-thirty a.m. I am awoken by a text:

Are u up yet? I want to come over and water the plants.

Jamie has been my friend for a number of years and, until this minute, I have never known him to be out of bed before midday.
   Full of beans and acting as if he springs joyously into life every morning at the crack of dawn, Jamie bustles around with the

watering can whilst I stagger about in the bathroom. Nearly all my eyelashes have fallen out now. I decide not to wear mascara today; I've lost more lashes on the right eye than on the left. So applying mascara creates a somewhat *Clockwork Orange* effect.

Once I've managed to struggle into clean clothes and apply make-up, Jamie has made tea. He squints a professional eye at me.

'If you're not going to wear mascara you should put some smudgy dark shadow along your eyelids.'

I nip back into the bathroom and try it. He's right, you know.

❖

Most of my time and energy today has been spent dealing with offers of help from all my friends. I may have to employ a full-time secretary to field their calls and emails.

Justin drops by to help me eat lunch. He brings a huge bunch of bright yellow chrysanthemums. There is nothing in this world more guaranteed to cheer me up than flowers.

Mum calls. 'Great news, Jess!' She goes on to tell me that her old friend Mr P has offered to pay my airfare to Australia when my cancer treatment is all over.

I'm really moved. I'm not used to being on the receiving end of so much spontaneous generosity and I don't know how to respond.

OCTOBER

Sometimes I wonder if my decision to have chemotherapy was the right one. After all, I don't have cancer. Mr Hadjiminas got it all out, yes?

It seems to me that the principle behind chemotherapy is this: they shoot one with a machine gun and hope to hit the correct targets, if there are any targets to hit.

The side effects I'm experiencing are niggly but, taken as a whole, rather debilitating. I'm fatigued beyond reason. Often I struggle to get out of bed before the afternoon. Everyday tasks seem insurmountable. The thought of emptying the dishwasher floors me. I have persistent ulcers in my mouth and under my tongue; they make it painful to eat or talk. My fingers tingle and my toes hurt. My nose bleeds a little, but often. I have spots on my face. Worst of all, my fingernails have started to go yellow and lift away from my fingertips. They're turning *manky*.

May calls me on the telephone. 'I just want you to know that you're doing the right thing,' she informs me.

'Why is that?' I query.

'I have a friend who was diagnosed three months ago with early-stage cancer like you. It wasn't aggressive. He said "no thanks" to the chemotherapy. Yesterday, he died.'

I would be eternally cross with myself if I declined the chemotherapy and then died. So I think I will spend more time in bed, eat more Manuka honey, carry packets of tissues and bottles of water everywhere with me, slap on the concealer and obsessively rub hand cream into my fingernails.

Only three more chemos to go.

❖

Today my cancer-busting diet starts well with a refreshing vitamin- and enzyme-packed glass of organic celery, lime and grape juice.

I take the bus to Harley Street.

Here is a testament to the power of addiction . . . I stopped smoking eighteen months ago. Four months ago I was diagnosed with cancer. I have had surgery to remove a malignant tumour and I am in the middle of a ghastly course of chemotherapy to be followed by radiotherapy. I am on my way to the hospital. The number 23 bus takes a route down Edgeware Road and as we pass by I gaze down on a tableau of men, some in crumpled suits, some in flowing white robes, all smoking *shisha* pipes. It takes every fibre of my willpower to restrain myself from getting off the bus, abandoning today's chemo session and joining them. Just for the one don'tyaknow.

❖

People tend to think that staying in bed all day is one of life's luxuries. But it's rubbish.

Today has been grey and drizzly so there wasn't really anything to get up for. And what with the sore toes, nosebleeds, a tongue ulcer and general fatigue, nothing seemed like much fun. I decided to stay under the duvet.

I don't have to get out of bed, I told myself. *No one can make me.* Cousin Ben came by and made me a cup of tea. I looked at him with a plaintive face, ready to defend my sloth, but he didn't try to cajole me out of my nest.

After Ben left I spent a few hours sleeping. This sleep is really additional to requirements. Rather than being soothing and refreshing, it is the kind of sleep where I toss and turn and have dreams about school and piles of tax returns.

I am woken up by the telephone, all bamboozled. It's Seraphina. She offers to come over and help me to do some paperwork. I fall asleep again. Next thing I know she's ringing the doorbell. I pull on a tattered cardigan. Seraphina has brought soup. I slump on the couch in my pyjamas with pillow marks on my face and a blanket wrapped around me, slurping a bowl of minestrone. I'm kind of glad that Nick isn't here at this very moment.

Seraphina writes a letter to send to the DWP, appealing against their assertion that I should get a job. She encloses yet another doctor's letter, this one from my oncologist, confirming once again that I have been diagnosed with cancer and that I am not well.

I would say that having to have so many fights with so many inhumane and just plain insane institutions is far more dispiriting than the effects of the chemotherapy ever could be.

From day one the DWP have taken the attitude that I may try to fool them into believing that I have cancer *but they are not falling for that old trick*. I am obviously a fraudulent, work-shy malingerer. Further, they know that all my doctors are in on the con too. They feel sure that some subcontracted pen pusher in Leeds is better qualified to assess my medical condition than a whole fleet of eminent surgeons and oncologists. And that they can do so without ever examining me or even speaking to me. Should I disagree with them, they will make sure that I pay for my impudence by forcing me to fill in 26-page forms, read meaningless and convoluted letters, and wait at home for telephone calls all day every day from now until it's time to begin filling in the claim forms for my old-age pension.

Next, Seraphina has a crack at the leaning tower of filing. She manages to wrestle a few pieces of paper from its clutches and slide them into various folders. In the end the filing mountain wins the battle but I give her points for tenacity and spirit.

As Seraphina puts on her coat I wonder why I'm crying. I finally have to admit that I find it incredibly difficult to ask anyone for help. And even if help is freely offered, I feel guilty.

It's as if I must do everything myself or I won't be able to justify my existence. I feel that somehow I don't deserve other people's generosity. I realise that I've always felt like this, deep down.

I'm telling you this because you might be feeling the same way as me. Flossie says that, far from being noble, refusing help amounts to a rejection of those who offer it. No matter what we feel, that is a very ungenerous and mean thing to do.

Tomorrow I'm going to rise and shine and say 'yes' to whatever comes my way.

❖

Since Mr P so generously offered to buy my airfare to Australia, I've started having anxiety about everything related to the possibility of actually going. *Will I be able to get there for Christmas? How will I get travel insurance? Who will look after my flat whilst I'm away? What will I do with my car? What if I never work again? Will the earth inevitably be swallowed up by a black hole?*

My phone bleeps. A text from May:

> Dear Jessy I am on shamanic course. The north whose spirit is condor, eagle. I asked my teacher, of course, about the feather. And she said that this is a gift from eagle, your healed piece yr healed self, a blueprint for u 2 hold. How great is that. She was in awe. In american indian, great steps follow when an eagle feather comes. Lvx xx

That sounds like an exceptionally positive outlook to me, whatever it may mean. I Skype Nick in Sydney.

'Honey, I'm coming home. Book tickets to Hobart and we'll go down to visit my mum.'

After days of lethargy, suddenly I'm all action. Suddenly I'm facing the future, not the past.

I can get on a flight on Christmas Eve. I send an email to Mr P I hope he hasn't changed his mind.

❖

Today is just the kind of beautiful autumnal day that makes me want to skip to the hospital. But it is chilly. I really feel for the first time that my head is very cold, even though I'm wearing a headscarf. It just goes to show how much protection our hair provides.

Standing at the bus stop, tears suddenly spring from my eyes. Lots of tears. But I'm not really crying. It's an automatic mechanism that kicks in because I've got insufficient lashes to protect my eyeballs. I jam on my sunglasses and make a mental note not to leave home without them from now on. Then my nose starts to run freely. This is because all the hairs have fallen out from inside my nostrils. I fish for a crumpled tissue in my handbag. It is all covered in snotty blood. At this point I notice that the girl who was standing next to me at the bus stop has moved away.

I'm trying my best to be Chemo Chic but I have to tell you it's a challenge sometimes.

❖

Nick has booked a campervan! He emails pictures. We are going to tootle around Tasmania for a week. I'm beyond excited. I have always wanted to go on holiday in a campervan, ever since I was a kid. I love neat little places where everything folds away and turns into something else.

In one of my former lives I used to do work that often involved travelling in giant deluxe Winnebagos. But we never got to sleep in them or have a shower. The truth is I haven't had a lot of holidays at all. I'm not fishing for sympathy here. My work has taken me all over the world. But I always had a job to do. Only rarely have I indulged in the traditional notion of taking time off work, going somewhere sunny where not much happens and just relaxing. In my youth, I admit, I may have viewed the idea of holidays as a tiny bit *bourgeois*.

Now I am ready for what is shaping up to be the holiday of a lifetime. Nick and I are planning to spend a week in Tasmania at my mum's place and then go off on our own in the campervan. Then I will stay on for another fortnight with Mum whilst Nick flies to Japan for a skiing trip with his children. After that I will fly back to Sydney and Nick and I will set off in his car to drive north along the coast to Queensland, camping here and there along the way. He has rented a house for us to stay in near his mum and dad's place in Noosa. Nick will spend some time in Queensland looking after his mother whilst I waft around the beach and the ice-cream parlours but we will have time alone too. Finally we will head back to New South Wales and revisit the shack on the south coast where we spent a magical week when we first met. We will again lie in one another's arms on the beach where we were blessed with the mighty eagle's feather.

Sunshine, beaches, family and friends, tropical fruit and fresh fish to eat every day! Sounds good? For me, the best part is that this will be a time just for living: to get well and strong, to rediscover happiness and vitality, and to strengthen my relationship with the man I have come to love.

❖

I ache all over. Yesterday I jumped out of the bath to answer the phone, slipped in the hallway, fell hard on my bottom, bruised my leg, scraped my foot and bashed my head against the wall. I saw stars for a minute or two.

This afternoon I tripped over a box of orange juice in the corner shop and stumbled wildly down the aisle, only just managing to avoid pulling the entire shelf of laundry detergent down on my head. I put all this clumsiness down to peripheral neuropathy. That is to say, numb toes. Which, as Dr Cleator warned me, is a side effect of the Taxol.

With a badly bruised ankle and worsely bruised pride, I limped straight home for a little lie-down. Sometimes the only thing for it is to wait for tomorrow and start afresh.

❖

This Thursday will be my last chemotherapy session. 'Hooray!' says everybody and I definitely agree. But, weirdly, a small part of me is not joining in the celebrations.

I have so much to look forward to. Nick will be arriving in London in less than two weeks. Then I'm going home to Australia for a long stretch in the sunshine and the arms of my lovely man. So why do I feel conflicted?

My guess is that I am afraid. Of the future. Soon I will be resuming my normal life (whatever normal is), but as a *cancer survivor*. I don't even know what that means in practical terms. But, psychologically, it's a label I shy away from. I don't want to identify myself as 'Jessica – cancer survivor'. I want to be 'Jessica – a fabulous friend', 'Jessica – chic chick', 'Jessica – sexy girlfriend' and 'Jessica – creative goddess'.

So far, I have been looked after every step of the way on this perilous road called cancer treatment. I'm flattered to have all those eminent doctors taking an interest in me. Above all, I have had the constant care of the wonderful nurses. I will miss them. I don't know how to make sense of all these mixed feelings.

I talk it over with Nick.

'Darling, you've just become a tiny bit institutionalised,' he informs me. 'You'll be like one of those people who goes out and commits burglaries so that they can get back into prison.'

'Except I will have to deliberately contract cancer in order to be readmitted,' I reply.

I wonder if I might go down the road of developing full-blown Munchausen syndrome.

'I could always take up smoking again?' I suggest with a hopeful lilt.

❖

Mondays seem to be the low point in the Taxol cycle. But there's only one more Miserable Monday to go.

I've spent most of today in bed. The graze on my foot has become inflamed so it's difficult to walk or put on shoes. I am now wearing socks and sandals, or to be more precise: Crocs 'n' Socks. Could this represent a new nadir in Chemo Chic fashion?

❖

Today I have my first appointment to discuss radiotherapy with my new oncologist, Dr Carmel Coulter – another top breast lady, I'm told. I wear what I think is a snappy get-up: a black trouser suit; a black jumper by Bella Freud with the words 'Ginsberg is God' knitted across the front; my 'red skulls' scarf and Crocs 'n' Socks.

'That's quite a lot of statements you've got on,' remarks Dr Coulter.

Something tells me she's a no-shit kind of a lady. I feel quite relieved that I haven't worn my Bella Freud jumper that has 'SEX' knitted across the chest.

Dr Coulter explains the radiotherapy process. First I have to go for 'planning'. This is when they get their microscopes out and measure my breast. Dr Coulter will then figure out exactly how to direct the cancer-busting rays so that they target my breast as much as possible and avoid zapping my heart and lungs. I completely trust that she knows what she is doing.

Then Dr Coulter and I have a small negotiation. I want to start the radiotherapy on the 16th of November so that I have maximum free time with Nick whilst he is in London. She wants me to start on the 9th so that I have maximum recovery time before I fly to Australia. We settle for the 12th.

Finally I ask, 'So why, exactly, am I having this radiotherapy?'

Dr Coulter looks a little puzzled. I can see what she is thinking: *Surely someone must have told her this before?* They have, but I like to be certain.

'It's the most effective way to prevent the cancer recurring in your breast,' she says. 'The chemotherapy is most effective at stopping it spreading in the rest of your body.'

Next I have an appointment with Mr Hadjiminas. (Yes, you've been missing him too, no doubt.) He gives me a thorough examination with his 'magic hands' (as good as any mammogram, in my opinion) and examines my scars.

'I hear you've been doing a lot of writing about us on your blog,' he remarks. Now, I'm not generally one to take on board what other people think of me but suddenly I feel very keen indeed to have the good opinion of Mr H. After all, I am going to have to rely on this man for the rest of my life.

'Do you approve? Or not?' I ask in a wavering voice.

One thing I've observed about Mr Hadjiminas is that he is totally deadpan. One cannot tell what he is thinking. He reflects for a moment, then says, 'I think it's good.'

Well, *that's* a relief.

❖

So, at last, I'm off to Harley Street for my final chemo session. I get up late, as usual, then stagger about getting dressed and making cards for the nurses. I like to print my own photographs onto cards for special people.

Nick Skypes: 'I just want to tell you that I love you and I hope it all goes well today.' I have to say I'm feeling very emotional.

I have been thinking about an appropriate gift for the nurses. I know that they get inundated with cakes and chocolates, yet it's difficult to think of another gift that they all can share. I brought them a bunch of flowers once to cheer up their front desk. They thanked me but the flowers were quickly 'disappeared' without ever being unwrapped. I guessed that they must have fallen foul of the no-flowers rule that is often in force in intensive care units, chemo suites and such places. (Apparently flower pollen can cause infections.) In the end I'm not imaginative enough to think of any alternative gifts. Patisserie Paul on Marylebone High Street does a lovely gift box of mini macaroons. If I had the energy I would go up to Harrods and get the Ladurée ones that Iris is always raving on about. But I haven't. Anyway, the ones from Paul are pretty damned delicious.

Macaroons on board, I walk up to Daunt Books and buy cards to replace all those that I left behind on the table at home. I don't admonish myself any more. It's just chemo-brain.

The unit is quiet today. I'm grateful for that. I don't feel like being surrounded by drama on the last day. Nurse Cara does my observations: weight, blood pressure, temperature and oxygen saturation. Nurse Karen looks at my feet.

'Crocs 'n' Socks will soon be on the runways,' she observes.

Karen wraps my arm in a heat blanket to aid the manifestation of a vein. The veins in my arm are pretty well worn out at this stage. But I'm truly thankful that at least one of them has held up to the end. I haven't had to have a central line installed in my chest, as I've seen many have. All in all, I feel that I have had a pretty easy ride of it with chemotherapy. I have read, heard and seen some real horror stories. It's been difficult and miserable at times but never intolerable. I haven't suffered major organ failure, I haven't been admitted to hospital, I haven't had to have a blood transfusion and my fingernails have not fallen off. What more can one ask for?

I attribute my relatively undamaged state to Suzy Cleator's weekly Taxol cycle and a regime of supplements recommended by Michael Thomsen.

With a few inadequate words of thanks, I hand over the macaroons. With eloquent and gracious words of thanks, Nurse Karen accepts them. Then she gives me a big hug. You might get the impression that this is the most beneficent gift that the nurses have ever received. I am sure it is not.

The chemo itself is uneventful. Sandra comes by and gives me a soothing reflexology treatment. I will miss those. Karen offers me a green macaroon. I recline in the big armchair, eating the macaroon and having my feet rubbed.

'It doesn't get much better than this,' I remark.

'Well, you could have George Clooney bringing you a glass of champagne,' observes Sandra.

'You're right.' I sigh. 'I knew there was something missing.'

Finally, the chemo is finished. Nurse Karen unplugs me and it's time to leave. She hesitates a moment before applying the mini plaster to the spot where she removed the needle.

'We just have to be a bit careful,' she says. 'Sometimes people have gone off and then come rushing back with blood pouring down their arms.'

'I'm sure that won't happen,' I say. 'It's never happened before.'

I put on my jacket and hug them all. I will be happy not to have chemotherapy any more but very sad not to see these nurses.

'Goodbye, goodbye.' I have to blink back tears. Then, as I reach for the doorknob, I feel a trickle on my hand. I rip off my jacket and throw it to the floor. Blood is pouring down my arm. I rush back in for a final dose of care and attention. It's a psychosomatically induced blood spout, I'm certain of it.

My last stop is to see Suzy Cleator. It may be difficult for you to comprehend that one can be genuinely pleased to see an oncologist. But I am. She has become a good friend to me. She is heavily pregnant now and will soon be stopping work.

Suzy confirms my opinion that I have tolerated the chemotherapy very well. I have to say that that is very much due to her expertise. The weekly regime of Taxol has been a big success. I hand over her card and start to choke up again.

Honoria comes in. She is heavily pregnant too. I will, however, be seeing her again in two weeks' time when I come for radiotherapy 'planning'.

Suzy raises the subject of Tamoxifen. It's a hormone therapy drug that she is recommending that I take every day for the next five years. I shift uneasily. I've read and heard all sorts of conflicting things about Tamoxifen, many of them quite scary. Of course I haven't got any of my facts straight.

'I am concerned about the side effects,' I say, in an embarrassed tone.

'It is highly recommended for you,' counters Dr Cleator. 'Your tumour was oestrogen receptive. So if there's still any lurking about the Tamoxifen stops it being fed with oestrogen. You can try it, and if you find it too difficult you can decide to stop.'

'I'm worried it will cause bone loss,' I reply.

'Tamoxifen has a bone-protecting effect,' she rejoins.

'Oh, I don't know. Of all the therapies, this is the one that I feel most uncomfortable with,' I say unconvincingly.

Suzy clears her throat. 'Of all the treatments for breast cancer, surgery is the most important. The next most important is Tamoxifen. Then chemotherapy, then radiotherapy.' I study the floor. 'I think the best thing,' says Suzy with one of her indulgent looks, 'is to discuss this after you've had the radiotherapy.'

She sure has learned how to play me.

I wish both Suzy and Honoria all the best with their births, bid them goodbye and leave.

Then I step out into Harley Street and into my future.

❖

I am sooooo tired. I'm too tired even to wear my wigs any more. Thinking that the chemo is all over and I would be back to normal, I booked in several appointments today. First, a committee meeting about a charity event, then a birthday lunch for my friend Sal and, finally, the movies with Sheldon.

Having fallen asleep at seven-thirty last night, I jumped out of bed at the crack of ten a.m. I made a divine fennel, grape and lime juice, ran the juicer parts under the cold tap and hopped in the bath. Ten minutes later I heard splashing. It sounded like it was coming from somewhere quite close by. I pondered for a while on what it might be. I was hesitant to get out of the bath because last time I did that I injured my foot and cracked my head. But finally I felt that I must investigate.

The kitchen sink was overflowing and there was a 2 centimetre deep puddle all over the floor. I skipped about chucking down every towel and tea towel that I own, emptied the bath and then piled the sopping textiles into the tub.

What has become clear to me is that the chemo has not yet left my body. Nor my brain.

I drive around to Mayhem Mansions. Smells of exotic cooking waft down the hallway as Hugo hurls himself in a frenzied attack at my ankles. The place is jumping. In the kitchen I find Muttiah, just returned from a long trip home to Malaysia and now cooking up a tempest: lamb curry, chicken curry, vegetable curry, rice and pappadums. Ted has just got in from work. He is baking a crumble or something. I hear a joyful 'yap, yap, yap,' and Chilli bursts onto the scene, closely followed by Iris and Jamie. Jamie is learning lines for his forthcoming starring role in a play.

Lounging on various sofas are Valentina, her husband, Tom, and Lydia, another acting friend of ours (I mean in the sense that she is an actress, not a stand-in friend). Over dinner Valentina announces: 'I am so hyappy. Now that I have my British citizenship I am going to buy a Kyasee Ooltimo* machine and open a beauty salon.'

'What's that?' we all ask.

'It is the latest, most scientific machine for gyving non-surgical facelifts,' Valentina explains. 'They devyeloped it for people who have had strokes and then they found that the side of their face that was being treated was looking younger than the other side. It's true,' she declares, 'it's better than buttocks!' By this time the whole table is fainting with delight at the idea of a machine that can give us a facelift and is better than Botox. Furthermore, that we should know someone who is about to own such a machine.

'I'll be your guinea pig,' everyone shouts at once.

'I need it the most,' hollers Lydia.

'Yes, but I've been the sickest,' I say.

'I was deeply traumatised as a child,' Jamie declares, in a melodramatic tone. Then, so as to deflect attention from our greedy graspiness we ask Valentina about her salon plans.

'I want to hyelp people, like abused women,' says Valentina with the magnanimity of Miss World.

'What, you want to give them facelifts?' asks Ted.

'No,' she explains patiently, 'I want to make a network of people who can help them.' I am still a little mystified by this aspect of Valentina's business plan.

The conversation naturally turns to ghosts and psychic mediums. Everyone tries to top one another's otherworldly experiences. Jamie and Iris, in their endless quest for the ultimate crazy fad that will make their lives complete, have recently attended the Spiritualist Church. There, Iris's long-deceased mother spoke to her. I am quite impressed to hear it. It has been

---

* It's called the CACI Ultimate.

my opinion that psychic mediums are a bunch of hoodwinkers but I am always willing to entertain a different point of view. We imagine what ghosts might be stalking us right at this very moment. 'The Murdered Maid of Mayhem Mansions?' Iris suggests. Spooked now, we decide it is time to leave.

'I think Valentina will make a wonderful beautician,' I remark to Iris in the car on the way home.

'Yes, she is so lovely and so kind,' agrees Iris.

Valentina is such a big presence that I have never really had a proper conversation with her husband, Tom. 'What does Tom do?' I ask Iris.

She thinks hard for a moment or two. 'Well,' she finally tells me, 'he has got some kind of a, um, ah, job!'

Iris and I fall about laughing. It's a concept that is totally alien to us.

I'm back at home now, feeling tremendously pleased that I have managed a full evening out with my friends without once throwing up or falling asleep. Even better than that, Nick is arriving in the morning.

❖

It's so much fun now Nick is here. I have missed him a great deal more than I've let on. All of my friends have been terrific. Nonetheless, it's been hard going through all the chemo without my gorgeous guy. I find it comforting just to share meals and watch movies with him. He loafs on my couch in just the right way. I sleep restfully in his arms. When I open my eyes in the morning his smile fills my new day with joy. Nick fits me like my favourite jumper. And it's great to have someone to help me water the plants and take out the rubbish.

That said, I was surprised at how distressed I became after Nick arrived. 'Compare and despair,' the wise ones say. What they mean is that longing to be who one is not is a hiding to nothing. Yet that is what I was doing. I managed to put a subtle spin on it by comparing myself not to Cate Blanchett but to myself, six months ago. When Nick met me I had long red hair; I was sexy, healthy and carefree. Now I'm bald and sick. I'm tired all the time. My greatest and most buried fear is that he will run away in horror from the new reality.

I finally pluck up the courage to let Nick know that I don't want to lose him. He reassures me, tells me that he thinks I'm beautiful and generally lays it on thick with all the stuff I like to hear. That cheers me up no end.

❖

I find tattoos fascinating. I'm intrigued by the idea of submitting to pain in order to create beauty. And I'm baffled by the idea of submitting to pain in order to create some kind of hideous blue splodge or gammily scrawled acronym on one's arm or, likely as not, one's face. And then having to live with it – forever.

Let's face it, the good ones are beautiful and the bad ones are moronic. My friend Cindy has a skull tattooed over her entire back. That may strike you as repellent but in fact it is a work of exquisite artistry. In a bikini Cindy is a subversive masterpiece. It takes vision and courage to transform oneself in such a way.

Most people, though, get an innocuous flower or some Chinese writing (why?) tattooed in a discreet spot and then watch it fade, stretch and become irrelevant as the decades roll by.

I have, on occasion, toyed with the idea of searching the world for the ultimate Zen Tattoo Master who will etch a delicate yet powerful image of a phoenix over my lower back. But I have never had the gumption to actually do it. So I have chosen instead to have no tattoo at all.

As well as being a yoga goddess and a great mate, my friend Tess is a committed football fan. Today she has taken Nick on a pilgrimage by train to her Mecca, Old Trafford, to watch Manchester United play Everton. Meanwhile I'm at the Harley Street Clinic for radiotherapy planning. This is when they take precise measurements in order to work out exactly how to administer the radiation. Apparently the rays will be sent into my breast at a very oblique angle so as to penetrate only as deeply as is strictly required. If they simply blasted me front-on the radiation would cook my heart and petrify my lung. And we don't want that.

In the basement Diane, a radiographer, greets me. She hands me a pack of leaflets to add to my extensive collection. These ones are all about radiotherapy and its side effects. There is also a schedule of twenty-five appointments, one every weekday for five weeks. I sign yet more papers exonerating everyone from everything in the event that I peg it on the table. After taking a routine MRSA swab (methicillin resistant *Staphylococcus aureus*, the dreaded hospital superbug), Diane leads me into a lead-lined room and asks me to strip to the waist. I assume this means wig and all.

I lie on a bench whilst Diane and her colleague Sam position my limbs and then make pen marks all over my torso. Diane and Sam are both Antipodean. I wonder if the hospitals of Sydney and Auckland are overflowing with British and French medical professionals? The radiographers shine some green laser beams on me. Diane makes mysterious calculations and calls out the results: 11.4, 109 and so on. Next, Dr Carmel Coulter bustles in. She asks me to confirm which breast they will be irradiating. I appreciate that kind of belt-and-braces approach to safety. Then everyone leaves the room and my body slides into the giant doughnut of the CT scanner. The scans will show the precise shape of my chest and ribcage, where my lungs are and suchlike.

Scan complete, Diane returns. 'I'm just going to spot some ink onto you and then prick it in with a needle,' she informs me.

'Okay,' I say, 'but why?'

'The marks will enable us to line up the radiotherapy in exactly the same way every day,' she explains. 'They are very small, like tiny blue freckles. But they are permanent.'

And thus I have my first tattoo. I can't wait to tell Cindy.

❖

Since Nick arrived I've been so preoccupied that I haven't had a chance to keep up-to-date on hair- and nail-related matters. An inspection shows my right big toenail has started to come away all down one side. This is most disappointing. I had assumed that since the chemo has ended, so would the side effects. Not so, apparently.

No sign of eyelashes or eyebrows yet. I manage to create an eyelash illusion by smudging a fine dark line of powder along my upper lids. As I study my eyes I catch sight of the top of my head in the mirror. It is covered all over with fine white fluff, like baby hair. I'm sure that's new.

Hallelujah! My hair has started to grow.

❖

It's my birthday. Nick wakes me up with a cup of tea and a box of chocolates. The chocolates are from Haigh's, a high-class chocolatier in Sydney's Strand Arcade.

'Shall we have one now?' he asks.

'Darling, I don't really want chocolate for breakfast.'

'Okay,' Nick replies with unusual restraint. I put the chocolates on a shelf in the kitchen.

It blows me away that Nick managed to bring the box of chocolates halfway across the planet without eating them. Leaving Nick alone with chocolate is akin to leaving Charlie Sheen unattended in the chemist's.

Today is also the date of a charity Hallowe'en party that I have been involved in organising. I've roped Nick into it too. With various friends, we spend most of the day hard at work shifting furniture, decorating, organising tombolas and raffles, setting up sound equipment and so on. I rather deplete my energy reserves and by four o'clock I am shattered. Nick takes me home to get some rest before returning to attend the party. I crawl into bed.

'How about a nice cup of tea and one of those chocolates?' Nick offers.

'Oh darling, that would be just lovely,' I answer in a tired whisper. I snuggle down and listen to the reassuring sound of Nick whistling and clanking crockery in the kitchen. He reappears with mugs of hot tea. I sip my tea and gaze at him expectantly. He gazes back at me expectantly.

Then he says, 'I think one of those chocolates would be lovely just about now, hey, darling?'

'Oh, yes, I agree with you,' I reply.

He disappears again and I lie back on the pillows thinking that life is just about perfect. A moment or two later Nick comes back into the bedroom. I perk up and look at him. I notice that he has a strained and slightly crazy smile on his face. I also notice that he is not holding a box of chocolates.

'Darling,' he says, 'I think a chocolate would go really well with our cup of tea.'

'Mmmm, absolutely,' I say, bemused.

Suddenly, Nick's composure seems to break down completely. He advances towards the bed. 'Right, Jessica, I've had enough of this,' he almost shouts. 'I really want a chocolate. Give me one.' He tears off the duvet and peers underneath. 'Where have you hidden them?'

'They're in the kitchen,' I squeak.

Rested and full of chocolate, we don our Hallowe'en costumes. As a miniskirted witch and some sort of chicken-bone voodoo man, we return to the party. Despite continuing numbness in my toes I wear shiny black high heels. Nick holds me in his arms and I dance for the first time since I was diagnosed with breast cancer. It feels good.

NOVEMBER

Nick can barely contain his excitement. He has booked tickets to see Dr John. All dressed up we drive to Soho, miraculously find a parking space straightaway and stroll along Frith Street. Inside

Ronnie Scott's it's all cosy with velvet seats, black polished tables and shiny brass railings. The warm-up act is an eccentrically dressed singer accompanied by two acoustic guitarists. Her voice is technically good but she just doesn't have the elusive quality of emotion that grabs one's heart. My attention wanders to other members of the audience.

There, sitting right in front of us, is an old acquaintance of mine, Toby. As the annoying singer leaves the stage I tap Toby on the shoulder. He beams at me.

'Jessica, how *are* you?'

Now, 'How are you?' is a tricky question. It is generally accepted that the question is asked merely as a matter of courtesy. The standard response is 'Fine, thank you', or 'I'm well'. Most people understand that the questioner is not really hoping for an honest and detailed reply, telling them of our marital problems or describing our bouts of premenstrual tension. But I also recognise that to reply 'I'm fine' when I am, in fact, in the midst of treatment for a life-threatening illness might be taken as blasé to the point of rudeness.

'I'm well,' I reply. Then I add, 'I've had . . .' and here I find myself mouthing the word cancer. 'But I'm well,' I say. 'I'm having all the treatments and I'm going to be fine.' Toby nods and squeezes my hand.

Why, I wonder, do I still spontaneously feel the need to mouth the word *cancer*? Instinctively, I don't want the people at the neighbouring tables to hear it. But why not? I don't know them. I will never see them again. I certainly don't care what they think about me. I suspect that it is because many still respond to even the mention of the word with irrational fear and shying away. And I don't think I could cope with that spontaneous rejection.

I only have a short time to ponder the question. Nick howls with delight as Dr John appears with his ju-ju stick, his dark glasses and his necklace of fangs. The band kicks into some true funky music and I'm so transported that for the next hour that I don't even once think about c-a-n-c-e-r.

❖

Head fluff continues to increase and thicken every day. It's exciting. Who knows how long it may take before actual hair will appear? I talk to Mum about it on the phone.

'It takes a few months for babies' hair to grow,' she speculates.

'And it may take longer for an adult,' I muse. 'After all, babies just grow everything like crazy.'

'But then again,' says Mum, 'you were born with a full head of hair.'

I try to picture what my new appearance may be. I can't imagine. Of course I haven't seen my natural hair colour since I was sixteen. In the intervening years it has been black, blue, purple, pink, deep brown, bright red and, mostly, auburn. Nurse Lottie told me that after chemo my hair might grow back curly. Or dead straight. Or black. Or completely white. Some kind of hopeful montage of Katharine Hepburn crossed with a shampoo commercial vaguely formulates in my head but then slips away. Looking in the mirror I see a bald old woman. I can hardly remember what I used to look like.

❖

Today I receive my first dose of radiotherapy. I have been in some denial about how scary that is. When I finished the chemo-therapy all the nurses assured me that, compared with chemo, radiotherapy will be 'a walk in the park'.

Last night I found myself sobbing for no apparent reason. Nick just stroked my tummy until I was calm again. I have to say that, even though he insists on stashing his dirty socks and pants behind the bedroom door, it is nice to have him here with me. Although he has been with me all along, his physical presence warms me in a way that Skype chats, no matter how intimate and kind, cannot. There is an unspoken conversation that continues between us when we're simply walking, eating or watching a movie. The sound of Nick's breathing gives me a sense of safety and belonging. Being alone at night with my fear has been hard.

❖

Nick and I are in the basement at the hospital, where they keep all the big medical machinery. An Australian voice calls my name. The voice comes from an attractive young woman whose name badge says *Bianca – Radiography Team Leader*. She leads the Jessy-and-Nick team into a small room and runs through a list of key points that I need to know about the radiotherapy procedure.

Apparently each session will take about fifteen minutes. The actual zapping will take about two minutes. Most of the time will be taken up with getting me into exactly the right position so that I receive a very targeted dose of radiation to just the correct area – that is to say, my left breast. Bianca shows me a CT scan of my breast with lots of coloured lines drawn on it, somewhat like isobars on a weather chart. This is a plan devised by Dr Coulter, mapping exactly how much radiation will be received in each part of my breast.

Bianca runs through the possible side effects: fatigue and sunburn-like redness that may make my skin dry, sore and itchy. But generally 'a piece of cake' compared to chemo.

After Bianca has explained everything, she asks me if I have any questions. As usual, I can't think of any.

'I have a question,' says Nick. 'Why is it that everyone who works here is Australian?'

With the Q&A session concluded we are introduced to a second radiographer, named Debbie. Debbie is not Australian. She's from New Zealand. She guides us back through the labyrinth of underground corridors. Then we arrive at the radiotherapy chamber. Outside is a control panel of computer screens with all sorts of scientific graphs and numbers displayed on them. Inside is a gargantuan machine looming over a small bench.

'Does it have a name?' asks Nick.

'No,' replies Debbie, 'but we think it's male.' Nick christens it 'Bruce'.

I strip to the waist behind a small curtain and emerge half clothed. I wonder why I always wish to disrobe behind a screen, even though all assembled onlookers will see my bare body in the next instant? Perhaps the act of undressing is more revealing than just being naked.

Wearing only black leggings, knee-length boots and a pink skull-print headscarf, I climb onto the table. Debbie and Bianca arrange my arms to rest into a set of stirrups above my head.

'How are you feeling?' enquires Bianca.

'A bit intimidated,' I reply.

'Well you look *fantastic*,' blurts Nick.

Next come the green laser beams, strafing my body this way and that. The two radiographers reel off numbers to one another whilst they press buttons that move the bench up, down and to one side and the other. Bruce rotates its big eye around my torso. Nick strokes my leg as they make their calculations. The gentle touch of his hand comforts me. Once the two radiographers are satisfied that they've prodded me into the correct position and cross-checked their readings, everyone leaves the room. Bruce whirrs into action. It beeps and then makes some clicking noises, rotates then beeps again.

'That's it,' says Debbie as she re-enters the room.

'That's it?' I repeat. I get dressed and we go home, stopping by Ainsworth's pharmacy to pick up some of their Emergency Cream for the treatment site.

'What's for dinner?' asks Nick as we cross our threshold.

'There's still some of that delicious fresh plaice. How about I fry that up and make some brown rice and salad?' I offer.

'Yum,' replies Nick, with feeling. I pull my boots off and lie down on the bed. I feel Nick's hand holding mine. I feel myself diving and diving into a dark pool of oblivion.

A long time later, Nick is shaking my shoulder. 'Jessy, it's half-past nine,' he says.

I stagger groggily into the living room. There on the table are two plates filled with freshly fried plaice, brown rice and salad. This is my definition of happiness.

❖

Radiotherapy will now be every day, five days a week, for five weeks. My concern is that, because I really don't want to do it at all, I will subconsciously sabotage the whole thing by forgetting to go. Hence I've set multiple alarms on my phone and computer for every appointment.

I had hoped that the end of chemo would coincide with the end of my worries and cares. What with everyone going on about how radiotherapy is such 'a walk in the park' and so on, I had imagined myself and my slightly pink breast bathed in rainbows, tiptoeing through the tulips hand in hand with Nick, pausing here and there to pluck a fresh chocolate éclair from the trees.

So I'm surprised to find myself regularly breaking down in tears, with Nick having to calm my frenzied bouts of anxiety. Of course, money is always a worry for anyone dealing with a serious illness. Those of us who are self-employed don't even get sick pay. Social Security won't cover the cost of organic groceries, let alone health insurance, home insurance, petrol, parking, clothes, phones, new tyres, broadband, Hermès scarves and a thousand other daily expenses. So, like many people, I've borrowed and gone into debt to get through. I am very lucky that my sister, Miranda, has been able and willing to bail me out.

Another source of anxiety is the prospect of long-term side effects of the various cancer treatments. A quick Google will throw up endless opinions that both chemo and radiotherapy cause other illnesses. Many of these are simply scare stories,

God only knows who originates them and for what possible reason. But then there are solid concerns too. Last week I read about long-term side effects of radiotherapy on the website of Cancer Research UK. Apparently it can cause fibrosis that leads to hardening and shrinking of the breast. It can also trigger lymphedoema.

I was quite taken aback. I feel as though I had not been fully aware of these possibilities. I don't know how commonly it happens. But it was enough to start the little hamster of anxiety running on its wheel. Pretty soon my mind worked its way around to the big looming unknown: Tamoxifen. When it comes to this drug, opinions are polarised. According to Suzy Cleator, Tamoxifen is the most important treatment for oestrogen receptor positive breast tumours after surgery. Those in the medical profession swear that it's a wonder drug that has changed the outlook for breast cancer sufferers. According to many in the alternative camp, it is a destructive and misogynistic treatment that wicked drug companies have peddled to credible doctors for their own greedy ends.

The inescapable fact is that Tamoxifen is known to cause blood clots, strokes, cataracts, hot flashes, headaches, fatigue, nausea, vomiting, dryness of the vagina, itching skin, rashes and cancers of the uterus. I still have a lot to find out and a lot of questions to ask. But I sometimes feel that I will inevitably have to make a choice between a disease that may kill me and a drug that may kill me.

The thing that really gets to me is that a few months ago I was told that Mr Hadjiminas had completely removed the tumour from my breast. The more I learn, the greater seem the risks associated with what I had understood to be a belt-and-braces approach.

All I can do is inform myself to a point where I feel comfortable with whatever decision I take – and then embrace the unknown. In the end, I tell myself, there are no wrong decisions.

❖

Today, I have a series of back-to-back appointments at the hospital.

First, I'm to see Mr Hadjiminas. In the past few weeks I've been doing some heavy lifting. Honoria warned me not to but I feel that I can't just sit around like a helpless doll whilst others fetch and carry for me. It started gently, with carrying groceries, and culminated with helping Flossie to move her bed. Since then, fluid has again started to collect in my back at the site of the surgery. Next, I have a massage. I've been looking forward to that since I booked in three weeks ago. Then I have an appointment to see Dr Coulter. I'm nervous about that because I intend to ask her lots of questions about side effects of radiotherapy and Tamoxifen. My final stop is for radiotherapy.

With such a schedule, I guess it's unrealistic to expect zero hitches. Mr H's clinic is running late. By the time Honoria calls my name it's already time for my massage. Nick asks the receptionist to let them know that I may be ten minutes late.

Mr Hadjiminas is full of smiles for me and handshakes for Nick. Once the niceties are complete, I disrobe behind the screen. Mr H prods a finger into the large bubble of fluid on my back.

'Ouch,' I say.

'Hmm,' he replies. 'I think we will send you down to see Dr Butler – she can get a better look at it on ultrasound.'

'What, now?' I gaze helplessly from him to Honoria.

'Yes, now,' replies Mr H in a firm tone.

'But I've got a massage booked.'

Honoria promises to call the therapist to see what can be done. Mr H fills out an ultrasound form. Then Nick and I jump aboard the lift to the basement.

As we arrive the receptionist is on the phone. I hand her the form as she replaces the receiver.

'Ah, Miss Jones,' she says. 'They've just phoned to say that you should reschedule your massage for another day.'

'Oh,' I squeak. I feel as though they cancelled Christmas. I keep my chin up and try not to pout as we take a seat in the tiny waiting room. But Nick can tell.

'Breathe, darling,' he says. 'In . . . two . . . three . . . four . . . hold . . . two . . . out . . . two . . . three . . . four . . .'

Half an hour passes by as we wait. I glance at Nick. 'I'm due to see Dr Coulter in five minutes,' I say in a tone of rising anxiety.

Nick strides out to have a word and in the next moment a nurse calls my name. I'm ushered in to see Dr Butler, the ultrasound doctor. She runs her magic seeing-eye over my back and pronounces that I have fluid build-up from under my arm right down to the small of my back.

'But what is it?' I ask.

'Oh it's just kind of . . . juice,' she pronounces. She inserts a needle to siphon it out. Breathe . . . two . . . three . . . four. It's no good. My back goes into spasm. She withdraws the needle and we start all over again. As Dr Butler begins to draw off the fluid she looks over to the nurse. 'Can you get me a bigger container?' she asks. Breathe . . . two . . . three . . . four . . . 'This isn't juice,' says Dr Butler, 'it's blood. You must have haemorrhaged into your back.' Breathe . . . two . . . three . . . four . . .

Eventually I dress and rejoin Nick in the waiting room. The nurse pops her head in.

'Can you wait?' she says. 'Dr Butler wants you to take a sample of the blood to Dr Coulter in case she wants to have it tested.'

'Oh Nick, I'm so late,' I say.

'Don't worry, I will go up and tell them,' he says.

Once I've got the pot of blood tucked safely in my handbag I walk up to the main reception desk on the ground floor. Nick isn't there.

'He's gone up to the second-floor waiting room,' the receptionist informs me.

The temperature in the Harley Street Clinic is usually about the same as it is in Dubai. By the time I've climbed upstairs from the basement to the second floor my spindly legs are buckling beneath me. I collapse into Nick's arms and he brings me a plastic beaker of iced water. We wait. And wait.

'Oh no, now I'm going to be late for radiotherapy,' I gasp. I've completely given up on the breathing. Nick leaps to his feet and heads to the desk.

'There we go,' he says, 'they've rescheduled your radiotherapy.' How I'm going to manage to make it to all these appointments without Nick I have no idea. At last my name is called.

Dr Coulter is no fool. Yet she has a caring, almost maternal side to her nature. She can tell that I'm stressed and incoherent. She talks to me in a calm tone. First, I hand her the jar of blood.

'I have no idea why they've sent me this. Your blood is perfectly healthy,' she pronounces. Smiling, she drops the jar into the bin.

'Yes, well,' I reply, 'I've heard that Tamoxifen can cause other cancers. I'm concerned about side effects.'

'It is true,' Dr Coulter replies, still smiling, 'that Tamoxifen doubles the risk of cancer of the uterus.' My face falls. 'But the risk is very small to start off with. So, the general occurrence of cancer of the uterus is about a half in a thousand. With Tamoxifen that risk becomes one in a thousand.'

'I went to a talk by this American woman who wrote a book about hormones and the menopause.' I mention the title of the book. 'Have you heard of it?'

'I'm afraid I haven't,' replies Dr Coulter.

'Anyway, she said she wouldn't take Tamoxifen under any circumstances.'

'Oh? And why not?' asks the kindly doctor.

'Well, she wasn't really clear about that. But she said that doctors are in the palms of the drug companies and that you should get in touch with an oncologist who co-wrote the book with her for more information.'

I'm surprised at Dr Coulter's immediate acquiescence to the suggestion. 'Of course; we can email her,' she says. 'This has to be your decision.'

I was warned that fatigue is a common side effect of radiotherapy but I didn't think it would be worse than after chemo or come on so quickly. Today I didn't get up until midday, again.

'Remember what Dr Coulter said,' Nick reminds me. 'Rest, good food and get some exercise. We must get out for a walk today.'

'Mmm-hmm,' is my non-committal reply.

By the time we've bathed and dressed and eaten some muesli, Daisy is ringing on the doorbell. Way back in June, when I started having treatment for cancer, my friend Daisy said she wanted to help by giving me singing lessons. *How will singing lessons help with breast cancer?* I wondered.

I've come to relish my weekly singing sessions. The breathing part of the lesson is most relaxing. Then letting rip and belting out a song is simply exhilarating. Singing in the car is a marvellous stress buster. That pushy f***er in the 4x4 who cuts you off at the lights? Just sing him away. Daisy says that singing is 'an invisible anchor for the spirit'. I have to say that I agree with her. I find it uplifting yet at the same time grounding, if that makes sense. Like most things, singing is largely in the head. Henry Ford coined a wise aphorism: 'If you think you can do a thing or think you can't do a thing, you're right.'

Buzzing after the lesson, it's time to head off to Harley Street for my daily zapping. Today I have a proper look at Bruce. It really is a gargantuan machine. If Bruce were in my flat it would fill the entire living room as well as busting through the ceiling for good measure. Dan, one of today's radiographers, tells me that to install Bruce they removed a part of the roof then lifted it over the top of the building and dropped it down in four pieces. Bruce was then assembled in situ, inside his concrete- and lead-lined basement room. In the room next door lives an identical machine, Bruce II.

It's dark outside by now and still we haven't had our recommended daily exercise.

'Let's go to Hyde Park,' I suggest.

The Serpentine car park is deserted. We walk down to the quiet water. In the lee of an island a small flotilla of ducks is sleeping. Tethered rowboats bob. Geese paddle silently behind us hoping for a bread crust.

At the end of the lake looms a huge Ferris wheel sparkling with white fairy lights.

'What's that?' asks Nick.

'It must be the Christmas Fair.' I gasp with glee. 'Oh Nick, let's go there!'

We stride on, aware that we have come out with no money whatsoever, yet drawn onward, mesmerised by the lights and distant music. Before we know it we are walking in the midst of Winter Wonderland.

It turns out to be a fantastic fair. We stroll past big swings that spin around, an inflatable monster that one can walk inside of, Waltzers, Bavarian sausage stands, a Ghost Train, a Hall of Mirrors, a wooden Helter Skelter, an Edwardian penny arcade and an ice-skating rink. We reach the front entrance by the Queen Mother's Gates at Hyde Park Corner. A young PR-type woman with a clipboard approaches us.

'Are you on the guest list?' she asks.

'No,' replies Nick. 'Where can we get tickets?'

'You can't,' she informs us. 'Today is for the media only.'

Not to be defeated, we cry out in unison, 'But *I'm* in the media!' and then look around sheepishly to see if anyone noticed us being such blatant hustlers. Nick flashes the girl one of his melting smiles. Under such an onslaught of foolishness she crumbles.

'Well, because I like you I'm going to give you two passes,' she pronounces.

We grab them with glee and run away before our good fairy can change her mind.

'Oh, honey,' I squeal, 'can we go on the Waltzer?'

'No, no!' cries Nick. 'The giant swings first.'

We go on the Waltzer *and* the swings. We ride the huge wheel and have our photo taken. We play games of chance and skill in the Penny Arcade. Nick is fascinated by a What the Butler Saw machine: full of saucy photos of Edwardian babes. We get lost in the Hall of Mirrors and fly on mats down the big slide. Nick finds a cash machine and then buys us roast beef rolls with mustard. At last we find our way to the Zippo's Circus tent and settle into plastic seats to watch a show of ladies being sawn in half, magnificent strong men and lithe 'African' tumblers. It's classic entertainment.

As we finally depart, all the stalls are closed up. The German fairground workers cluster around in little groups, smoking and quietly chatting. The big monster lies deflated on the ground. We walk back along the shimmering Serpentine arm in arm and I lean my head on Nick's shoulder.

'That was the most fun.' I sigh. And it was. After cancer, every gift seems like a treasure. Every day is special. Some are simply magical.

❖

Having radiotherapy treatment is very different to having chemotherapy. On the plus side, it doesn't make me feel like I want to lie down on the floor and vomit. It doesn't make my hair fall out, nor attack the linings of my mouth, throat and other orifices (no, I'm not going to describe that for you). It doesn't threaten to necessitate a blood transfusion.

A sane person would favour radiotherapy over chemo any day of the week, given the choice.

But there are downsides too. The chemo treatment was only once a week, or once a fortnight. And, strangely, I felt more cared for. The whole chemo unit was set up to make you feel as comfortable as possible. There were the big easy chairs to snuggle into, blankets and pillows and, above all, nurses. The nurses were always there to hold my hand if I got frightened or to make me a cup of tea or just to have a chat.

Radiotherapy is more impersonal. I arrive each afternoon.

'Take a seat,' says the receptionist. Then five or forty-five minutes later she calls my name and says, 'Please go on down.' I take the stairs to the basement and sit in another small waiting area. It is always hot and stuffy with a medical smell. My name is called again. Every day I see a different pair of radiographers. They are pleasant and professional but they're not interested in chatting. They see patients every fifteen minutes all day long. The job requires a high level of concentration. There is no room for mistakes yet they must try to stay on schedule. They don't know *me* at all. My main interaction is with Bruce or, on one occasion so far, Bruce II. The whole procedure makes me very aware that I am on a cancer conveyor belt.

My radiographers du jour are Patti and Laura. I strip to the waist and assume the position on the bench with my arms above my head. They reel off their readings, adjusting the bench until my body is perfectly aligned in the crosshairs of their green laser beams. Then they leave the room. Once again I'm alone with Bruce and the ever-playing Elton John CD. It seems just like Groundhog Day.

'Hello Bruce,' I say. Bruce says nothing, just stares at me with its big eye. Elton, however, pipes up. In a concrete- and lead-lined basement he sings to a woman on a bench and a giant machine.

❖

Last night I said goodbye to Nick at Paddington then stood on the platform watching the Heathrow Express slip away westward. I thought that I might cry but I didn't. I have learned that crying often happens when I somehow feel that I'm being deprived of something. But I know that I will see Nick again. And quite soon, really. The past few weeks have cemented our relationship. I feel secure in Nick's love. Now I'm just counting down the days until this cancer business is officially 'over' and Nick and I can spend carefree, joyful time together.

Being with Nick has taken up a lot of my time and attention. I'm alone again. It seems like a good moment to catch up on where I am with treatment and future plans.

Money continues to be a worry. But, so far, everything has worked out somehow or another. So perhaps I should give up the worrying. It doesn't contribute anything to the situation. The Department of Work and Pensions have been unfailingly unhelpful. Since the beginning they have bombarded me with paperwork. Last month I received seven separate letters from them in a two-day period. Last week they sent me a fifty-page form asking me for all the information that I have already given them. They assessed me as fit for work when I was recovering from surgery and having chemotherapy. I have had to fight them every step of the way for my benefits and it has been exhausting. Six months of illness has generated a file of paper four inches thick. Each of their mad missives necessitates a telephone call, a long period on hold, an inane conversation with yet another person who doesn't know what they are talking about and cannot help and, finally, a wait of indeterminate length until someone more qualified calls me back. Or, more likely, does not. During that time I cannot leave the house nor even use the phone for fear of missing the call and having to start the whole hellish process over from the beginning again. It is not the kind of help one needs when one is ill.

The tax people, by contrast, have been marvellous. In July I contacted the Inspector of Taxes to explain my situation. After waiting three months I received a letter in reply. The inspector informed me that, as a writer, I am able to spread my earnings over two years. Thus, at a stroke, he halved my tax bill.

When the chemotherapy ended I thought I was fine and fit as a flea. With hindsight I can see that I was actually quite sick and very weak. In the past week or so I've begun to feel stronger, although I'm still immensely tired. Yesterday was my twelfth radiotherapy session out of twenty-five. So I'm nearly halfway through. Since I injured my back a couple of weeks ago there has been quite a lot of fluid collecting there. I'm quite distressed about that. It feels like I've taken a step backward. Parts of my arm, back and breast are still numb following the surgery.

On the whole, though, I continue to be really pleased with my progress. I got through the chemo very well. Although I felt sick and all my hair fell out, I did not have to be hospitalised at any stage. And now my hair is growing back.

But I'm still concerned about whether or not to take Tamoxifen. Every day I change my mind five times before breakfast. I am swayed in one direction then the other each time I read something new or get another opinion. However, I am gradually marshalling all the information I need to make a decision.

In the meantime I think about what else the future might hold. Cancer has turned my life inside out. Disintegration holds the possibility of regeneration. 'Everything happens for a reason.' How many times have you heard that glib phrase slip from the lips of a well-meaning friend at a time of difficulty? But if you question your friend about what it actually means, they will mumble something about 'life lessons'. Pressed further, they will admit that, really, they haven't got a clue.

Are we are all naughty schoolgirls who somehow need to be taught our lessons? I do not believe that in some karmic way I deserved to have cancer. I cannot accept the notion of an inter-ventionist God sitting up above, moving the chess pieces around, pronouncing, 'She has to get sick so that she will learn patience.'

Yet the more I have thought about it the more I have come to the conclusion that everything *does* happen for a reason.

Here is how I interpret 'everything happens for a reason': things happen but the reason is not pre-ordained. The reason is what we make it. Every situation in life has a positive aspect. It is up to us to examine our difficulty and draw the benefit from it.

Here are the things that I have gained in the last few months:

understanding that Nick won't run off and leave me when the chips are down has renewed my faith in romantic love; I have become truly aware of how many loyal, loving friends I have; I have learned how to ask for help, even in small ways; I have discovered that there are people who will step in to support me financially; I have been told that I have a 'good-shaped head' and can get away with very little hair; I have found that I can endure extreme emotions – the fear of death and the anxiety of financial insecurity – without needing the crutches of drugs and alcohol.

All of these gains will be advantageous to me in my future life. I'm sure there will be more entries on the pro side of the balance sheet before this is all over.

I cannot change what has happened but I still have a choice: to gain some benefit from it – or not. It's only twenty-six more days until I leave for Australia. Only twenty-seven days until Nick and I are together again.

❖

With Nick gone my days seem vaguely pointless. On Saturday I slept until six in the evening. I hauled my bum out of bed just in time to get over to Marylebone for a full-on Thanksgiving dinner courtesy of Ted, who is a native of San Francisco. Chilli the chihuahua greets me at the door with Iris following on her heels. Unlike me, Iris is not Nick's biggest fan so I haven't seen much of her in the past few weeks. Well, every cloud has a deep purple lining, so I hope that Iris and Chilli will reappear in my social windscreen between now and Christmas.

On Sunday I had morning tea with Flossie.

'How're you doing?' she asked. I took this as an invitation to let rip with a mudslide of whingeing . . . from 'I'm so tired' to 'I'm worried about not having any work, how am I going to afford to be away in Australia for so long?' to 'I don't know what to do about Tamoxifen'. As a professional psychotherapist Flossie is able to let all that kind of nonsense wash over her. But the decent thing to do would be to bung her £50 for the 30 minutes she endured. Instead, Flossie told me that I shouldn't be thinking about working whilst I'm recuperating from cancer treatment and then paid for my tea.

After that I retreated to the couch. I slept through Everton v. Liverpool and Arsenal v. Manchester United, woke up, Skyped Nick and then went to bed. I awoke at ten this morning to the phone ringing. It was Ben.

'I feel so bad for sleeping all the time. How am I going to get my life back together?' I said.

Ben suggested that I stop worrying, sleep as much as I like but get some exercise. 'Put on those crazy walking shoes and get out of the flat,' he said. I pull on my red beret, buckle up my MBTs and stride out into the rain-lashed streets. I stride on as far as the Oporto café on Golborne Road and then break for mint tea and a custard nata. *Got to build my strength up gradually,* I sensibly advise myself.

The walk perks me up, though. I decide to revert to my proven modus operandi of time commitment. That is to say, small actions taken on a daily basis. I have a daunting list of things to do before I leave for Australia. Just looking at the list is enough to propel me straight onto the couch. But if I commit myself to doing just two things a day, then I will easily have it all completed in time.

❖

It's Monday so it's back to Harley Street for me. Today I am ushered into the presence of Bruce II. I strip to the waist and in a trice I am on the bench with my arms aloft. This is the thirteenth session so I'm more than halfway through the treatment. To celebrate, radiographers Laura and Susie are going to take an X-ray of my chest.

The green laser beams flash, the readings are cross-checked and the radiographers leave the room. I listen as the lead-lined door whooshes and clunks shut. Bruce II extends an arm with an X-ray film plate attached to it. There is a click, followed by a long silence. Nothing.

Then I hear the chunking of the heavy door mechanism disengaging. Susie rushes in.

'Don't move,' she says. 'The X-ray arm won't retract so I'm going to have to do it manually.'

I do not move my head but out of the corner of my eye I can see that Susie is fiddling and pushing and getting nowhere. I feel an itch on my right temple. Laura comes in to assist Susie with the fiddling. The itching strikes up all along the underside of my shoulder.

'Why don't you get a big stick and give it a whack?' I suggest in a helpful fashion.

'That's exactly what I was thinking,' replies Susie.

As if to pay me back for my unkind thoughts, stabbing pains begin shooting up my left arm followed by pins and needles in my hands. I close my eyes and visualise myself walking on the beach with Nick. I hear the rhythmic swooshing of waves gently breaking. I feel the dry sand scrunching beneath my toes. Warm sunshine caresses my shoulders. Unaccountably, I see myself dressed in a long, turquoise-print silk robe by Diane von Furstenberg. I'm told that I will have to protect my breast from exposure to the sun for the rest of my life. When I get to Sydney Nick is planning to take me out shopping for a rashie. That is a 'rash vest' or nylon t-shirt with added something that apparently has the quality of protecting one from UV rays. I've looked at some rashies on the internet. The one thing that they all seem to have in common is being hideously garish and covered in logos.

I silently recite my sankalpa, a technique that I've learned from listening to Tessa's Yoga Nidra CDs: *I am healthy, I am happy, I am whole, I am sexy, I am prosperous, I am loving, I am loved, I am free!* It's no good. My arm is definitely about to drop off.

'Please may I put my arms down?' I squeak.

'Oh, go ahead.' Susie sighs and as I do Bruce II glides the X-ray plate back into its cavity. We start the procedure again from the beginning.

❖

Back in Aus, Nick is jetlagged. He Skypes me at seven a.m. Sydney time, full of beans. After he has showed me the view from the window (sunny), his new thongs (flip-flops to you) and a fat, perfect mango that he plans to eat for breakfast, he gets out a bright blue ukulele and plays 'Twist and Shout'. I sing along in a freezing cold London winter's night.

'Please bring that ukulele in the campervan,' I beg him. 'Oh, if you insist, darling,' he replies, 'but only if you bring your red wig.'

DECEMBER

Here's a tip. If at all possible, schedule your radiotherapy for the mornings. The drag about having most of my radiotherapy appointments in the late afternoon is that delays often pile up throughout the day. They keep me waiting for nearly an hour today. I top up the pay-by-phone parking three times. To pass the time I play pinball on my iPhone. I switch the sound off so that the receptionist and the other cancer victims can't tell that's what I'm doing. Then I forget to switch it back on again and miss loads of calls.

Today is an important day for me. I'm going to see Mr Hadjiminas to talk to him about Tamoxifen. Because I have several appointments back to back, Jamie has offered to drive me to and from the hospital. And because I get all tongue tied and forget to ask important questions and then forget to write down the answers, Wanda has offered to accompany me to the appointment with Mr H.

This morning I missed two calls and received two messages. The first from Jamie telling me that his car needed three new tyres, so he wouldn't be able to drive me to the hospital. The second was from Wanda telling me that she had been called back for an acting audition, so she couldn't accompany me after all. Oh, well. I called Tess. She willingly accepted the position of No. 1 henchman and agreed to come to the hospital with me.

'My question is this,' I say to Mr Hadjiminas, my tone defiant, 'if I don't have cancer, why do I need to take Tamoxifen?'

At this moment Mr Hadjiminas has the demeanour of a man who has gone to ground. Holed up behind his desk. Hunkered down with ballpoint pen, flak jacket and helmet.

But I think I've got a fair point. The possible side effects of Tamoxifen are legion, and I don't understand why I need it at all. The cancer has been removed, first by surgery and then any lurking cell anywhere in my body was poisoned by chemotherapy. Finally, any tiny bit of tumour that thinks about rearing its head is currently being nuked with radiation therapy. So with Suzy Cleator having a baby and Carmel Coulter on holiday, I am bearing down on Mr Hadjiminas again, giving him both barrels of my panic and anxiety. I've brought Tessa with me for moral support; poor old Mr H only has Honoria on his team. She is about ten-and-three-quarter months pregnant and can barely stand up.

'The thing is this,' explains Mr H. 'If we had a big scanner we could put Jessy in and say, "There's not one speck of cancer remaining in her body", then we certainly would never give you any Tamoxifen. But we cannot be sure that the chemotherapy got every single cell of cancer in your body.' He continues, 'Statistically after ten years we find that out of a hundred women similar to Jessica, who have had surgery and chemotherapy, twenty-five will relapse. So in retrospect we see that there must have been some cancer cells left behind in them.' I nod. Tessa grabs a pen and takes notes. 'But with Tamoxifen for five years we might find that only eighteen women relapse.'

'So, um, that's seven per cent fewer?' I ask, calculating in my head.

'Yes,' agrees Mr H, 'I think it's a significant difference.'

'But if I've endured five years of hot flashes and itching skin, had a stroke, gone blind in one eye and got cancer of the uterus, I might not want to be alive,' I retort with an air of empty triumph.

Mr Hadjiminas steeples his fingers. 'The risk of cancer of the uterus is increased but it is still very small compared to the risk of recurrence of your breast cancer. And we would monitor you all the time, so if you did develop it we would pick it up straightaway.'

'Yes, but I would still have the cancer,' I reply.

'That's true,' says Mr H, 'but it is 100 per cent curable.' I don't want to ask him what the cure involves. 'The risk of stroke in a woman your age is about one in a thousand. That would be doubled to two in a thousand. The same goes for blindness. The risk increases by 50 per cent so it would go from maybe two in a thousand to three in a thousand. Macular degeneration is an old person's disease. It's unlikely to affect you.'

'Is there anything else you're worried about?' interjects Honoria. 'The early menopause, perhaps? Some women worry that they will suddenly start to look old.'

'No.'

The menopause is my persistent, unspoken fear. It is a natural part of every woman's life. Yet I have seen people, both women and men, physically recoil at the mention of the 'M' word. And there it is: that buried fear of being rejected for something over which I have no control.

'Well, yes,' I say. 'I don't want to be old. I don't want to look all wrinkled and fat.'

'But you won't,' says Mr Hadjiminas.

'But I've read that Tamoxifen thins your skin and so you start getting wrinkles.

'Where is the evidence?' cries Mr H. 'Did someone take a piece of skin from a woman taking Tamoxifen and compare it with another woman's skin? No!' I love Mr H's enthusiasm for his work. 'Some women come back after taking Tamoxifen for five years and complain that they look older. I tell them, well, you are five years older.'

I spring a surprise ambush from left field. 'What about this ER-alpha S118-P? I read that Tamoxifen is effective in people who have high levels of that but not in people with lower levels?' At this point I'm shooting in the dark because I left the article that referred to this on the dining table at home. I have no idea what ER-alpha S118-P is.

'Where did you read that?' asks Mr H.

'*Science Daily.*' I hesitate. 'I think. Can you test for that?'

'Yes, we can do a test. But the studies are not certain by any means. And if you found you had a low level, would you decide not to take the Tamoxifen?'

'Oh, I don't know,' I reply wearily. 'If I had a high level, I might decide in favour of taking the Tamoxifen.'

By now my head is spinning and I don't think I can absorb any more Tamoxifen information. I ask Mr Hadjiminas to have a look at my back. It has filled up with fluid again. It's painful but, more than that, I find it very distressing. Mr H says that if it hasn't settled down by next week he will give me a steroid injection. I don't even ask him what the side effects of that might be.

I change my mind about Tamoxifen twenty times a day. I talk about it all the time, to everyone. It spills over into my thoughts and dreams. On the one hand is the undeniable cool logic of Mr Hadjiminas's approach: try it and see. On the other hand is my deep and instinctive terror of this drug. The jury is still out.

Daisy arrives at my place for our singing lesson. After a good old warble I feel relaxed and revived. She asks me how I am and I tell her about my dilemma. I run through the arguments for and against. I give her all the angles.

'It comes down to this,' Daisy states flatly. 'Do you feel lucky?'

❖

I've just returned from Harley Street and my final radiotherapy session.

It was a strange farewell. I shook hands with today's radiographers, gave Bruce a little pat and then left. I will be back there next week for final chit-chats with Dr Coulter and Mr Hadjiminas. And then in three months' time. And then every three months for a year, every six months for another year and then every year for the rest of my life.

I feel I will celebrate with a big glass of carrot and lemon juice and a tofu fry-up.

Thank you, Jesus. Thank you, Tinkerbell. Thank you, Ganesh.

❖

Now the countdown is on . . . Only six days until I depart for Sydney.

A friend of a friend has broken up with his long-term partner and is facing a rather miserable Christmas. So I've offered him my flat. Actually, it really suits me to have somebody to take care of the place whilst I'm away. The only issue is that I have so much *stuff*. James will not be able to hang up so much as his t-shirt unless I sort some of it out. I've spent the last two hours folding winter clothes into four big plastic boxes. And yet my wardrobe is still bulging. Who can explain the physics of fashion?

I've told you before about the complicated and far-flung structure of my family.

Eloise flew to Australia this week to spend some time with her father and stepsisters before returning to Moscow for Christmas. Because Eloise is only six, Miranda flew with her and took the opportunity to cram a quick holiday in the sun into her relentless schedule of mysterious and important diplomatic work. I can never figure out what Miranda does exactly, so all my friends assume she's a spy.

Miranda and Eloise met Mum and they all spent a week at my Aunt Flora's place near Noosa. By chance, Nick was in Noosa at the same time, helping his father with the heartbreaking work of taking care of his mother. He was very keen to hook up with Miranda, Mum and co. whilst they were all in the same area.

This morning Mum emails me some photos of herself, Miranda, Eloise, Nick and Aunty Flora all having coffee together. She tells me that not only did they meet for coffee but Nick hustled them round to his parents' house afterwards. I find it a little awkward that Nick should invite half my family to meet his mum and dad without me. At the same time, knowing that Nick is so keen to be a part of my family gives me a good feeling inside.

The phone rings:

'Hello, Jessy, it's May. How are you? When are you going to Australia? You must be so excited!'

A pause . . .

'Whilst you're away, who is going to look after your eagle's feather?'

Thank heavens she called. In all the turmoil and excitement of preparing for my trip, I hadn't even thought about appointing a feather sitter.

❖

My head is awhirl with of visions of *Love in a Campervan* and other forthcoming sitcoms starring Jessy and Nick. The red wig is packed and the suitcases are zipped shut. The fridge is clean. Jamie is on his way over to lug the cases and drive me to Heathrow.

I feel as though I'm wrapping up my year of cancer too. On Tuesday I had my final appointment with Dr Coulter. To make her day I wore a Bella Freud knitted dress with 'GIRL' written across the front.

'Yes, well, we won't forget what you are, Jessica,' said Dr Coulter, dry as ever.

I'm still wavering back and forth about the Tamoxifen. 'Did you get an answer to the email that you sent to that American oncologist?' I ask. 'The one who co-wrote the menopause book?'

'Yes, we did.'

Dr Coulter shows me the reply. The gist of it is that the oncologist in America thinks that I must have *misunderstood* her co-author's warnings about the dangers of Tamoxifen. She has never heard so much nonsense. Furthermore, if I were her patient she would strongly advise me to take the Tamoxifen.

Yesterday I saw Mr Hadjiminas for the last time this year.

'Your DNA test shows that you have both the pairs of genes that indicate that Tamoxifen will be good for you,' he announced, beaming.

I already have the dreaded drug in my suitcase. Dr Coulter suggested that I start taking it two weeks after I get to Australia.

'At least have a bit of a holiday first,' she kindly advised. I intend to.

Mr Hadjiminas then drained some bloody fluid out of my back.

'Bring a pot, Honoria,' he cried, 'there's plenty here.' I tried not to wince. Mr H squirted the liquid into the pot. 'At least a quarter of a pint. Terrific,' he pronounced with a satisfied tone.

'I've read *Your Life in Your Hands* by Professor Jane Plant,' I told him.

'I'm giving up dairy. What do you think about that?'

'You're asking the wrong person. I like cheese.'

'What should I do if my back swells up again?'

'Nothing. Don't let anyone touch it,' shot back Mr H. 'If it's really bad you must see a plastic surgeon. Your chest wall is about this far from your lung.' He held his forefinger and thumb very close together. These top surgeons are very territorial about their patients. It's endearing.

I went around the hospital saying goodbye and distributing Christmas cards. Bess and Karen gave me big hugs and showered good wishes on my head.

This year has been interesting but I'm not wishing for another one like it. Bring on the new year. Bring on the sunshine. Bring on the love.

THINGS FALL APART

My general outlook gets brighter. I was upgraded to first class on the flight. Heaven-*ly*. I slept and slept most of the way to Sydney. Only problem is, now I never want to travel any other way.

I texted Nick from the lounge at Seoul airport:

> Happy Christmas baby. I'm in Korea. J x x x

> Oh my goodness. Hope you have a restful flight. You'll need all your energy when I get hold of you. N x x x

The 747 took off from Heathrow on Christmas Eve. Now, as we taxi toward the gate at Kingsford-Smith airport, it is Boxing Day. For me, Christmas was simply squeezed out of existence. But I am ready to receive the only gift that I have wanted: my beautiful holiday of recovery. Through the months of horror I have longed for sunshine, good food and love. I've dreamed of getting strong and back on my feet both physically and emotionally. I sink back into my seat and gaze at a rain-veiled Botany Bay, savouring the seconds of anticipation that thrill my body like the drops of water that squiggle across the small, round window pane.

Two helpful young men lift my cases from the carousel onto a trolley. I canter for the exit. As I slide through the doors to the terminal I experience a brief but familiar moment of arrival anxiety.

When I was a little girl my mother, Sally, my father, Julian, my sister, Miranda and I lived on a tiny dot of an island off the north coast of New Guinea. Formed by a now-extinct volcano, the island was fringed with mangroves and surrounded by a technicolour coral reef. Every vestige of the modern world – powdered milk; oblong tins of corned beef with little silver keys attached to their sides; everlasting black pumpernickel bread; rubber thongs; batteries; glass beads and us, came to Unea Island by way of a long, sick-making passage on a stinky old fishing boat. On the boat lived a wild and fluffy tree kangaroo with eyes like moons.

Coconut palms creaked and waved their fronds in the breeze. Giant rhinoceros beetles patrolled the garden. Fragrant frangipani flowers plopped onto the lawn. Miranda and I played in the white fluff under the kapok tree with our dogs, Blacky and Tanny, and two scrawny cats, Tanny and Blacky. As well as being a sometimes Irish republican sympathiser my father was, at various times convenient only to him, an anarchist; an atheist; a Roman Catholic; a communist; a fascist; a colonialist; a chef; a musician; a restaurateur; a newspaper publisher and, at all times, an alcoholic. His creed seemed to be this: 'Whatever causes maximum irritation to my fellow man.'

The scam that my father had embarked upon at that time involved stealing a coconut plantation from its rightful owners. Apart from being a con man of magnificent grandiosity, Julian was a relentless womaniser. After he moved his mistress into our house, my mother packed up and went back to Sydney, taking my baby sister with her. The deal was that Mum would find a house for us to get settled in and then my father would send me on to join Mum and Miranda. But he didn't do that. Instead he spirited me off to the green, misty highlands of New Guinea.

There I travelled from place to place with my father's mistress, a blonde German woman named Agatha. There were no roads in New Guinea. We landed on a grass strip at Simbai and then walked all night up to the remote mountain village of Kaironk. At Kaironk we slept in grass huts. The toilet was a deep, dark pit over which one squatted at one's own peril. From my perspective the high point of our stay was when a chicken fell into the shit pit and all the tribal elders gathered around in long, earnest discussions about how to rescue the precious bird from its dire situation.

Another time I stayed with some friends of Julian's who owned a motel. One of their troupe of children reported me to her father for swearing. He washed my mouth out with soap. Sometimes Julian and the mistress left me in the care of the Country Women's Association. With them I ate a lot of cake.

I later learned that my father was sending telegrams to my mother all the while, telling her that I would be arriving on this flight or that. I did not arrive on those flights. Eventually, he and Agatha gave me a fake birthday party, told me I was six (I think I was four years old) and despatched me unaccompanied on a flight to Sydney. Only this time he neglected to send a telegram to my mother.

When the plane landed there was nobody at the airport to meet me. I kicked my heels, sitting on one of those high desks. A lone stewardess waited along with me. We stared across the vast, shiny floor of the empty terminal painted with oblongs of sunlight that spilled through the glass panels of the distant doors. Eventually my mother burst through those doors, running full tilt.

Consequently, throughout my life I have experienced a certain level of anxiety when arriving at airports, especially Sydney.

What if Nick doesn't recognise me? It's been a whole four weeks since we've seen one another and since then I've grown almost a centimetre of hair. What if he isn't here? I scan the milling mob of expectant husbands, anxious mothers and bored taxi drivers holding up signs.

Nick's face is not amongst them.

Bewildered, I circle the terminal, pushing my trolley. *Maybe he's at the coffee stand – it is very early. No! He's not coming. Stop freaking out Jess, he will be here. People can be late sometimes you know.* I call him.

'Jessy! What? Is that the time already?' Half an hour later he arrives. He gives me a big hug and a ravishing smile.

'My kids can't wait to meet you,' says Nick as he loads my suitcases into his car. He has a daughter and a son, both in their early twenties.

Contrary to my expectations, it is chilly and raining in Sydney. We go out for delicious yum cha (Chinese dumplings served from roaming trolleys) and then to the cinema to watch *Avatar*.

This 3D spectacular is the perfect entertainment for a jet-lagged body and mind. It is beautiful to watch and not complicated or difficult to understand. Unlike real life.

After cuddles and kisses and yum cha and the cinema, we drop by the mobile phone shop. I haven't been able to get my phone unlocked but Nick has an old phone of mine that I had loaned him back in London. Since then he's bought a new phone.

I propose a solution: 'Nick, give me back my old phone and you can use your new phone.' I buy a SIM card. Because the phone had been mine before, it still has all my numbers stored in it. With Nick by my side I send a text to Mr P to tell him I've arrived and am looking forward to seeing him.

We go home to Nick's place.

Some things that Nick and I both love: swimming; sex; good food; cricket, and a nice cup of tea. I put the kettle on. Nick picks up my mobile phone handset. 'I'll call my daughter and ask if she will lend you a phone. She's got two.'

'Oh, don't bother, Nick, I'm happy to use the old one. I know the screen is cracked but it's already got all my numbers in it.'

Nick sits on the couch, holding my mobile phone. I watch from the kitchen as his hand slides to the couch by his side. His fingers work the buttons. He stares straight ahead, ignoring his hand, as if it doesn't belong to him.

Through the kitchen door, should he care to glance that way,

Nick would observe his girlfriend with her centimetre of brand-new hair standing rod-straight in the middle of the narrow galley. Should he hold his gaze a moment longer he would see her eyes drop and her shoulders sag forward. I try to block out my comprehension of what I am seeing, to make it mean nothing, as if it is not happening. I feel myself folding up inside, crumbling from within, as if my body has been turned to ash. But he doesn't look at me. He keeps his eyes trained on the opposite wall, studying it with fixed intent, as if some unique species of insect has suddenly materialised there. And all the time his fingers work the buttons.

The kettle reaches a throaty crescendo and then clicks off into silence. Like an automaton I reach for the teabags and then carefully pour the boiling water into the mugs, spilling not one drop.

I walk back into the living room. My eyes dart from wall to wall. I take in the tropical fish in their vibrant underwater world; the tall, dark hoop pine through the window; the oatmeal-flecked rental carpet; the cheap blond-wood dining chairs; the tired Bali batik wall hanging. I look everywhere, anywhere but at Nick and his beautiful eyes and his hand and the mobile phone.

'Here's a nice cup of tea,' I warble and hand it to him. Nick takes the tea, walks into his bedroom and closes the door.

I stand in the living room. I stand there a bit longer. My thoughts cannot formulate. They present themselves as a rushing sound in my head. My ears begin to sing. My vision closes down to a narrow tunnel. The world goes grey.

I walk across and tap on Nick's bedroom door. Then I open it. Nick is sitting on the side of his bed with the phone still in his hand.

'Nick, what are you doing?' I ask quietly. And he tells me.

'Jessy, I'm seeing someone else. I'm not in love with you.'

❖

So, contrary to my expectations, Nick and I will not be going on holiday in a campervan, nor driving up to Noosa to meet his parents, camping along the way nor any of the other lovely things that Nick had planned for us just recently when he *was* in love with me.

You make sense of it. I can't.

After Nick chucks his revolting hand grenade into my heart, I run from the flat. It is still raining. I run and run into the rain until I reach the end of the road. It ends in a car park on a high sandstone cliff edge that drops away into the not-so-Pacific ocean. Surf beats at the rocks. The rain sweeps my face and hair. It is dark now. I sit down on a bench. A pair of headlights slowly approaches across the car park towards me.

Is it Nick? I want it to be Nick coming to tell me that he's got it all wrong, that he's called his new girlfriend and broken it off, that he realises he doesn't want to live without me, that there is no girlfriend, he just made it all up, she's dead anyway, that he developed a brain tumour last week and is now prone to making irrational and wild pronouncements.

But what would I say to any of that – *It's okay, honey, I under-stand* or *Get away from me, you repulsive bastard?* It is plain to the tiny rational spark that glows dimly in the back of my mind that what Nick has done is irrevocable. Not even so much that he has had an affair but that he has done it at a time when I have been hanging on by a thread to my very essence of who I am – as a woman, as a lover, as a partner, as a friend. When looking forward to seeing him again was sometimes all that kept me going. When we have planned and dreamed of this time together. When he told me that he loved me. And now he wants me to know that he doesn't love me at all. Has never loved me. How could we find a way back from that? It is too huge. Too monstrous. Too cold. *Too cruel. Too cruel. Too cruel.*

I hold my head in my hands. I don't want him to see my tears. The headlight beams approach slowly, raking through raindrops.

Is it Nick? I want it to be Nick. The car slows to a crawl and I lift my head a fraction. It's not Nick. It's some fucking guy cruising the car park. My whole body tenses. *Just think about getting out of that car, my friend, and I swear you and I are both going over the edge of this cliff.* My hostility obviously zaps through the ether. The unidentified man drives on.

Clearly I cannot stay here or there will be a major incident of some kind.

So now I'm back at Nick's flat. I've nowhere else to go. A hotel? It's Boxing Day and I don't have that kind of money. My old school friend Lulu is staying at her dad's place nearby but I know how stressful her Christmas has been already, what with her elderly father, her snarky sisters and her teenage son. Mr P lives way up at Palm Beach, a considerable drive away. He also has a house full of family visiting from all over the world. I don't want to be ringing people up on Boxing Day night with some insane drama. Instinctively I don't want to tell anybody. I feel like I need to hold this tight to myself, as if I am holding a huge, gaping wound together, preventing a fatal haemorrhage with the pressure of my bare hands.

Nick puts his arms around me. I stand stiff like a wooden fence post and let him hug me. *I don't want to hit him.* He tries to kiss me. *I just want the world to go away.*

I have no recollection of what we talked about that evening. Here is what I do recall: we go to bed, in Nick's bed. I lie there with my eyes open, clenching my jaw so that I will not whimper with pain. In the end I can't bear it. I moan and slide from the bed onto the floor like a loose sheet of paper slipping from a folio. Nick gets up and asks me if I would prefer to sleep on the couch. I nod and he pulls out the folding bed and fetches some sheets and pillows.

In the darkness I punch my stomach as my mind races in loops. *He doesn't mean it. That's irrelevant – there is no going back. Call somebody. It's two o'clock in the morning. Go straight to the airport in the morning and get on the next flight to London. You can't do that, you have to make a reservation, it's Christmas, the flights are all full. Call Mum. You don't want to upset her. If only I had not asked him for the phone. But he still would have been betraying you. Maybe he'll change his mind. It's too late, the damage is done. Call someone in London. Stop being so dramatic, you'll only run up a huge phone bill.*

At four a.m. I call Tessa in London. I tell her what has happened. Just the facts.

'What do you mean?' asks Tess. I repeat my story, like a robot.

'That can't be right. When did this happen? Who is she?'

'I don't know, Tess. I don't know.'

Only a few weeks ago Tess invited Nick as her guest to watch her beloved Manchester United play at Old Trafford. They went up to Manchester on the train and spent a long day together. I was so happy to know that he was developing independent friendships with the people I love.

'How did you get on with Nick?' I'd asked Tess the next day.

'Oh, he is *lovely*. So kind. And Jess – he totally *loves* you.'

Tessa is one of the most well-liked people that I know. She is no pushover but she is straightforward and honest in a kind way, unfailingly generous with her time and friendship. I have rarely heard her speak harshly of anybody. There is a brief silence on the line.

'Right now,' says Tess, 'I would like to punch his head in.' And, in a way, that seems like the most loving thing anybody could have said to me.

❖

I must have dozed off after dawn. Now, as I open my eyes, it is about eight a.m. on a clear, blue-sky day. Nick is setting a cup of tea down beside me. He lifts the covers on my sofa bed, hops in, throws his arms around my body and snuggles up next to me. I feel reality lurch sideways.

Suddenly I am compensating for Nick. I can't comprehend the idea of being at odds with him. He has been my constant companion through every day of my illness. I have shared my terrors and my dreams with him. I have awoken each morning to his laughter and gone to sleep with him by my side, either holding me in his arms or talking to me on Skype. Not once have we ended a day in acrimony. How can Nick not be a part of my life? I never think of a future with him not in it.

'How was your night?' he asks.

'Pretty rough,' I laugh and stroke his hair. This is insane. After breakfast and a shower I am thinking more clearly. I must begin to climb out of this vortex of denial before I lose myself completely. I still don't want to tell anybody what is happening, but I can't just stay here in this flat alone with Nick. I call Mr P and give him a brief sketch of the situation.

'Please don't tell Mum,' I implore. *What is with this 'tell no one' policy?*

During my teenage years, from the age of ten until I was nineteen, Mum and Mr P had an ongoing love affair. Mr P was married. He treated Mum badly with his to-ing and fro-ing. Obviously he treated his wife badly too. Mum loved him and so did I. Miranda may have been less keen but that girl was born a diplomat, she kept her own counsel.

During those years Mr P was the only father figure I had. I cherished the secret fantasy that he and my mum would marry and live together. When he finally left his wife he turned around and married his secretary. That betrayal drove Mum to some dark sadness that I don't think she ever fully recovered from. We all felt it. I still love Mr P but in much more of an arm's-length way. That's just the way human beings are made – there is no getting away from the fact that, even though he was rubbish, he was more of a father to me that my own father ever was.

Anyway, what I am getting at is this: I think I may be concerned that it will be very painful for Mum to know that her daughter is going through the same kind of cruel betrayal and abandonment. On reflection that may be why I have never wanted to take any of my boyfriends home to meet my mum – until Nick, that is.

'Christ, Jess!' says Mr P. 'Stay there, I'll come over.'

I put the phone down and wonder how to get through the next hour of my life.

Mr P rings the intercom. As I answer it, Nick disappears into his bedroom and closes the door. Mr P enters and gives me a hug.

'Where is he, then?' asks Mr P, looking around the empty living room. I tap on Nick's bedroom door and open it a crack.

'Mr P is here.'

'I'm on the phone to my therapist.'

I have to say that I have always been a little baffled by Nick's relationship with his therapist. He sees her twice a week. On top of that she seems to be available to him at all times, including on a Sunday morning two days after Christmas. Nick says she is 'a brilliant therapist' but to my mind it demonstrates a distinct lack of healthy boundaries. Iris, on the other hand, says that Nick is unwittingly buying his therapist a house.

Mr P and I leave him to it and go out to lunch.

Over oysters and salad Mr P kindly offers to batter Nick with a baseball bat.

'You can watch, Jess. Then you can comfort him afterwards,' he says with a wry laugh. Pretty soon I'm laughing too.

My phone rings. It's Mum. With breezy bravado I tell her that Nick has dumped me but, not to worry, I'm still coming down to visit her and everything is fine.

Mr P doesn't think that Nick is for real. 'That prick will soon snap out of it. He clearly loves you, Miss Jessy. By this time tomorrow you'll be getting married.'

I'm not so sure. 'Up to now, everything that Nick has said and done shows me that he loves me. But, you see, he's told himself that he doesn't love me. He has to believe that in order to justify having an affair with another woman whilst his girlfriend has cancer. He's painted himself into a corner.'

❖

It's Monday and it's another bloody public holiday so I'm stuck. I can't *do* anything. I have yet to open a bank account, do some shopping, sort out Medicare before I fly down to Tasmania on Wednesday morning. That will all have to be done tomorrow. At least I've got a phone! I call Lulu.

'Jess! You're here at last. How the hell are you?' We're back to this again. *I'm fine. Oh, you know, life has its ups and downs.* I screw up my courage and tell her the truth.

'What kind of crap is that?' she says.

Lulu scoots round in her car and whisks me off to have tea in Centennial Park. Beneath the spreading branches of a Moreton Bay fig she tries to cheer me up by relating the details of her disastrous relationships with her sisters, her ex-husband and a clutch of former lovers. She gets me laughing in a grim, painful kind of way.

Then Lulu takes me back to Nick's place and accompanies me inside. She presents Nick and me with a box of Christmas chocolates and Nick presents each of us with a cup of tea.

'So,' says Lulu to Nick, 'what's going to happen now?'

Good question.

Nick looks at me. 'Jessy, I've been thinking. We can still go to Tasmania together. It's all booked.'

'Right-o, Nick. Let's go down there and then you can tell my mum that you're sorry that her daughter has had cancer and all that but, gee, isn't she looking well now? And, by the way, I don't love her – in fact, I'm seeing someone else but I thought I'd just come down here to your house for a bit of a holiday and some free sex. If that's okay with you?'

Lulu explodes in giggles. Nick looks as though he's been punched. I simply don't care. I'm so tired.

I spend another long night of jet-lagged anguish on Nick's put-U-up. In the morning Nick gets into the bed again. This time he doesn't attempt to kiss and cuddle me. I've gone into soldier mode. The only way I can go on is to be completely matter of fact about everything. I have to get to the bank. I have to buy a rashie. Nick has to cancel the campervan and his aeroplane ticket.

'And another thing, Nick – I haven't got much money. I've come here to live with you for three months, in your flat. I don't have enough to stay in a hotel or even pay rent. I suppose I will have to rent a room.'

'Jessy, I think maybe you should go back to London.'

'Nick, I don't give a fuck what you think. I'm going to need a car as well.'

We drive to the bank. When we get there Nick offers to give me $2,000. I have been very cautious about getting financially involved with Nick. I've noticed that he has a compulsive tendency to try to 'save' people by giving them money – his children, his previous girlfriend, his friends with dubious business schemes – and then he resents them for not giving him the respect and love he expects in return.

Equally I have my own issues about money. Childhood poverty has left me with a strong sense of *dis*entitlement. At home our clothes came from op shops and our furniture was rescued from tips. I'm not saying that I grew up in squalor, far from it, but I was definitely inculcated with the belief that poverty is virtuous. 'Make do and mend' could have been our family motto. My relationship with Brendan was horribly entangled in every way, notably in the area of finance. We worked together and all of our income went in to Brendan's bank account. Although I contributed greatly to the profitability of our endeavours, Brendan controlled the money and gave me hand-outs. He was breathtakingly profligate and got through vast piles of unidentifiable cash. On top of that, he had a terror of paying bills. We regularly received threatening letters from the Inland Revenue and the mortgage company. One day we were having lunch in a restaurant and I asked him for some money.

'What for?'

'Brendan, I just need some cash.'

He produced a handful of coins and dumped them on the table. That was pretty much the bitter end. Since then I have been wary of being financially indebted to a man.

But I don't see what else I can do. And it is, after all, a gift.

'Thank you, Nick. I will take that.'

❖

Now it is Wednesday morning and we are at the airport.

'Well, goodbye, Nick.' *Should I kiss him on the cheek? Shake his hand?* I turn and walk away.

❖

Mum is at Hobart airport to meet me. *Hide. Run back onto the plane.* I don't want her to see my despair. I have looked forward so much to showing Mum how well and happy I am.

I force a smile onto my face. It actually hurts. 'Hi, Mum.'

Mum gives me a big smile. A real one. And a hug.

Mum grumbles about the newfangled airport parking charges as we load my suitcase into the back of her little red car. We motor out of the car park and pass the campervan rental company. I quickly turn my head away but I feel as though I might throw up.

After driving for an hour we arrive at Mum's idyllic waterfront home, where I am greeted by Aunty Noni, who lives next door, and Cousin Eve, who lives next door to Aunty Noni. The whole place is an eccentrically gorgeous artists' compound. Apart from the three houses there are various studios and a gallery. The gardens merge into one another and are populated with sculptures by Mum, Noni and Eve, dotted amongst the gum trees and native shrubs. Parrots and cockatoos abound, squawking and carrying on in the branches overhead. Wallabies mooch across the lawns.

Echidnas occasionally stomp out of a hedge. Exquisite lizards sun themselves on rocks. And there is wild samphire growing at the edge of the pristine turquoise bay that lies only a few metres from our door.

In Tasmania it is thirty-six degrees. Unheard of! All around Mum's house grow spiky sand-grasses called 'sags'. I know from experience that I am allergic to sags. They bring my feet out in an angry, itchy rash. So on the way through from the airport we stopped off in Sorrell to pick up a pair of knee-length pink-and-lime stripy socks. Teamed with my new steel-grey rashie, Crocs and a pair of 1970s boy's orange swimming shorts, I think this outfit explores a new frontier in beach Chemo Chic.

THURSDAY 31 DECEMBER

Oops. After a two-year separation I am back in the arms of my first true love: cigarettes. It really came down to a straight choice between jumping off the cliff or lighting up. In order to maintain a semblance of chic I am smoking Sobranie Cocktails, those rainbow-coloured sticks with gold filters. I'm sure they don't count.

Here at Sommers Bay the year is going out in style. There are no street lights to pollute our view across the bay and the King George Sound beyond. Often the water glows softly green in the moonlight but tonight is overcast, so the stars and the full blue moon are occluded. The blue moon, I learn, is when there are two full moons in a calendar month. Iris says the blue moon is also known as the 'goals moon' – it's an opportunity to set out clearly what one wants for the future. I am pretty clear about my goals for this year. I've said it often enough in my sankalpa: *I am healthy, I am happy, I am whole, I am sexy, I am prosperous, I am loving, I am loved, I am free.* Beyond that it all gets a bit vague.

After dinner we gather on the front verandah; the neighbours start exploding sky-rockets. 'Ohh', we all exclaim, and 'aaah' I wonder if they are going to start an out-of-control bushfire. In my mind I plan my escape route to the beach. *Whizz, wheee* go the fireworks and then CRAAAKABOOOOM the sky simply explodes. Huge orange sheets shoot across the horizon. Molten white daggers strike the opposite Tasman Peninsula again and again. Piercing jagged branches of light arc horizontally from one side of the sky to the other above our heads. It's a lightning storm of gargantuan might and magnificence. With each flash the bay lights up, bathed in a blue-green luminescence as if it's a giant swimming pool lit from below. The show is at once mesmerising and terrifying. The neighbours continue letting off their fireworks against this backdrop of majestic splendour. The effect is comical.

As the lightning advances around the bay towards us Mum and I rush into the house to unplug all the computers and phones. We hear shrieks at the door. Cousin Eve with her friend Matt and Noni's stepson Malcam have bowled up. They crack open a bottle of champagne, popping the cork off the balcony and into the jaws of the storm.

Goodbye cork! Goodbye cancer! Goodbye Nick!

It's an exhilarating finale to a strange and pivotal year for me.

JANUARY

I have been in Australia only seven days.

After ending our relationship Nick wanted us to go ahead with our holiday as planned. I couldn't see how that would work.

Yesterday I relented. Us breaking up is all wrong. I love Nick. Nick loves me. If we work through this together it can be a stepping stone on a path that will lead us both to deeper self-understanding and ultimately a stronger bond. Surely we can sort things out? I called Nick and talked it over. I agreed that he should join me in Tasmania, albeit a week later than planned, and we would see what could be salvaged between us.

I know that his behaviour has kicked off 'International Despise

Nick Week' but I also try to understand his difficulty in having a girlfriend who lives half a world away and has gone through cancer. The campervan has been cancelled but we can still go fishing, swim in the bay, explore the locality, laze about and eat fresh vegetables from the garden. Mum is most magnanimous about it all. She is pleased for me and has started making revised plans to welcome Nick into her home. I am happy to have hope. I am looking forward to seeing him again.

This morning Nick calls to tell me that he has changed his mind yet again. He won't be coming.

'Jessy, I don't want to hurt you any more,' he says. What a walking cliché.

'Okay, Nick, well, that's that,' is about all I can muster. At this stage I am exhausted and wrung out. I feel sick. It's as if a big elephant has come along and sat – *splat!* – on my dreams.

❖

At this time of year the twilight lingers. Across the bay orange and pink slashes glow, vibrant behind black clouds. I turn my head to the east and take in the stars and the white belt of the Milky Way. I love the southern sky, the sky under which I was born. *Thump, thump* – a small black wallaby is nosing its way across the lawn. It's all so beautiful. I feel so miserable.

Suddenly the tears come. Mum rushes to put her arms around me. Poor Mum, this is most distressing for her. I can't speak. On the outside I just cry and cry but on the inside I'm thinking, *It's really true. I've had cancer and I've survived it. It might come back one day. I don't know. I don't know what to do. All I want now is a holiday, some joy and love. Why has this happened? FUCK YOU, NICK.*

❖

When Mum is not making me a cup of tea she is rubbing my back with liniment or slipping hot water bottles into my bed.

Today we are off to Bream Creek to see Mum's masseur, Debs. Debs lives on a high hill with panoramic views of the coast. She is a practitioner of Ka Huna, a full-body massage that originates in Hawaii. Debs works up and down with firm, sweeping strokes of her forearms. In the past few days I have experienced the return of severe neck and shoulder pain. It is a tension that I haven't felt since before my breast surgery. As my body relaxes I begin to cry again. I just don't know what kind of therapy can heal the sadness that I feel.

Here's what I've learned through having cancer: every day is magical. Live life. Love what comes your way. Take your happiness wherever you find it. Sad to say, *some people* don't feel truly alive unless they are enduring a painful, messed-up emotional melodrama.

In Nick I thought I had found a special man, one who could tolerate my foibles as well as enjoying my fabulous points. Not perfect – who would want that? But the right man for me. I don't think I was fooling myself. Every relationship has wobbles, but on the whole Nick's words and actions led me to believe that he genuinely loved me. I mean, for heaven's sake, he was so keen to introduce me to his parents and his children. He seemed to delight in my company, as I did in his. Our affair was drawing me back home to Australia. I followed his beckoning without fear.

Now I feel lost, foolish and betrayed. At night I lie awake trying not to recall this time last year, when Nick and I spent our time talking and laughing, luxuriating in one another's presence. Life seemed filled with promise.

I have come across several cruel stories of women whose husbands and partners left them whilst they were going through breast cancer. I just didn't think it would happen to me. In my darkest hours I battle with the notion that the break-up is all my fault.

I have lost trust in my body – after all, it did try to kill me. I am no longer strong and fit. My glorious red hair is gone. Then there is the looming shadow of Tamoxifen, which I must start taking soon. That will put me into early menopause. I imagine that in

Nick's eyes I am not a woman any more.

People keep telling me, 'That's men for you.' But these are the actions of one man – a man who couldn't or wouldn't step up when the going got tough. It's Nick who has let me down, not the entire male species. I don't believe that all men are bastards any more than I believe that all women are doormats. People are unique. Each of us has the choice to be who we want to be in every moment of our lives. It requires courage and faith.

Then again, I wonder if lesbians are so quick to sprint for the exit when their partners get breast cancer?

❖

I was determined not to call Nick. I found myself staring into the computer for hours late at night, hoping his face might appear. Unlikely, seeing as how I was too chicken to turn Skype on.

This afternoon I cracked. Mum had gone to Hobart for the day. I paced and paced going over and over recent events, round and round. Then I rushed to Mum's computer, flicked on the Skype and called him before I could reason with myself. Nick's profile appeared on the screen.

'Hello, Nick.'

Ohh. Aahh. Aahh. Aaaahhhhhh. Is there a bug in Skype? A crossed line? Nick looks at me in confusion.

'What? Who is that?'

'It's me, Jess.'

'Jessy! Let me call you right back.' Black screen. A couple of minutes later Nick calls back.

'Nick, were you watching porn?'

'Jessica, it's what I do. It's a way of holding myself when I'm distressed.'

Holding myself? I bite my tongue.

'Sweetheart, I am going out of my mind. I don't understand any of this. I can't find any peace of mind. Please tell me the truth about what you've been doing, Nick, I really need to know.'

Here is the story, as told by Nick (and retold by me):

Once upon a time, in September last year, Nick sat next to a 'beautiful girl' on a plane. They got talking. The girl's father had died from Alzheimer's disease, the same dreadful condition from which Nick's mother is now suffering. They had a common bond. Nick pursued the beautiful girl (I shall call her Kandy). He wanted to screw the girl but he couldn't because he knew that everyone – even his own children – would think him a scumbag if he did that. He didn't want to lose the opportunity of a fresh dalliance, nor did he want to show himself up as a greedy, self-serving sex addict. What to do?

He devised a scenario . . . Nick and Kandy were star-crossed lovers who were meant to be together. But that could not be because, Nick told Kandy, he was trapped in a loveless relationship with a poor suffering cancer victim called Jessy and he was too noble a man to break Jessy's heart in her time of need. Also, Kandy was in a relationship herself, enslaved by love until she chanced to meet her saviour, Nick.

Are you with me? It's not complicated.

Nick selflessly made a pact with Kandy that they would have no contact for six months. During this time Kandy could pine for Nick and Nick could go to London to spend time with Jessy, tell Jessy that he loved her, organise a three-month holiday that involved introducing Jessy to his parents and his children, and then break up with Jessy at the end of the holiday.

Then Nick and Kandy could be together as they knew that they were destined to be after three dates and a grope in his car.

But on Christmas Day, the day before Jess arrived, Kandy found her longing for Nick too great. She broke the embargo and called him. Tears were shed. Promises were made. Nick decided that he could wait for his true love no longer. His life thus far had been but a sham. Now he knew his truth.

He dumped Jessy the next day.

THE END

It is shattering to hear this from the lips of the man I loved and respected. But at least I know what's what. I now understand what a truly mediocre human being I have been dealing with. I just wish he had been straight enough to tell me upfront instead of leaving me in pain and confusion to wonder what on earth was happening to me, trying so desperately to piece it all together.

I'm ashamed of Nick. I'm ashamed of myself for having had anything to do with Nick. It is possible that he is ashamed of himself. I wouldn't put it past him. He is so, shall we say, *multifaceted*.

I should not feel anything for Nick at this point but I do. My heart is broken. And I'm angry with him for involving my family in his tawdry scheme.

Nick has hurt my mother as well as me. After going through the fear of her daughter having cancer, she had hoped to see me strong, and full of life and love. Instead she comes home today to find me curled up in a ball, shaking and sobbing my guts out.

I tell Mum the story.

'How banal,' says Mum. 'Well, I was prepared to love him. Now I'm NOT.'

I couldn't agree with her more.

❖

All this emotional distress is not good for my recovery. I have made a decision: I'm not going to take the Tamoxifen. Not never, but not now. Amongst its side effects, Tamoxifen is known to cause depression. I don't think that I can face being alone in Sydney, feeling sick, with a drug-induced depression on top of everything else.

Mum thinks that I should get some input on the Tamoxifen question from somebody she trusts. We drive down the Tasman Peninsula to see a naturopath, Nancy Haywoode.

Nancy is a very open and welcoming person who speaks in no-nonsense terms. She does not offer advice on whether or not I should take Tamoxifen: that decision is for me alone. She does, however, give me some very useful information to aid me with my decision.

First she builds up a picture of how my body has produced and handled oestrogen in the past. She asks all about my history. Was I ever on the pill? What were my periods like? Did I ever have PMT? Pregnancies? Based on my answers she ascertains that I have not been overproducing oestrogen.

She explains that there are different types of oestrogens: those we manufacture in our body and those we ingest from other sources. Tamoxifen blocks the uptake of all oestrogen. Unfortunately it inhibits uptake throughout the body, not just in the breast tumour. I have never been able to quite get past the idea that the rest of my body must need that oestrogen for some important purpose.

If I am not taking Tamoxifen, Nancy explains, then I must do two things: reduce any oestrogen from outside sources and also ensure that my liver converts enough 'good' oestrogen to occupy the receptor sites, thereby blocking the uptake of the 'bad' oestrogen.

So she asks questions about my liver. Have I had hepatitis? Do I drink alcohol? Take drugs? Were my liver function tests at the hospital okay?

Having established that my liver is up to the job, Nancy tells me the most common sources of 'bad' oestrogens: plastics and pesticides. The substances released by plastics and pesticides are not real oestrogen but the human body does not have receptors for plastics and pesticides (yet) so it treats them as strange oestrogen – xenoestrogen – and sends them to the same places.

'Avoid all soft plastic and non food-grade plastic in contact with your food and drinks,' says Nancy, 'especially if the plastic is heated in any way.' What I understand this to mean is: don't wrap food in cling film or plastic bags, don't drink water out of plastic bottles and *never* eat food that has been microwaved in plastic. I have already replaced my plastic water bottle with a glass lemonade bottle that I refill from the tap.

She continues: 'Tupperware is food grade, which means that it does not leach PVC molecules, but don't put it in the microwave. And don't eat food out of tins. The lining is plastic and they heat the tins to seal them.'

I visualise the shelves of my local supermarket. Every single edible item is enveloped in a sheath of soft plastic. Avoiding plastic is going to be difficult.

Next, pesticide. That is more straightforward: eat organic food wherever possible. I have already done so ever since I was diagnosed. The shame of it is that it has precluded shopping for lovely fresh veggies on Portobello market and forced me into the supermarkets where all the produce is wrapped in plastic. If organic is not available, she advises me to reduce my intake of meat, chicken and dairy.

I have lugged my extensive array of supplements along with me. 'Which of these can I live without?' I ask with a pleading eye. I find it tedious to force all those pills down my throat each morning. The supplements that she recommends for me are: selenium (200 μg daily) and omega-3 fish oils. I have been taking an expensive high dose co-enzyme Q10 capsule.

'That was important to protect your heart whilst you were having chemo,' she says, 'but you could reduce it now. Resveratrol is a powerful anti-oxidant. You should definitely continue that as long as you are smoking.'

Finally, Nancy wants to inspect the fluid build-up in my back. I take my top off.

'Oh my,' gasps Nancy, 'that is the most beautiful surgery I have ever seen.' The way that other medical professionals universally celebrate Mr Hadjiminas's handiwork is a source of continuing delight to me. She continues: 'It takes time for your lymph vessels to re-establish after surgery. The white pith of citrus fruit helps in the strengthening process.' I am pleased to hear this. I regularly chuck half a lemon, with the skin on, into my juice extractor along with the carrots.

On the drive home Mum and I stop at several roadside stalls. People in Tasmania just grow everything and then sell it from outside their house or the back of their ute. We buy cherries, sylvan berries, pink-eye potatoes, onions, snow peas and carrots. Every single thing is organic and plastic-bagless.

❖

I have wrestled with the practicalities of what I should do next. Go back to London? I have a friend ensconced in my flat (he is also going through a relationship break-up so it would seem harsh to give him his marching orders). It is mid-winter in London, bitterly cold, dark and economically depressed. Besides, going back would feel like utter defeat. I came here for a holiday. I can still spend time in Sydney and maybe drive up the coast to Queensland on my own.

But where will I stay? How will I go on a driving holiday with no car? How will I cope with the aftermath of cancer alone? So here I am, again, on the brink of making a decision that may well have profound implications for my physical and mental recovery with no real understanding of how to make that decision.

One of my suitcases is still at Nick's place. He wants to know what my plans are. We have surreal Skype conversations, mixing up mundane practicalities with bitter recriminations and further cruel revelations. Nick keeps trying to rescue me. He offers rooms that I might rent, one at his friend's girlfriend's place, another in the flat of an elderly friend of his parents'. *I don't want to stay with anyone Nick knows.*

I ask him why he changed his mind about coming to Tasmania when it was he who proposed the idea in the first place. He tells me that his conscience wouldn't let him go through with his secret plan to break up with me at the end of the trip. He tells me, in a confessional kind of way, that he has never ended a relationship before. *Like this is some big therapeutic breakthrough in Nick's development as a man.* Then he tells me that another friend of his has a spare car. I can rent it from her for $75 a week. Well, that sounds practical. I do need wheels.

This is all horrible, though. I want Nick out of my life. But if I am to spend time in Sydney it seems that I will have to rely on him to some extent. *And, anyway, I don't want Nick out of my life – I want Kandy out of our lives. I want Nick to come to his senses. I want everything to go back to how it was. I want to be loved, to be joyous, to be free.*

I want to disappear into a hole in the ground.

❖

From: Jamie
Subject: Tamoxifen
To: Jessica

Jessica, I think you need to wake up and smell the coffee here. Naturopathy and food are no match for a virulent cancer and even if they were (which they are NOT) you cannot be vigilant on all of the areas you outline. Frankly, I think you are messing with your life. Tamoxifen dramatically reduces the risk of relapse and your genetic tests show that you are suitable for it. And yet you refuse. I'm not sure you realise the consequences of your decision . . . and I am certain that your doctors will be worried if you persist with what I think is an insane decision, in the circumstances. Be grateful that this option is available, follow the suggestions of your doctors, stop playing God, and start to take the bleedin' thing . . . otherwise, you could die. You know me. I say this with love and as a fellow cancer survivor. I have never agreed with this decision of yours and it worries me greatly. When my doctor gave me my diagnosis, he said I had no choice but to have intensive chemotherapy. Then he corrected himself and said 'Well, yes, you do have a choice. You could choose not to do it, but then you would die.' You have had a very traumatic few months not only with the cancer, but emotionally too, and I seriously do not think you are thinking straight at the moment. Please give what I have to say some serious reflection.
Love
Jamie

From: Iris
Subject: Tamoxifen
To: Jessica

It's up to you what you do in the end but this level of avoidance of materials (even if its merits are true) is impractical/impossible in the UK. Sadly cancers like yours tend to return if you take this approach there is a possibility that you will spend the last few years of your life trapped in a paranoid world of fear and control – like those poor women who dedicate themselves to punishing Gerson therapy routines. Just saying. x

From: Jessica
Subject: Re: Tamoxifen
To: Jamie, Iris

Dear Jamie and Iris,
I really appreciate your concern. This is not a decision that I take lightly by any means. It is my life that we are talking about, after all. I have been doing a lot of reading and finding out about different approaches to cancer treatment. There is no doubt that many of them are paranoid or just plain mental. I am, at the moment, impressed by Jane Plant's book *Your Life in Your Hands*. Jane Plant had breast cancer that came back four times, despite chemotherapy, radiotherapy and a host of alternative regimes. The last time it reared its head she was given 3–6 months to live. Undaunted, she decided to do her own research and came up with what, in my opinion, is a relatively easy-to-follow regime. That was sixteen years ago and she is still alive! It seems common sense to me to do everything that one reasonably can to minimise harmful substances in one's diet, cancer or no. At this time my mental health is my priority. I don't want to add a drug-induced depression to the turmoil that I am already going through. I do feel, however, that I'm getting stronger day by day. I have discussed my decision with my oncologist and intend to do so again. The Tamoxifen issue is not closed. I intend to keep my decision under review.
    Lots of love to you both and thank you for being such good friends,
Jess.

❖

I must do these blue moon prayers more often.

I called Lulu, my friend from school. She lives in Armidale, a university town far away in the north-west of New South Wales. Lulu got on the phone to Samantha, another friend from school. Samantha called me.

'Come and stay at my place,' she said without a moment's hesitation. Samantha lives at Watsons Bay, one of Sydney's loveliest harbourside locations.

I am in Sydney now. Samantha is at a health farm in Byron Bay. Before she left, Nick collected the spare keys to her house. This morning he met me at the airport with Samantha's keys and my suitcase in his friend's 'rental' car. He was dressed in the smart new clothes that we had bought together a few weeks ago in London.

'You look great,' I said.

In the car Nick said, 'Jessy, I think this car is a bit of a heap. I want to lend you my car instead. I'm worried that in your state of mind you might have a crash. I will keep this car and you can pay the rental.'

He took me to lunch – at the same restaurant that he took me to when we first met. Over lunch he reiterated his desire to be with Kandy.

'I love you, Jessy, but I'm not *in* love with you.'

This is the last straw. 'Nick,' I say with venom, 'you don't know what love is. You cannot tell the difference between sex and love. You only want to be with Kandy because you're not with her. You think you're in love if you're experiencing pain and longing. Your last girlfriend treated you like shit.'

I go on, my words spraying him like machine-gun bullets.

'Please correct me if I'm wrong – you went on three dates with this Kandy, then you embargoed her with the plan of spending the following six months with me and then breaking up with me at the end of our holiday?'

Nick nods.

'How old is she, Nick?'

Nick doesn't want to answer that one but I hammer away at him.

'Thirty-six.'

Another blow to my pride.

'Does she have children?'

'No.'

'Have you considered that it is quite likely that she will *want* children?'

'She does.' *They've talked about that already?*

'But, Nick, you don't want to have any more children.' Nick told me once that one of the things that he found so attractive about our relationship was the fact that I don't want children either, 'And you've had a vasectomy!'

Nick nods again.

'So, Kandy is prepared to sacrifice her desire to be a mother in order to be with a man she sat next to on a plane? Am I also correct in thinking that she is already in a relationship and she is planning to leave her partner for you?'

'Mmm-hmm.'

'Nick, have you at any stage questioned this woman's mental health?'

'Well, yes,' he mumbles. 'It has crossed my mind.' I burst into tears.

After the most painful lunch of my life – one that seemed to go on for a week – we collected Nick's car and drove to Samantha's place. I didn't sleep at all last night.

Now here I am, wandering around a big, beautiful, empty house in Watsons Bay. But I honestly don't know what I am doing here. I feel more desolate now than I have at any time in the last year.

At the same time I am continually astonished by how life changes from moment to moment. One minute my boyfriend does a runner, leaving me marooned and devastated on the other side of the world; the next, new people appear, like angels, to help pick up the pieces. That is my experience anyway.

The phone rings.

'Hi, this is Mike, Angeline's husband.' Angeline is the sister of Deirdre, a friend of mine from London. 'I may know of a room to rent.' Mike continues. I tell him thanks, but I am fine for now. 'Well, I must get you together with my friend Jack,' he says. 'He's great fun and he'll take you out for lunch.' *Accommodation and a lunch date, wow.*

Mr P calls: 'Lunch and a movie on Monday?' *You bet.*

A text. It's from Deirdre.

Come over. Let's go to the beach.

I drive round to Bellevue Hill. A short while later Deirdre, her young son, Eddy, and I are promenading at Bondi. I go in for my first proper swim. How I have missed the luxury of bathing in the Pacific Ocean. The water is warm. The surf is gentle. There are plenty of waves to catch but it's calm enough for swimming too. My body feels alive, at home in the sea.

An email arrives. It's from Desmond, another friend from school:

Are you in Sydney? Come and stay with me.

We go out for dinner instead and we chat, chat, chat. The phone rings.

'It's Nick,' I gasp.

'Who is Nick?' asks Desmond.

❖

I have been thinking a lot lately, about love.

I once wrote that I 'fell head over heels' with Nick. But I acknowledge that as a lazy kind of shorthand to describe our early infatuation. I don't believe that people 'fall' in love, as one might fall down a hole in the road. I made a choice to love Nick based on the deepening intimacy between us. I renewed that decision every day.

There is a feeling, familiar to you as well as to me, that one will surely die if one cannot immediately and utterly possess the person who is the object of one's desire – if one can't, as Samantha puts it, 'climb into their stomach and live there.' That feeling, I can confidently say, is not love.

So what is love?

Here is my current perspective on the matter. First of all, one must be prepared to take a risk. Love is not a feeling; it is an action. My friend Sheldon and I regularly have long talks on Skype. Such conversations are often called 'heart-to-hearts'. Think about it. 'Love is time,' says Sheldon. I agree with him. Love is time; it is intimacy; it is desire; it is trust; it is courage; it is commitment; it is tolerance; it is respect. Above all, love is kindness. And it takes two people. Love is not something that just happens to us – rather, it is something that we do.

My recent experiences have left me shaken but, I hope, not broken. I hope that I will love again; I don't know how or when but I am determined not to allow myself to become bitter or un-trusting in the future. I don't yet know who my new lover will be. But I do know two things for certain: that he will be a man who knows himself and that he will have a connection with my country.

I walked into love, with my eyes open. And now, I am walking back out of love.

But not away from it: I have the love of my friends and my family always. And I trust that I will take a risk on romantic love again. Maybe tomorrow? Maybe one day.

❖

Samantha has blown in from Byron Bay like a tropical cyclone. She is nonstop nervous energy. Samantha had breast cancer last year and she has heartache troubles of her own – she broke up with her boyfriend on Boxing Day. When it comes to health and romance we seem to have a grim synchronicity, Samantha and I. She tells me all about what a bastard her ex is and how appallingly he's behaved.

'Well,' I observe, 'he kind of puts Nick in the shade.'

'Oh no,' says Samantha, 'I met Nick when he came here to pick up the keys. Did I tell you about that?'

I shake my head.

'Jessy, it was utterly bizarre. He positively bounded in the door, all smiles: "Hi, I'm Nick." He was so charming, vibrant – and handsome; I'd go as far as to say flirtatious. We chatted for quite a while. I have to say, I was a little bit entranced by him. "He's really lovely," I thought. And he seemed so protective of you, "but – *oh hang on* – he's just dumped Jessy and torn her heart out,"' Samantha hoots. 'And then,' she squeals, 'and then, Jessy, he went around and meticulously rearranged my house in preparation for your visit. "Jessy will want to sleep in this room. Jessy will need this many pillows . . .'" By now we are both crying with laughter.

❖

When Nick left me, so suddenly and unexpectedly, I was pitched into a time of shock and panic. Here I was in Sydney with limited resources, nowhere to stay and few friends. In London I rely heavily on my infrastructure of friends for conversation, company and love.

Tess was on the phone immediately, calling up the long-distance reinforcements. 'You must ring my friends Bernadette and Nigel and Madge.'

I called Bernadette and we went out for dinner and a long, heartfelt chat. 'What a bastard,' she concluded.

I called Nigel. We met for coffee. 'What did you expect?' said Nigel. 'All my friends are getting divorced. I don't like Nick anyway.' I didn't ring Madge straightaway. She lives in Byron Bay, about 800 kilometres north of Sydney. I felt it would seem a bit odd for her to receive a phone call from a stranger in faraway Sydney, looking for emotional support. But, then again, I call people in London and lean on them almost daily. So this morning I decide to make contact with Madge.

'Hello,' I announce awkwardly, 'this is Jessica speaking, I'm a friend of Tessa's. I'm visiting from London.'

'Oh yes!' Madge practically screams. 'Tess has told me all about you.'

'Well, I know you're in Byron Bay . . .' I begin.

'But I'm not,' Madge cuts in. 'I'm in Sydney today. Come to dinner. I'm meeting some friends.'

'Oh, I would love to but I've already made a date to go to the movies.'

'What a shame,' Madge replies and then motors on. 'Anyway, London! Do you know Adrian A?'

'Yes, I do.' We chat about Adrian A for a moment.

'And do you know Janet Q?'

'Of course, Madge, I know her quite well.' The conversation continues in this vein. It turns out that I happen to know most of the people that Madge cares to mention.

'Okay,' I say, 'how about this? I'm looking for a friend of mine in Sydney. I've lost her number. Her name is Mandy B.'

'That's who I'm having dinner with tonight!' exclaims Madge. 'You have to come.'

I collect Deirdre from her home and we take in dinner and a movie. After dropping Deirdre home I call Madge.

'We're in a restaurant in Paddington,' she informs me. 'Come over. I won't tell Mandy that you're coming.'

Ten minutes later I walk in to a crowded pizza joint. The table goes quiet. Then Mandy nearly eats her napkin.

'Oh my God. Oh my God. Oh my God. Jess!'

Mandy and I have been travelling on parallel but ultimately different roads. She has been dating a gorgeous man, Tony, who lives in London. By chance, I am also independently acquainted with Tony. So in the course of the past year, Mandy and I have crossed paths several times, first in Sydney and then whenever she visited London to be with Tony. On each occasion Mandy and I had got together to have lunch and gossip about our lovely men and long-distance relationships.

And now, here is Tony, sitting in the restaurant in Sydney. I take a seat next to him.

'How long are you here for, Jess?' asks Tony.

'I go back on the twenty-sixth of March,' I reply.

'Can you change your flight?' he asks.

'Why?' I look at him, puzzled.

'Mandy and I are getting married on the twenty-seventh,' Tony quietly tells me.

❖

I regard my mobile phone with murderous rage. I want to pulverise and smash it, jump up and down on its carcass and then run over it a few times in the car. *Look what you've done, you bastard phone!* At other times it feels as dangerous as a lump of plutonium my hand.

Because we have both had possession of it, the phone contains Nick's contact numbers as well as my own. Nick deleted all of his text correspondence with Kandy but her number is still in the phone. It rings. The name on the display is 'Sebastian'. Sebastian is Nick's friend; I met him last year when he invited Nick and me for a day of sailing Sydney Harbour on his boat. He and his girlfriend made me very welcome. I warmed to Sebastian; he seemed like a straight guy. But why is he ringing me now?

There is only one way to find out.

'Hello?'

'Oh hello, Jessica. This is Sebastian, Nick's friend. Look, Nick has told me what he has done. I imagine that you must be feeling terrible. Would you like to have a talk? Can I take you out for dinner?'

Is Nick's friend trying to make a move on me? No, he's got a girlfriend. But Nick told me that they keep having rows. Yes, but who doesn't have rows? That doesn't mean he's not a decent bloke. Not all men are like Nick. Oh, aren't they?

I decide to give Sebastian the benefit of the doubt. 'Yes, that would be nice,' I say. I am further reassured by the fact that he doesn't offer to pick me up but, rather, asks to meet me at Bondi. 'Okay. And I promise I will try not to bitch about Nick all evening,' I say.

We meet for dinner at a cheap Thai restaurant. That also bodes well. He's not trying to impress me. I make small talk, trying to avoid the 'N' word.

'How's business? Tell me more about what you do. How is your girlfriend, Linda?' *But why are we here? What is his motive?* It seems false to not talk about Nick at all. Nick is the only person Sebastian and I have in common. In the end it is he who broaches the subject.

'Jessica, I think the way Nick has behaved is appalling. But I want you to know that you're better off out of it with him.'

'How do you mean?'

'Nick is the most selfish person I have ever met. I put up with him because he's fun but I'm a man. Nick got together with one of my female friends before he met you and he really hurt her.'

This is news to me. According to Nick he was on his own for eighteen months before he met me. He told me that he took the time to heal from his previous relationship break-up. He told me that he didn't have any involvements with women at all. Why would he say that? But I don't press Sebastian for further details. I don't get the chance.

'I wouldn't introduce Nick to any of my friends. He hardly ever works. He doesn't even read the papers. If you asked Nick about what is going on in the world he wouldn't have a clue. His only interest is in himself. He is a human wrecking ball. Nick doesn't care who he hurts.'

He goes on in this vein, with scant encouragement from me, for an hour. I feel that Sebastian had not intended to launch into a tirade but it would seem that he might have been bottling up his opinions about Nick for some time. It's like somebody shook a can of pop and ripped the stopper off.

After Sebastian has let it all out he looks a mite embarrassed. We go for a walk on the promenade to cool off but the polite chit-chat peters out. It is clear that we're both uncomfortable. I do like this man and I appreciate his kindness and courage in reaching out to me but I don't think we can become friends. It would just be too awkward.

❖

When Nick and I were blessed by an eagle's feather falling from the sky I took it as an augur of far sight and longevity. Later, I made a decision to love Nick for who he was. I would stick with him. I thought that love and commitment would get us through.

Of course, I never factored in a devastating illness.

Now, every time I see a campervan, my heart turns over. I eat in amazing restaurants and only think, *Nick would love this*. I go sailing and picnicking with amusing people and I wish he were there to enjoy it too.

Towards the end of my six years of solitude I realised that I had been alone for long enough. Too long. I had prayed to meet a wonderful man who would be my lover and my friend. I met Nick. He and I seemed to be having the relationship I had dreamed of. Not the white-picket-fence, let's-get-married-and-live-happily-ever-after relationship. Not in a tick-all-the-right-boxes sense. But a relationship in which we could both dare to be vulnerable, kind and honest. A relationship in which we didn't need to change or improve one another – we could just relax, enjoy a cup of tea and be ourselves; a relationship in which I could build trust.

Why would I turn my back on that? Why would I not want what I already had? Nick told me that he too had prayed for such a relationship. And he met me. So he got what he had prayed for. Why would he throw it back in God's face?

And this brings me to what is, for me, possibly the most devastating aspect of this situation. It has shaken my faith in God.

Please settle down and exercise a modicum of tolerance whilst I elucidate a little on my understanding of my personal higher power: in matters of religion my father, Julian, careened from extreme to extreme: from atheism to Roman Catholicism. When we lived on the island in New Guinea, he sent me to the mission school. The school was a palm hut on the beach containing maybe fifteen children of varying ages. It was run by a couple of starchy nuns under the supervision of a priest. My father and the priest were locked into a fiery battle for the hearts and minds of the plantation workers so there was some background tension surrounding my attendance at school, apart from the fact that I was only three years old and I had to lie and tell them I was four. The nuns made me sit on my own because I was, despite my dodgy provenance, a white girl. In their view it would not do for me to be fraternising with the natives. I hated that school from the very first day. One afternoon the nuns invited me up to the mission house for tea and a little chat about what's what in the world of Christianity. I informed them, as Julian had taught me, that a virgin birth was a straight impossibility and that 'Jesus came from a sperm.'

After that there was no more school for Jess. Hooray.

A while later Mum, Miranda and I moved from Sydney to Queensland to be near my grandparents. My mother didn't have much time for religion. Nanna however was a regular attendee at the local Presbyterian church. On Sunday morning she took me with her. After we had settled into a pew and Nanna had convinced me to stop talking and asking questions everybody struck up singing. I love to sing! So I joined in with one of the songs that my father had taught me – a drinking song: *Oh the more they try to keep me down the better I live in Sydney town; I've got ten stubbies in the fridge and I pay no toll on the Harbour Bridge* . . . Nanna hustled me from God's premises quick sticks.

I guess the upshot of those early experiences is that I don't regard church as a very welcoming place. And yet . . . I have always been deeply convinced that there is *something*. I searched for a spiritual connection.

Living in a squat, Craig and I often had nothing to cushion us from this harsh world but a prescription for Mogadon that we could regularly manipulate from our local GP. For a brief respite from cold and hunger we would visit the Radha Krishna temple in Soho Square. In order to qualify for a free lunch we were required to chant for half an hour and then endure a Q&A session. I have to say, I always rather enjoyed sitting on silk cushions in that perfumed room singing 'Hare Krsna, Hare Krsna, Krsna Krsna, Hare Hare, Hare Rama, Hare Rama . . .' I genuinely liked the Hares. They were a congenial lot. I still break out in a smile when

I see them dancing their way down Oxford Street. But I declined their invitations to go and live at their ashram in Hertfordshire. I preferred the mean streets of Soho.

In my twenties I became a devotee of a sect of Japanese Buddhism. I loved the contemplation, the chanting and the underlying philosophy of tolerance and connectedness. But there was an organisation that had developed to deliver and safe-guard the wise teachings. Sad to say, this organisation fostered a pronounced attitude of: 'if you're not with us, you're against us'. In my experience this is the common failing of most religions – their basic philosophies are kind, loving and tolerant but the organisations that support them tend to become self-righteous, paranoid and self-serving.

My search continued.

I count myself fortunate to be amongst those whose lives have disintegrated so spectacularly that we have stumbled into the sanctuary of a twelve-step programme. When we enter recovery from addiction, we are asked to allow for the possibility that a power greater than ourselves exists. I was a smart, sometimes rational, educated (up to a point) woman with everything going for her and yet I was driven to obliterate myself with drugs and alcohol on a regular basis. In order to gain some insight into this paradox I had to examine my beliefs.

One day I was doing the washing up and a programme came on the telly about quantum physics. I listened with one ear. The first conclusion was that we will all, inevitably, be swallowed up by a black hole. Then the boffins went on, piling one mind-boggling scenario upon another. Here is my (possibly incomplete) understanding of the predicament in which we find ourselves: 84 per cent of all the galaxies consist of dark matter. Not nothing but something that we cannot see, measure, or detect. If it wasn't for that dark matter the galaxies and everything that's in them would fly apart into infinity because they're spinning way too fast for gravity to contain. But wait – there's something else lurking in between the galaxies: a menacing and spooky dark energy. Not matter at all but 75 per cent of the entire universe nonetheless, which, perversely, is pulling all of everything apart. And if it has its way the ever-increasing dark energy will 'pull space and time asunder so rapidly that the galaxy clusters will scatter, followed by the disintegration of individual galaxies then solar systems, until finally matter itself will be shredded into nothing by accelerating space.' You and I will fly apart, crash into one another and then disappear as the universe ends in one final 'big rip'. So they say.

In the face of such profound cosmic mystery I tend towards the conclusion that there might be a god. I mean, who else could pull off such a crazy stunt as that?

Is there a god? My balance sheet:

In favour	Against
The awful ecstasy of living	Cruelty
Miracles that happened when I was paralysed	Religion
Trees	
The joy of creativity – it must be modelled on a primary force of creation or else why would we do it?	
Empathy – why do living things empathise?	
The miraculous results of small positive actions indicates the interconnectedness of all things	
The power of prayer	
Coral reefs	

I believe that God is empathy. I believe that God is connection. I believe that God is love.

But now I'm just not so sure.

FEBRUARY

I drive to Centennial Park, one of the glories of Sydney. This enormous park contains grasslands, a paperbark swamp, reservoirs, playing fields and trees of awe-inspiring magnificence. I park in the shade of a gargantuan Moreton Bay fig. These cathedral-like trees can grow up to 60 metres tall. Mandy and Tony meet me by a lake populated with flocks of black swans and cormorants. We find a bunch of their friends lunching in the shade of a glade of casuarina trees. We spread out our rugs and picnic provisions then spend a lazy afternoon lying in the shade, chatting.

I take a moment to myself. Lying on my blanket with my hat on my face I can just see Mandy and Tony in the sliver of vision beneath the hat brim. They are laughing and touching one another, smiling flirtatiously, their eyes flashing. I am so happy that they are to be married. And I am utterly sad that the story of Jessy and Nick just petered out so pointlessly. Don't get me wrong. I harboured no secret dream of Nick and I marrying. I just enjoyed his company. I do not long for an all-consuming enmeshment. I grieve for the small, private moments of togetherness: cooking and eating meals; Nick teaching me how to snorkel; chatting about the day; sharing the bathroom; buying clothes with him . . . simple stuff, really.

Mandy senses my sadness and comes over to talk to me. 'You are such a gorgeous, beautiful, sexy woman, Jess. You know that man is not good enough for you. Everyone knows that. I have no doubt that an incredible future is in store for you. You just can't see it yet.' She's right: I cannot see it. But I do know that I am exceptionally fortunate to have such caring friends.

❖

I keep calling Nick. Asking him questions. Why did he beg me to take him back after he broke up with me in the hospital? Why did he tell me that he loved me? Why did he organise this holiday?

'Nick,' I rationalise, 'so many things you did were acts of love. How can you say you didn't love me?'

'That's your reality, Jessy.'

Well, of course we all experience things differently but surely one cannot ignore plain facts? Have I been living in denial? Has it been obvious to everybody but me that our relationship was phoney? In a desperate search for some kind of consensual reality I quiz my friends: 'Did you see this coming? Did Nick give off any sign?'

'He fooled me,' says Sheldon. 'Nick gave green lights all the way. He fooled everybody.'

'All I ever got from Nick was how much he loved you and how crazy he was about you,' says Tessa.

'He is a disgusting twat with a Napoleon complex,' says Iris. Friends tell me to let go. 'Let go' – it sounds freeing but how, exactly, does one do that?

I give it some thought. Here is my conclusion: acceptance is truly the key to freedom. If I accept myself as I am and I accept others exactly as they are, I can resign my resentments and truly let go. But acceptance requires understanding. And understanding requires insight. And insight requires honesty. That is why people whose loved ones have been disappeared by General Pinochet or the IRA go on looking for their bodies for decades. That is why Nelson Mandela invented the Truth and Reconciliation Commissions. In order to be reconciled we need to know the truth.

I just don't think that Nick has been honest, either with me or with himself. The things he says now are so at odds with the things he has said and done in the past. None of it adds up or makes sense – to me or to anyone. So I keep calling him and asking, coming at the puzzle from different directions. Chipping away at him like bird trying to break open a snail.

Now, at last, Nick feels that he owes me an explanation.

We arrange to meet at Nielsen Park on the shores of Sydney Harbour. I don't really want to meet him there. It is one of the few places that I love that is not despoiled by painful memories. But I can't think of anywhere else and at least I can get a swim in at the same time. It's twilight and I'm backstroking up and down when Nick's silhouette appears on the grassy bank. Even through the lenses of swimming goggles at a hundred metres distant I know it is him. Every line and curve of his body is familiar to me.

I towel myself off and paste on a smile. We sit on a bench and chit-chat, both sidestepping the reason for our meeting. Thus far Nick's explanation is not forthcoming.

'So, what did you come here to say?'

'Well, I know I've been avoiding your calls so just ask me any questions you have and I will try to answer them.'

'Okay. Why did you beg me to take you back after you broke up with me in the hospital?'

'I was conflicted. I wanted you to give me another chance. I thought I could make our relationship work.'

'And I did give you another chance,' I say quietly. 'Nick, you seem quite conflicted now. You seem to be just running away from everything. I love you and I care about you. You're my best friend. I think that at this point we can either just completely fall apart or we can use this conflict to make our relationship stronger. After all, this is how people grow together. They don't just get married and live happily ever after. Relationships are annealed in the flames of adversity. I gave you another chance when you asked me for it. Will you now give me, give us, another chance? Will you come to couples counselling with me? Maybe we can get through this?'

Nick shakes his head and looks at the ground.

'But, Nick, our relationship has been so good. What happened to you?'

'When you got ill, Jessy, I felt like there was no one taking care of me. You weren't there for me. You didn't understand me.'

Nick, I had cancer. I couldn't take care of you. And how do you say that I didn't understand you? We spoke every day. You shared your secrets and fears with me and I with you. We were so close in every way, apart from physically.

'So why did you want to have this holiday at all?'

'I just felt that I couldn't get out of it.'

'That may be true. But you didn't have to book a campervan. You didn't have to make arrangements for us to go to Queensland to meet your mum and dad. I didn't ask you for any of that. I was just happy to spend time with you.'

Nick shrugs.

I'm aware that, although Nick has come here to give me his explanation, I'm now the one doing all the talking.

I try another tack. 'So you tell me now that it has been your intention all along to break up with me at the end of the holiday. If that is so, why did you pursue my family to meet you in Noosa then drag them round to your dad's place only two weeks before I was due to arrive? Why would you do that?'

That episode has had me crazy. I questioned Mum about it. She said that she felt reluctant to go to Nick's parents' house, having never met them before and knowing that Nick's mother is suffering from Alzheimer's disease. Encountering strangers can be most distressing for those with dementia. But Nick insisted. Mum found the whole visit quite embarrassing. 'But why do you think he wanted you to go there?' I'd asked her. Mum had looked thoughtful and said, 'I think he was showing off.'

'I wanted my niece Scarlett to make friends with Eloise,' says Nick.

Nick, I thought you said you were going to answer my questions honestly

'What! So the little girls could become friends and then never see one other again? So you could fuck their lives up as well?' I'm no longer speaking quietly.

Stop now Jess. You're beginning to lose it. This is my default reaction: lecturing; confronting; cajoling. Trying to force Nick to see sense. I want to grab my words and stuff them back down my throat. But I have already unleashed the whirlwind. Reason is engulfed by a familiar, self-destructive compulsion to rampage on until there is nothing left but a blasted landscape of carnage.

The more I ask Nick questions, the more he closes up like a clam and repeats his lines. 'You didn't *see* me. You didn't *mirror* me.'

I'm your girlfriend, not your therapist.

It is dark now and we are going around in circles. I still don't feel that I've had much honesty from Nick, but it is apparent that I'm not likely to get any by railing at him.

He walks me to my car (oh, all right, it's *his* car). I say goodbye and drive. When I get as far as Double Bay I turn around and begin to double back. One single brain cell of sanity screams in my head: *Don't go back! There's nothing there for you! This is not love, it's compulsive behaviour! This is naked neediness! This is insanity.*

I'm not listening.

Nick is still standing in the darkness where I left him.

'Nick, why did you tell me that you loved me?'

'Jessy, I never said I loved you. You just believed what you wanted to believe.'

And here it is – the reality switch. You may have experienced this yourself but not been able to put a name to it. You may have suspected that your partner was having an affair. You may have challenged your partner. Your partner may have reassured you and told you that you were imagining things. You may have let the matter drop. But then you may have been presented with irrefutable evidence that your partner was having an affair. Your partner may have denied everything with a totally implausible rationale and then begun to suggest to you that you are crazy, jealous and losing your mind. You may have found that upsetting but your partner simply stuck to that line and then, over time and despite real evidence to the contrary, you began to accept that your partner was not having an affair and that you were indeed crazy, jealous and losing your mind.

Maybe this is the truth. Maybe I just imagined that Nick loved me. Maybe I trapped him in a romance that he never wanted. Maybe I'm so desperate and needy that I invented all those loving words, those kind actions, those shared intimacies.

That is the reality switch. It is a most insidious form of manipulation and mental cruelty.

Feeling as though I have been slapped in the face I drive away again, heading for Samantha's house. Abruptly my fragile mind shatters. I begin sobbing hysterically. My vision reduces to a narrow tunnel in the blackness. I'm heaving and smashing my forehead on the steering wheel. I can't drive. I can't go forward or back. *Is this what they call a breakdown?* I make a mental note to ask somebody.

I phone Nick. *He is the only one who can rescue me.*

'Where are you?' asks Nick.

'I don't know.'

'I want you to walk to the nearest corner and read out the name on the street sign.'

Five minutes later Nick arrives. He calms me down and then asks me to follow him. We drive very slowly back to his place.

Nick makes me a cup of tea and pulls out the sofa bed. 'I think you should get some sleep.' I'm a wreck. I feel ashamed of myself, embarrassed, desolate and empty. But I also feel a perverse glimmer of comfort being back in Nick's familiar orbit again.

❖

I am so confused now. The more Nick stonewalls me, the more I cling to him. The more I cling to him, the more he wants to push me away. We are locked in the dance of love avoidance and addiction that Flossie spoke about back in the hospital.

Why am I reacting like this *now*, though? When Nick broke up with me before I had every excuse to fall to pieces. I was in a hospital bed after recently being told I had cancer and then having most of my breast removed. I would have been well within my rights to scream and beg. But I didn't. I have done so much therapeutic work in the last decade, twelve steps, psychotherapy, personal development workshops. Why is none of it kicking in to rescue me from this deep, dank prison called love?

This isn't love. This is a desperate reaction to abandonment triggered by childhood trauma – you've done enough therapy, Jess, you should know that. I do know that, but the information does not help me one little bit. I can't even seem to find the walls of my mental trap, let alone the door handle.

Last year I had to focus my attention on the daily matters in hand. I had to cope. I had all my friends around me, and all the doctors. Everyone was on my side. Nick could leave but I would not be abandoned.

Now I am far from my friends and my support networks. Having cancer has ravaged my confidence and self-image. It seems that Nick's killer blows are always delivered at the times when I am at my lowest. He sure can pick his moments. 'I've never ended a relationship before,' he said. By Nick's own account his last girlfriend used him, spent his money, cheated on him and then left him. This time *he* has the upper hand.

And I am now fully playing my role in this twisted melodrama. I have crossed the line from victim to volunteer.

We are sitting on Nick's couch.

'Nick, I know you're going up to your mum and dad's tomorrow for a week. I would like to stay here whilst you're away.' *No, you wouldn't, Jess. That would be utter self-abasement.*

'Jessy, I don't think that is a good idea.' *Of course it isn't.*

'Look, Nick, I'm having a horrendous time. Samantha's place is great but it is really frenetic there. I can't think straight. My room is damp. I can't afford to get ill, I'm still recovering from chemotherapy.' All of that is true. Samantha's daughters, Lyla and Lily, have returned from their Christmas holiday with their father. Samantha keeps having wild rows with her ex-boyfriend. The place is like Bedlam-by-the-sea. Also she recently had a flood in the basement, hence my bedroom and the bedding are damp. I have developed a nasty cough over the past few days. *But is staying at Nick's place the solution?*

'I need you to help me, Nick.' *This is out-and-out manipulation.*

Nick leans in close. 'Right now, Jessica, I would like to punch your face in.'

He runs from the building. I stare at the floor for a while then I leave and sit in the car. *He's quite right, you know.* You might be thinking that I should feel horrified or afraid. What I actually feel is a sense of relief that Nick has finally said something real.

Nick's nice-guy façade has finally cracked. That can only be a positive thing.

Text to Nick:

> Well it seems I have met the real Nick Davis at last.

Four hours later . . .
Text from Nick:

> I'm sorry. Do you want to come over?

I know the drill. *Don't answer. If you don't answer Nick's love addiction will kick in and he will come running after you. The boot is on the other foot now. You will be the winner.* The winner of what? I just don't want to play that game. I love Nick. I don't want him to go to Queensland for a week of feeling terrible about himself.

I finish my coffee and drive to Nick's place. He is crying. I give him a hug and reassure him that wanting to punch my face in isn't the world's most heinous crime. Not a patch on the other shit he's pulled, I add, not wishing to let him off the hook entirely.

'You can stay here if you like. Just whilst I'm away,' says Nick.

It feels a very hollow victory indeed.

So here I am, ensconced in Nick's flat. Sleeping in his bed, watching his telly, drying myself with his towels.

Nick's possessions carry a mournful echo of the security that I experienced when I was with him. And I feel safe here in my solitude. I am actually experiencing serenity for the first time since I landed in Australia. My mind is peaceful and calm. I make myself cups of tea and simple meals and spend a lot of time reading Marianne Williamson's wonderful book *A Return to Love*. The phone doesn't ring. I don't have to make any decisions. I feel as though I am having a little holiday from reality.

Jess. You are one messed up chick.

No, you're not. You're just doing whatever is necessary to get through this with your mind and body intact.

A benefit of feeling peaceful and secure: I have started taking the Tamoxifen today. I am still quite scared about it.

❖

Last week was a temporary hiatus. I'm back at Samantha's and sinking further into despair. I seem to have completely lost enthusiasm for pretty much everything. My interests just about stretch to pacing, smoking and swimming.

I had anticipated this year ahead as being one of the happiest of my life: to have survived cancer; to leave behind the dark, gruelling days of surgery and chemotherapy; to be alive and to be in love with a man whom I thought was so wonderful, a man whose company was delightful to me – these were prospects that held nothing but joy.

Now, I can't stop crying.

Instead of lazing on the beach with my lover, I am spending all my time and money going to see a psychotherapist and reading self-help books.

I've been pondering – anguishing: What am I going to do? I haven't worked for nearly a year. My lover has left me for some passing fancy. I'm alone on the other side of the world, far from my friends and the infrastructure of my life. My resources are limited. Oh no! What is to become of me?

And I have been praying – meditating: *Let . . . go . . . let . . . god . . . let . . . go . . .* But I can't see the path forward. I am adrift in a fog of pain and confusion.

It is high tide. I am swimming in the old Vockler's Baths at Watsons Bay. Vockler's is a harbour pool enclosed by concrete arches with a boardwalk running around the top. From here there is an uninterrupted view across Sydney Harbour to the city skyline and the Harbour Bridge. The sun is shining. The water is warm. I slip into a lazy backstroke and after a few moments my mind empties. *Let . . . go . . . let . . . god . . . let . . . love . . . let . . . go . . . let . . . god . . . let . . . love . . .* stroking back and forth across the water. And then a voice in my head speaks clearly: *Jessica – sell your flat in London and move to Sydney.*

Ha! It's that simple.

❖

I call Nick. He doesn't answer. I call him again. He doesn't answer. I call him three more times . . . *Like a starving child returning to an empty cupboard.*

After a few hours Nick calls back. I feel like a fish with a hook in its mouth. We have a very long and pointless conversation during which I keep going over the same ground, trying to come at it from different angles, trying to break through Nick's carapace of self-justification. The longer we speak, the more incoherent I become.

Eventually Nick says, 'Jessy, I think you need more help. Maybe you should consider going to a rehab. I know a very good place.'

'Why don't you go there, Nick?'

'I don't feel I need it.'

'Really? Look at the horrendous mess you've made of everything.'

'Yes, but it doesn't affect me. You are the one who is suffering.'

'So you think it is okay to wreak devastation in my life as long as you can walk away scot free?'

'That's not true, Jessy. There have been consequences for me. I lost $400 on the campervan deposit. Then my friend charged me more than the $75 a week that I thought we had agreed for the car so I have to pay her an extra $200. I'm not asking you for that.'

'Are you for real?'

'Yes, Jessy, I'm doing fine. I've been going to therapy for seven years.'

'Fat lot of good it's done you.'

MARCH

To cheer ourselves up, Samantha and I have been buying bikinis. Lao-Tzu once said: 'if you can't fix the plumbing at least repaint the house' (not really). Because I am extra miserable I bought two. One is a padded halter style in a red-and-white Ikat print. The pants have a sash that ties at the hip. Very good for diverting the eye from any tummy wobbles. The other has a cute balconette bra in dark blue with a vivid print of large pink roses.

I'm in my late forties, I've lost a stack of weight (six kilos since arriving here in December) and had part of my breast removed. I still have to take care to cover up with the rashie at all times. But the right bikini makes me feel hot! To my mind, feeling good on the outside can go a long way to boosting a woman's internal esteem.

❖

Little by little, friendships are beginning to be established in Sydney. They are tenuous, like the delicate roots of tiny plants. And I am still living with Samantha, her daughters Lily and Lyla, Felix the cat and Lola the pug puppy. We've only known one another for a few weeks but the girls and I have definitely formed a mutual fan club. Yet I am still wading, swimming, drowning in the pain of breaking up with Nick.

Repetitive questions circle in my head, as monotonous as stuck CDs: *Why did you fly halfway across the world to be with me? Why did you burst into tears when Mr Hadjiminas told you that I was safely out of surgery? Why did you beg me for a second chance? Why did you book flights and a campervan and make all those plans with me? Why did you tell me how excited your children were to meet me? Why did you lie to me from the very beginning? Why did you abandon me when I needed you so much? Why do you think it is okay to hurt me like that? why? why? why? why? why?*

And then I found a lump under my arm.

I made an appointment to see Dr Warren Hargreaves, Sydney's answer to Mr Hadjiminas. I spent a week waiting, barely able to eat or sleep. I didn't tell anybody.

'How are you?' Dr Hargreaves enquired, beaming at me. Well, he did ask. So I told him: about the lump, about Nick, about crying all the time. 'Oh dear,' he said, frowning, 'well, the Tamoxifen will definitely be contributing to feelings of depression. Let's have a look at you.' He examined my neck, chest, breasts and armpits. I have always maintained that Mr Hadjiminas's hands are better than any mammogram. I get the impression that Dr Hargreaves has the same kind of magic fingers. After all, these top breast surgeons feel women up all day, every day.

'It's just scar tissue,' Dr Hargreaves proclaimed. I expelled a breath that I seemed to have been holding since the beginning of time. 'After surgery and radiotherapy you will get these lumps and you are bound to freak out. You have to get them checked up.'

This morning I am driving to see my therapist. It is rush hour and I'm in a slow crawl along Old South Head Road. I divert onto a side road to take a short cut. Ten minutes later I'm lost and hopelessly snarled in a gridlock situation. Then I begin to scream. It's weird. I have never screamed in my life before, not even as a child. I feel as if I have grown two heads. One head is observing: *What is that extraordinary noise? Where is it coming from? How are you capable of producing it?* The other head is simply screaming; deep, loud and vibrating with horror, the sound fills the car. And it will not stop. It screams and it screams. The first head remembers a song by the American folk singer Dory Previn, about 'Screaming in the Car'. She sings about being pulled over by the cops for screaming in the car in a twenty-mile zone. My screams convulse and metamorphose into sobs of laughter.

❖

I am beginning to understand that I made a big mistake right at the beginning of my relationship with Nick: I did not know who he was. Yes, we spent a lot of time together and we talked to one another about everything. Then, suddenly, we were hurled into the crisis of my cancer. Because of our shared intimacy in adversity, I trusted that I was safe with Nick. But in reality all I knew of Nick was what he chose to present to me. I never saw him in the context of his family, his friends and his daily life.

I was really taken aback by the vehemence of Sebastian's unexpected anti-Nick outpourings. Now, revelations are coming thick and fast.

I'm having coffee with my new friend Marcus and a couple of his friends. A dark and handsome man strolls up to our table, plops himself down and lights a cigarette. Conversation around the table continues and eventually I begin to chat to the stranger.

'Are you English?' he asks.

'No, I'm Australian but I live in London.' *I really must revise my accent.*

'What brings you to Sydney?' *What is the appropriate reply to that?* I'm amongst friends; I don't feel that I can just lie outright.

'I came here for a holiday to get over treatment for cancer and to spend time with my boyfriend. But it hasn't worked out too well.'

Suddenly the man is agog. 'I know who you are! I'm Anwar.' He extends his hand. 'We have to talk.' And now, upon hearing his name, I know who *he* is: Anwar is Nick's closest friend. Nick has spoken about him often.

'Okaaay,' I reply, with more than a touch of apprehension. Anwar beckons me to a separate table and I join him.

Anwar does not beat about the bush: 'Nick is a little shit. The way he has behaved is despicable. He keeps ringing up my partner, Joe, and going on and on about himself. Joe doesn't want us to have anything to do with Nick any more.'

I receive this information with puzzlement and, it has to be said, a thrill of schadenfreude.

A few days later I meet a woman named Abi. I hear that she too is less than keen on Nick. It seems that Nick has been romancing her. Apparently Nick has confided in Abi that he has been having a relationship with a woman in London but that he wants to leave the relationship because his girlfriend 'doesn't understand him', whereas Abi *does* understand him. Furthermore it seems that, a week before Christmas, Abi was at home sick with the flu. I'm told that chivalrous Nick visited her with flowers and chocolates and then tried to get into bed with her.

And then I find out about Liza. Who the hell is she? Well may you ask. Nick, I learn, was seeing Liza when he met me.

My body burns and churns in rage and confusion. I call Nick and insist on meeting him. This time he senses that 'no' is not an option. Face to face I confront him: 'Nick, who is Lisa?'

An expression of contempt crosses Nick's face and he lets out a spiteful little laugh. 'Lisa is my ex-wife!'

That throws me. For a second I wonder if I have allowed myself to become emotionally derailed to such an extent that I'm suspecting Nick of having an affair with his former spouse. But, no, I was just so flustered that I misspoke the name. 'I got that wrong. It's Liza, Nick. Who is Liza?'

This time Nick looks thunderstruck. I can see him mentally casting about for the right answer. He composes his face – the face that I am containing an urge to spit on.

'When we met, Jessy, I was seeing Liza at the same time. After you went back to London we had sex a few times but I realised that I wanted to have a relationship with you, so I ended it with her. She was pretty angry about it.' Clearly Nick believes that the fact that he chose me over Liza will make the situation acceptable to me.

'Nick, do you remember that day when we were walking on Bondi Beach and we met those people? I asked you directly if you had a girlfriend.'

'Yes.'

'You lied right in my face?'

'Yes.'

'So you lied to me from the very beginning? You used me?'

'Yes.'

'Nick, I want to be absolutely clear about this: if I had known that you were seeing somebody else I never would have got involved with you. Some years ago I made a conscious decision that I will not knowingly harm another human being in that way. I've done that and I never want to do it again. Furthermore, had I known that you were prepared to hurt her, I would have understood that you would also hurt me. By lying to me you deprived me of my integrity and my choice to live according to my own principles. What do you think gives you the right to do that?'

'I made a mistake. I'm sorry.'

'Right, Nick, this is it. I need you to be honest now. Do you have anything else to tell me?' I am wondering what he will say about his involvement with Abi.

Nick looks at me. He opens his mouth and this comes out: 'I went to my work Christmas party and I was dancing with a woman. I went home with her and we had sex.'

'What was her name?'

'I don't know. She was just some woman at a party.' *So not Abi, then.*

'Did you use a condom?'

'No.'

'Did you go for a check-up?'

'No. I don't think I need to.'

'Why ever not?'

'I haven't had any symptoms.' *Lord, give me strength.*

'Nick, I have been having chemotherapy. My immune system is shot to pieces. You know that. What you did could have put my life in danger.'

Nick thinks about that for a minute.

'I made a mistake, Jessy. I'm sorry. That was the only time. All the other times I used protection.'

All what other times? I don't even raise the subject of Abi. What is the point?

And then, guess what? Nick agrees to go to couples counselling with me. I am beginning to get an inkling of how Alice must have felt when she crashed through that looking glass.

I was just starting to come to terms with the idea of Nick's 'relationship' with Kandy. Now I find that he was betraying her too – even before she was permitted to spend any time with him. Despite reeling from this shocking onslaught of information, my heart grasps blindly for a crumb of hope: *Nick is coming to counselling. Maybe we can work things out after all. Maybe I can have my happy ending.* There is one thing that I might finally have to admit that Nick is right about: a spell in rehab could be just what I need.

❖

I long for a peaceful night of sleep. But I'm awake again at four a.m., clenching my teeth and whimpering. At six I go upstairs and make fruit salad from organic papaya, rockmelon, blueberries, lime and mint. I eat the fruit salad. I drink a cup of organic tea with organic soya milk. Samantha and the girls still slumber. It is dark. What am I going to do now? Smoke a cigarette. But I've run out.

I drive to the nearest petrol station in Rose Bay. They're just unlocking the door as I storm through it, a fiendish addict on the rampage.

I drive back up the winding S-bends to Vaucluse and then down to Nielsen Park. This place has become my church. Australia's smallest national park runs down to the harbour, where there is a little sandy beach with a netted swimming area. The bay itself is properly called Shark Bay. Obviously we are all grateful for the netting. The foreshore is grassy, shaded with banksia trees and magnificent Moreton Bay figs. In the middle of the promenade is a simple but elegant building housing a café and restaurant. I come here frequently to swim, to walk, to read books and to meet friends.

I sit on a bench and smoke one of the cigarettes. I feel less than virtuous. A soft pinkness is beginning to infuse the darkness. A ferry slides across the harbour with all its lights aglow, heading for Manly. It seems that I could almost reach out and touch it. I am surprised to find that I am not the only person here. Figures waft here and there in the gloom. Each person seems to be enclosed in his or her own cocoon of silence, alone.

Who goes swimming in the dark at six-thirty in the morning? These are not the body-conscious babes and beautiful boys of Bondi Beach.

A silver-haired lady breaststrokes gently by. As I sit I hear a shuffling noise approaching. It is a man who has obviously had a stroke. He slides his feet in small, mincing steps. His right arm does not swing as he walks to the water. A handsome blond man swims toward the shore. But as he emerges from the sea I notice that he has a withered leg. A single girl does yoga stretches on the sand. The dawn frequenters of Nielsen Park are the old, the crippled, the damaged and the broken. The people who really embrace life. The people who find their peace and freedom in the sea. People like me.

I walk back to the car, don my swimming costume and slip quietly into the water. I feel like I belong here.

❖

Mandy and Tony's wedding was beautiful. They were married at Shakespeares Point. The vows they spoke were profound, moving and real. I wept and wept, for happiness and for sadness. I felt joyful to see my friends so happy. And I felt so overwhelmingly sad for the love that I have lost.

I have not been coping well with the avalanche of grief that I am experiencing for Gaby's death, for my cancer and for Nick's cold indifference. I cry too much. I shake too often. So I am going away for three weeks, to the rehab that Nick suggested, for some emotional, spiritual and physical healing. I have been to rehab before, for drug and alcohol addiction. Yet somehow this feels more shameful to me. I imagine that people will think worse of me for not coping with a relationship break-up than for being a lush. After all, everybody who is anybody is an addict these days. I feel that the world would have sympathised if I'd had a breakdown when I was diagnosed with cancer. But when it comes to life crises such as divorce or bankruptcy, we are somehow expected to take it on the chin. One thing I do know is that trying to stand up to the blows that I have been subjected to is in itself a kind of madness. In the end the only sane thing to do is to put myself into the nuthouse.

APRIL

I have booked myself in to a highly regarded place. As rehabs go, it is on the swanky side. Set in one of Sydney's beautiful northern beaches, it has ocean views and vaguely edible food. The programme there is based on the model developed by Pia Mellody at The Meadows in Arizona. It focuses very much on codependency.

When Nick left me, my world became like a mirror that had broken into a thousand shards. Everything that I had trusted and believed now seemed insanely distorted, upside down and back to front. I had believed that at last I had met a man on whom

I could rely absolutely. A man who knew what he wanted and would be by my side in the darkness and in the light.

And I was horribly duped.

Nick told me that when I got cancer he felt that he was no longer the centre of my attention. He was compelled to seek solace in another woman's arms. In order to justify his behaviour it was essential for him to convince himself – and anyone else who would listen – that he had never loved me in the first place.

Once Nick had taken up that position it became impossible for our relationship to heal or grow. I do believe that in times of doubt and crisis we can reach inside ourselves to find the courage, honesty and love that will ultimately create a deeper bond and understanding between two people. But for Nick to admit that he ever did love me would have shattered his ego.

I blamed myself. In my head I went back in time and tried to reshape the past. I became trapped in obsessive thoughts about how I could have done things differently. Could I have focused more on Nick and his needs when I was going through the terror of chemotherapy? Whilst my hair fell out? Whilst I felt sick all the time? Could I have been a stronger person? A better girlfriend? Could I have just loved him a little bit *more*?

I tortured myself with these questions. I tried to *make* Nick see that his new 'love' was in fact textbook love addiction. I covered up for Nick in many subtle ways. I did not reveal the full extent of his cheating and lying to people who knew him. To others I spoke honestly about what had happened but I concealed Nick's identity from them. I allowed his shame to become my shame.

For three months I tore myself apart, desperately trying to figure out what was wrong with me. I thought that if only I could find the faulty gene, the broken fibre, the original fatal flaw, I could fix myself. I wanted to fix myself so that I could be sure that this would never happen to me again. Instead, my self-doubt brought me to the brink of despair.

That is codependency.

In a state of high anxiety I arrive at the rehab. I sit on my dormitory bed surrounded by a blue hospital curtain and burst into tears. I continue to cry for three days. It is a busy time though. Up at six-thirty a.m. A walk on the beach. Breakfast. A community meeting. A lecture. Morning tea. Group therapy. Lunch. Group therapy again. A workshop. Dinner. A twelve-step meeting. Supper. Bed. Up at six-thirty a.m. . . . In amongst this hectic schedule there are appointments with a GP, a nurse, a therapist and a psychiatrist.

I diagnosed myself as being severely depressed. To my surprise the psychiatrist did not offer me anti-depressants.

Rebecca, my therapist, has the compassion of Mother Teresa combined with the insight of an MRI scanner. She explains the shrink's opinion: 'You are suffering from an enormous amount of grief. The only way to deal with that is to feel your feelings and go through it. It will take as long as it takes. Anti-depressants would only put a lid on your grief and store up trouble for the future.' So much for Dr Jessica's diagnosis. 'You need to cry a lot,' she adds. 'You have experienced an extraordinary amount of loss in such a short space of time.' That helps to put things into perspective for me. I have assumed that I am just being melodramatic and hysterical.

We have lectures about codependency; lectures about boundaries; lectures about feelings; lectures about addiction; lectures about open communication; lectures about recovery, and therapy, therapy, therapy.

During the second week I go through an intensive programme-within-the-programme. This involves being shut up in a room for a week with four other traumatised wrecks. We do a lot of screaming at chairs.

After all the cathartic shouting I feel more settled and relaxed with the whole thing. Next, I present my 'trauma egg'. This is an illustration of all the ghastly experiences of my life from babyhood to now; it takes quite a long time. As my presentation concludes

I look around at the group. Everybody's jaws are hanging open. Rebecca turns to me with her marshmallow X-ray eyes.

'Are you going to write a book?'

Despite the intensive work I still hate myself. I still feel that it is all somehow my fault.

In despair I do the only thing left to me: I pray for a miracle.

Halfway through the third week I am sitting in a workshop listening to a beautiful young woman named Cecilia tell us how her older, divorced boyfriend had asked her to marry him. Cecilia accepted. The boyfriend then went abroad. That was three months ago. He has not returned.

'What is wrong with me?' she wails. 'I need to fix myself so that I can fix our relationship.' The therapist gives her a kindly look and holds out the palm of her left hand.

'Here is the evidence that this man has run off and abandoned you,' she says, then holds out her right palm, 'and here is what you are making up about yourself.'

Bam! I leap to my feet. 'I get it! At last!' I cry. 'What Nick did was an arsehole thing to do. He is a man who would cheat on his girlfriend when she had cancer and then abandon her. That is simply the kind of arsehole Nick is. His behaviour has *nothing to do with me.*' The whole room bursts into wild applause.

So here, in a nutshell, is what I have learned during my three weeks in rehab: the only thing wrong with me is that I keep thinking that there is something wrong with me.

Could I have done anything differently? Could I have been younger? Could I have been kinder? Meaner? Could I have been more beautiful? Smarter? Less smart? Warmer? Colder? A better cook? Could I have not got cancer? Could I have loved Nick more than I did? NO. And no matter how good I might have tried to be, our relationship would always have ended the same way. Nick's addiction to sex and romance is a gaping hole in his soul that cannot be filled. It means that he will endlessly search for the perfect woman, in the belief that when he finds her he will be complete. And he will never find her. Because that woman does not exist. The only person who can ever heal Nick is Nick. Until he is prepared to do the painful and courageous work that is required, his addictive patterns will not change. And so long as those patterns of behaviour perpetuate he may well continue to damage every woman that he comes into intimate contact with.

For the first time I experience a brief flash of gratitude that I got out of it when I did. I still feel pain at the loss of my dreams. I still feel loneliness when I wake up in the morning. I still love Nick. Love is not something that I am prepared to deny. But I am no longer prepared to be in the orbit of a man who is predestined to hurt me again and again. And in a strange way I feel great sadness for Nick. He has demonstrated to the world and to everybody he knows that no matter how dire the circumstances, no matter how close the relationship, Nick will always put Nick first. People pull away from that. It is not his fault. He is an addict. But he is truly alone.

❖

It has been four days since they let me loose from the rehab. This afternoon, Nick and I have our session booked with a relationship counsellor. In the last couple of days we have had some conversations on the phone that have been, if not loving and caring, at least honest. Nick says that, for what it is worth, he is truly sorry. He thinks that he may suffer from Narcissistic Personality Disorder.

I relate this insight to Sheldon. Sheldon laughs: 'Nick does love a grandiose label. He's obviously Googled that up — but it suits his purpose at this time. If anyone had suggested to him three months ago that he has a Narcissistic Personality Disorder he would have been outraged.'

Narcissistic Personality Disorder is pretty much untreatable so, of course, Nick's self-diagnosis exonerates him from ever having to do anything about his behaviour. But, in the light of our recent conversations, I am feeling conciliatory towards Nick this morning. I send him a text:

Would you like to have a coffee beforehand or maybe lunch afterwards?

No reply. Much later my phone beeps:

Hi Jessy. I've been very busy this morning and I would prefer to just meet you at therapy. I am going to see a friend after who has just come out of hospital. N

What did I really expect? Every small rejection feels like another body blow. Why do I put myself up for it?

The footpath of Macleay Street in Potts Point is cool under the dappling shade of its graceful plane trees. I ring the bell and Vanessa, the relationships therapist, buzzes me in. With my confidence on the floor, I enter a small room furnished with a couch, two armchairs and several strategically placed boxes of tissues.

Nick is already seated on the couch. I give him an awkward smile and take my seat next to him. Vanessa asks each of us some basic questions and jots down notes

'So, let's begin: Nick, what do you want?'

Nick begins to speak and then changes his mind. He gets up from the couch, takes two steps across the rug and seats himself in the vacant armchair. My heart breaks all over again. Nick does not look at me but I look at him. When Nick smiles he is beautiful. But when he doesn't, like now, his face takes on the expression of a kicked dog. He resumes.

'I have been very cruel to Jessica. I have been selfish. I have cheated on her from the beginning. I was seeing someone else when I first met her and I lied about that. I wanted sex. I pretended to be a kind, loving boyfriend. When Jessy got cancer I wasn't the centre of attention any more. So I started a relationship with another woman whilst she was having chemotherapy. On the day that Jessy arrived here she saw me deleting texts from my mobile phone. When she confronted me about that I broke up with her. I don't care about Jessy's pain. I want her to leave me alone. I never want to see her again.'

Vanessa stares at him, slightly agog.

'Okaaaay,' she says, turning to me, 'and, Jessica, what do *you* want?'

My throat constricts.

'I want a loving, committed, exciting, mutually supportive relationship with a man who knows himself. If I'm honest, my hope is that Nick will spend time working on his issues and I will spend time working on mine. Then we might try to heal our relationship and give it another go.' It sounds absurd. 'If that is impossible then I want to get to a place where I don't care about Nick any more. Not where I pretend to not care but where I genuinely don't care at all. I want to be happy.' I fumble for the tissue box and then weep uncontrollably for the remainder of the session. Nick spends the next fifty minutes manning the barricades of his vehement self-justification.

Vanessa looks pretty disgusted and then quite relieved as our therapy session draws to a sorry close.

❖

I will still be attending the rehab for three days a week as an outpatient. Before I went away I gave Nick back his car. Last night I found myself sucked into an internet vortex, trying to figure out how to get from Watsons Bay to Curl Curl by public transport. I searched. I looked at maps. I printed out lengthy timetables. Here is the lowdown: if I get on a bus at Watsons Bay at 6.48 a.m. I can connect with a ferry from Rose Bay to Circular Quay. Then, if I elbow my way through the throng to be the first to leap ashore from that ferry I can leg it down the quay and scramble aboard another ferry departing for Manly. Then it's one more bus ride to Curl Curl, arriving at 9.04 a.m. Two hours and fifteen minutes. The return journey will be the same thing in reverse only it will take longer.

I am seething with resentment at the very idea of it.

In the soft early morning I walk to the bus stop at Watsons Bay. The bus departs on time and swings right towards the harbour. I catch my breath as the vista of Sydney opens up before us. The water is smooth and green. The city towers reflect the gold of the rising sun. The Opera House glows like a pearl in the early light. The bus meanders down through the leafy streets of Vaucluse. Between ranks of luxury homes I catch glimpses of yachts and water.

I stand in the sunshine on Rose Bay Wharf for a few minutes. A sea-plane glides elegantly onto the bay and then roars into the terminal beside the ferry wharf. A sleek, twin-hulled white ferry approaches and I climb aboard with the early morning commuters. We speed past the grand villas of Point Piper, cut across Double Bay and skirt the expensive high-rise flats of Darling Point. Rushcutters Bay is crammed with yachts. I strain my eyes towards Elizabeth Bay, trying to catch a glimpse of the apartment block where I misspent my teenage years. In the foreground is Fort Denison, otherwise known as 'Pinchgut'. This is a tiny fortress-island where unlucky convicts were once sent for a punishment of solitary confinement and starvation. A perfect spot for a rehab, really. Finally we skim beneath the soaring white sails of the Opera House. With the iron-grey structure of the Harbour Bridge looming on our right, we glide into Circular Quay. I dash for the gangplank.

In minutes I am seated on a varnished wood deck seat aboard *Queenscliff*, a fine, old green-and-gold Manly ferry. The thrusters thrust and we churn back out onto the harbour, retracing the route to the east and north. Some time later the ferry passes Watsons Bay, where my odyssey began over an hour ago. I can see the hotel, Doyle's restaurant and the strip of white sand at Camp Cove. We sail right past and onward, the ferry now dipping and rising on a gentle swell that washes through the harbour mouth. I gaze through the Heads at the Pacific Ocean and the distant horizon. We could chug right out there and just keep going. I recall that the Manly ferries of my childhood originally came under their own steam 12,000 miles from Glasgow. They plied the harbour for nigh on fifty years. So we could do it. Next stop Santiago, Chile. Will I survive the journey on a soy latte and half a sausage roll?

Soon we are tying up at Manly wharf. There's time to buy a pineapple, mango and fresh mint juice before boarding the bus. This route takes me along Manly Beach with its boulevard of tall Norfolk pines. We skirt the delightful Freshwater Beach and then round the headland to Curl Curl. A sweeping view of surf, sand and spray stretches on for a kilometre. I alight the bus and stroll the last 50 metres to the hospital.

This has to be one of the most glorious commutes on earth.

MAY

I am flying to London tomorrow morning. Sheldon and Doug will be there to meet me at Heathrow. It will be good to see their smiling faces again. Yet I am also filled with dread. I know that my relationship with Nick is over, but leaving Sydney will mean finally shutting the door on all of my dreams. I am flying away from something that I wanted so much. And I am flying back to something that I don't want at all – namely, my first round of follow-up scans to find out if I am clear of cancer. My appointment is scheduled for Monday.

The spectre of those scans is stalking the dark back alleys of my mind. If I could run to Harley Street and have them RIGHT NOW I would. I want them out of the way so I can get on with my life. And if the news is not good . . . ? Well, I would rather know than not.

I have lost a lot of weight. I tell myself that it could have been caused by emotional distress and smoking. I wake up sweating in the night. Fear? A side effect of Tamoxifen? I find myself fingering a lump under my arm. Dr Hargreaves said it is just scar tissue.

In all likelihood I am well and clear of cancer. *My chances are excellent. **But am I jinxing myself by saying that?*** And so the obsessive thoughts go around.

I try not to worry. How, exactly, does one do that?

In the rehab I met a very funny woman called Vic. She had a great technique; we named it the 'Vic Flick'. Whenever a self-defeating thought crossed her mind Vic said, 'Thanks for the information', and flicked a finger, like a windscreen wiper, across her forehead.

My forehead is becoming a touch chafed.

I called Nick to say goodbye. You may think that was a love-addict thing to do; you may be right. I didn't want to depart from Australia leaving behind only a memory of bitter emptiness. Imagine how surprised I was when Nick suggested that he take me out to dinner. It took me a moment to comprehend what he was saying.

They say that home is where the heart is. My heart is in two places. I will miss Mum, Samantha, Lyla and Lily, Mandy and Tony, Marcus and all the new friends that I have made in Sydney. And I will be overjoyed to see all of my friends in London.

It is going to be hard to go to the airport and get on the plane alone.

However, it is also time for me to allow the possibility of new dreams. All I can do is pray and try to live in the moment. Tomorrow is tomorrow. Right now it's a warm Sydney Sunday morning. Samantha and I are off for our ultimate swim at Bondi.

❖

It's my last night. Full of nerves, I wrap my new hair in a pink skull-print headscarf and head off into a balmy Sydney night in Samantha's 1976 Alfa Spider, with the top down.

I stop for two young women at a zebra crossing. As they pass in front of the car one of them shouts, 'You look fabulous!' That gives my self-esteem a boost.

I meet Nick in Darlinghurst, at one of our favourite restaurants. Nick is nervous too. Our conversation is bumpy. I cry. At one point it seems that Nick is going to get up and leave. But we both manage to steer ourselves away from the brink of anger or emotional disintegration and navigate back into calmer water. Then another surprise: Nick offers to take me to the airport. Tunnel anxiety prevents Samantha from driving to the airport. The prospect of leaving in a taxi, alone, has been filling me with sadness. I gratefully accept.

A few fitful hours later, I creak out of bed to do my final bit of packing in the dark. At five-fifteen a.m. the doorbell rings – Nick is as good as his word. As he loads my suitcases into his car Samantha and her eleven-year-old daughter Lily arise and make cups of tea. Samantha's other daughter, Lyla, manages a brief appearance at her bedroom door – 'Goodbye, Jessy. Love you' – before tumbling back into her sleepy nest. She is thirteen, after all.

Lily hands me a home-made card. Inside it is a poem she has composed herself. With brimming eyes we all hug. I will miss Samantha and her girls a great deal. They have been unwaveringly kind and generous to me in one of the most difficult periods of my life.

In the car I read Lily's poem aloud to Nick. Tears stream down my face.

Lily's Poem

Dear Jessy,
We don't want you to go,
You make our household glow, We'll miss your smile
    and laugh.

We love you so much,
You have a very special touch,
Felix and Lola will miss you too, Goodness Jessy we'll
    miss you.

We hope you have a good time in London,
Being with you has been lots of fun,
We really enjoyed the swimming,
Good luck with your fabulous writing.

So thank you again for staying with us, And thank you
    for your kindness,
We'll miss you and hope you have a good time,
We'll see you again soon but to us it will feel like a
    long time.

All the love in the world from Lily, Lyla, Samantha,
    Felix and Lola xoxoxoxox
We love you and miss you!

GOOD FRIENDS
I'VE HAD,

GOOD FRIENDS
I'VE LOST

TUESDAY 11 MAY

What do I love about London? The freezing cold weather in the middle of May? The £185 gas bill? The honest and fair banks who have increased my mortgage repayments by THREE percentage points? The matey mechanics who swear that my car needs a new petrol tank at a cost of just £1,300? The dog excrement that gaily festoons the footpaths? The exciting Con–Lib coalition government? No, I love the people.

Sheldon and Doug meet me at Heathrow. The sight of their faces fills me with joy.

The last time that I knew happiness was as I passed through the exit doors at Sydney airport on Boxing Day with my luggage piled high on a wobbly trolley. Two minutes later I knew that Nick was not there.

Sheldon and Doug know all about my arrival anxiety and they were determined to meet me when I landed. It is in these small acts that we are truly shown love.

After they've lugged the cases upstairs I make tea and half-heartedly throw a few things into the washing machine. Then we begin the melancholic task of removing all traces of Nick from my home: there are photographs; cards; some clothes – little souvenirs of times shared – all to be consigned to the dustbin.

⁕

I have two scans scheduled this afternoon, a mammogram and an ultrasound. These are to be the first of the scans that will monitor my health from now on. Scans that, on every occasion, will address the question that fills me with dread . . . has the cancer returned?

After four months of sunshine and harbour views I find it pleasing to lay my eyes upon the grey flagged footpaths and yellow London Stock brick façades of Harley Street.

Iris comes with me to the hospital. If you're not sure who your friends are, here is a clue: they are the people who are prepared to spend half a day sitting around in stuffy waiting rooms reading dreary magazines and just . . . waiting . . . whilst you try to look all breezy and unconcerned, and they try to mentally devise what they are going to say or do if you happen to receive the worst news of your life in the next ten minutes. Iris, it has to be said, makes the best of the situation.

'I just love drinks machines,' she enthuses. 'I could stay here all day zipping these little plastic capsules into the slot and watching the coffee come out.'

The receptionist raises a wary eyebrow.

Tracy, a pretty radiographer, calls my name.

'Come with me, Iris,' I plead in a whisper.

We proceed down the hall, Iris clutching her coffee and magazine. Tracy bars her at the door.

'You can't come in here. It's an X-ray room,' she says.

Oh.

I enter alone. I remember the drill from the first time I had a mammogram. Strip to the waist. Get prodded, poked and pulled into a position that would probably land me a leading role in some kind of gymnastic-porno movie. Have right breast squashed flat between a metal plate and a plastic paddle. So far, so good; now the left breast, the one that had the cancer, the surgery and the radiotherapy. I twist and turn. The paddle descends. The squashing commences. I scream uncontrollably.

'Sorry. Sorry. Sorry,' gulps Tracy and releases the vice. Gasping for air, I bound across the floor and pull my jumper on.

'Just two more images to do,' says Tracy.

Trembling, I disrobe again and step back up to the plate.

A few excruciating minutes later we exit the room. Iris is loitering outside the door.

'Was that you yelling?' she asks and rolls her eyes.

Then it's down to the labyrinth where the ultrasound lurks. I lie on the bench in a blue patterned hospital gown. Iris flicks the pages of *Elle*. Dr Wang bustles in. I can tell he has something to say. I stare at him as he advances across the tiny room, in much the same way as a rabbit stares at the headlights of an oncoming truck.

'Your mammogram looks fine,' he announces.

Here is something I've learned about medical professionals: if everything is fine, they tell you straightaway; if it's not fine, they stay tight lipped.

'So, are you worried about anything?' the doctor asks. I tell him about my worries: feeling lumps in my armpit; stabbing pains under and around my breast; anxiety; shortness of breath; the continued swelling in my back. I consider adding in my fear of losing my home and dying alone or the earth being consumed by nanoparticles.

Dr Wang interrupts quickly: 'Okay, let's have a look.' He runs the magic wand over my breasts as I stare wildly about the room. Very soon he reassures me with a 'Nothing to worry about here.'

In the pit of my stomach I feel that spinning sensation that you get when they finally let you off the giant Ferris wheel.

Next stop: Mr Hadjiminas. He is all smiles. I hand him the mammogram films and he clips them to the light box.

'These look perfect,' he says. The image of my left breast is peppered with tiny white shapes; they look like arrowheads.

'Perfect? What are those?' I exclaim.

'Oh, titanium staples,' replies Mr H. Life is full of little surprises. Mr H is equally happy with the ultrasound scans. 'Now, let's have a look at your back.'

Behind the screen, Mr Hadjiminas inspects the wobbly cushion of fluid that has taken up residence in the space where my latissimus dorsi muscle used to live.

'Hmm. This seems to have got worse. I think it might need more surgery.' He looks at the scar that runs down my side. 'It will be tricky.'

I gulp.

'For me, not for you,' he adds hastily.

Well I should hope so; I will be unconscious.

'Let's give it to the end of the summer,' he says. Fine by me.

'So, next time,' I begin. 'Can I not have the mammogram, just the ultrasound scan?'

Mr H almost snorts. 'Do you think we are giving you these mammograms just for fun? Of course you have to have the mammogram.'

It was worth a try.

❖

Samantha calls on the phone. Skype is a techno-evolution too far for Samantha. She asks about my scans.

'My mammogram and ultrasound were both fine.'

Only three months ago I accompanied Samantha to St Vincent's in Sydney for her own first set of breast cancer follow-up scans. I sat in the corridor and pretended to look interested in the framed flower prints whilst my friend was ushered away to the mammogram room. She was gone for a very long time. Much longer, it seemed to me, than it should have taken. When she eventually emerged I tried to compose myself but the smile I gave her was strained. For a moment I feared the worst – then an inane grin spread across her face and that was all I needed to know. Samantha started laughing and shaking, gabbling at ninety miles an hour. 'It's clear,' she squeaked, 'I've never felt so high in my life.'

I have anticipated feeling that way too. But I don't. *Why not?* It occurs to me that lately I have been grappling with the fact that, for me, the loss of hope feels more distressing than the fear of death. At the time that I was diagnosed I was happier than I had ever been. I was in a wonderful new relationship with Nick but, more than that, I had reached a point in my life where I felt relaxed and confident. For the first time, I truly knew myself. Even though the surgery was shocking, the chemotherapy was hideously debilitating and the radiotherapy was weird, through-out all of that time I maintained a fundamentally optimistic position. Deep down, I always believed that I would get through the treatment and then get back to my beautiful life that was so rudely interrupted by cancer. Breast cancer would be an episode in my life, it would not *be* my life. It wasn't until Nick left me that I lost hope. I became convinced that God was out to punish me; that the cancer would slowly strip me of everything. It had taken my breast, my hair, my femininity and my lover.

I no longer feel that I can trust my own judgement. *If I was so wrong about Nick, what else am I wrong about?* Everything that I believed in has been undermined, including my belief that I will get well.

Hence, in an attempt to contain my out-of-control emotions, I have been smoking – I've tried to play it down but the fact probably hasn't escaped your attention. Now I do not advocate smoking as a positive lifestyle choice – it is a foul and insidious addiction. It all started the day that Nick told me about his betrayal. I reached for the cigarettes in the hope that they would alleviate my distress and they did, for a minute. But since then they have served to fuel my feelings of fear and self-loathing. Furthermore, it has proved annoyingly difficult to maintain the moral high ground with my friends – to lecture them about organic food, natural beauty products and the dangers of plastics – with a fag dangling from my lips. Speaking as an addict, smoking was my first refuge in a crisis. As I stood on a cliff top after running from Nick's flat my subconscious belief was that if I did not smoke I might harm myself in some more drastic manner. Since then I've been on a nonstop roundabout of stopping and starting. I wish I hadn't picked up that first one; but I did.

'Are you smoking?' asks Samantha.

'I've stopped this morning. The cigarettes are in the bin,' I reply with a self-satisfied air.

'And have you taken the bin out?'

After I've caught up with her news, I hang up. Then I race out the front door, tear open the rubbish bag and fish out the three putrid Marlboro Lights. The front door slams. I am locked out. No keys. No phone. No coat. No lighter.

This may teach me a lesson.

With admirable prescience I bought a flat that is 50 metres from a fire station. I trip around there and tell the officer in charge my sorry tale.

'We're not meant to break into people's houses,' he informs me. I bat my newly grown eyelashes and simper. 'Oh, go home,' he says kindly.

Two minutes later a shiny red fire engine pulls into the driveway. One minute after that four burly firemen pile up the stairs. They insert a flimsy square of plastic into my doorjamb and wiggle it. Five seconds later the door pops open.

I am in equal parts grateful and remorseful – also horrified at how easy it is to break into my home. Relieved, I light up.

❖

A friend of mine died a few nights ago. We were good friends for many years. Then we fell out. The reasons were trivial. During the time that we weren't speaking I missed him. I am glad to say that I saw him just before Christmas. We made up our differences and had a good chat. But then I went to Sydney and you know what happened there. Since I've been back in London I've been avoiding all but my very closest friends. Not because I don't like people but because they inevitably ask, 'How are you?' It's a question that I find so hard to answer without crying. So I hadn't called my friend. Now he is dead and I will always miss him.

This sunny London morning, in a narrow Soho street, two magnificent dusky horses with black ostrich plumes on their heads stand harnessed to a glass carriage. The horses snort softly and occasionally toss their flowing manes. A quiet crowd is gathered here, mostly dressed in black with the occasional flash of scarlet or hot pink. We chat in subdued tones. Inside the carriage my friend lies in his coffin. The coffin is made of cardboard, covered with red sparkly paper, decorated with ruby crystals and paper flowers. An outlandishly huge, black top hat wobbles on the roof of the carriage.

The funeral cortège sets off and the crowd fall in behind. Following the carriage, we process slowly around the streets of Soho for about an hour in our high heels until our feet nearly drop off. Eventually we arrive at St James's Church, Piccadilly. The church is already packed to the rafters. After everyone has squeezed onto a pew the coffin is carried in. The service is moving, joyful and elegant. Everything about the funeral is perfect: the glass carriage; the sunflowers; the readings and tributes; the press photographers; the eye-catching outfits; the circus atmosphere. Of course the one person who would have enjoyed it the most is not here to share the experience. At the end my friend's coffin is carried out to the music of his beloved Marc Bolan singing '20th Century Boy'.

It is unutterably sad to see a coffin carried away for the last time and to know that a kind, infuriating, contrary, funny, morose, witty, messed-up, sweet human lies inside it, his body about to be burned to ashes.

The mourners regroup in the churchyard for drinks. Later the wake moves to a club in Soho where there is more chatting and the showing of a funny and touching film.

At five p.m. the wake is still going strong but I have to leave. I have an appointment with my therapist.

I sit on the therapist's couch and cry for an hour. My friend wasn't my lover, or my brother. He was not the most important person in my life, nor I in his. But he was my friend, for better or worse. His death is yet another loss.

My friend didn't please everybody in this world. He didn't try to. What I can say for certain is this: for all his foibles, he was loved.

❖

Recently I've been finding it so hard to wake up in the mornings. Maybe this is a sign that I'm falling into depression. Or maybe I'm just physically and mentally exhausted after a year of seemingly nonstop knockdowns. The more I sleep and sleep, the more I never want to get out of bed again. *Just another half an hour*, I think and sink back amongst the pillows. The pull of oblivion grows stronger.

So it's good that there has been someone every day to disengage me from the arms of Morpheus. On Sunday, Iris and I went to the movies. On Monday, Antony came over and we went down the road to the Persian Café for lunch. Yesterday, Justin took me to the supermarket. This afternoon I have an appointment with Mr Hadjiminas, so I shall have to get out of bed for that.

The swelling in my back has not improved. I'm finding it impossibly uncomfortable to sit in a chair or lie on my side in bed. Like Mr Hadjiminas says, it is time to deal with it. Tomorrow I will be returning to the Harley Street Clinic for surgery.

❖

The surgery went well. I am back at home now. I slept through yesterday and most of today.

Nurse Tiziana cared for me a year ago. She was genuinely pleased to see me again and to hear that I am recovering well. Ben, Iris and Sheldon took turns visiting. But my stay in hospital was unsettling. Apart from the fact of having a general anaesthetic and being cut open – never at the top of my list of fun things to do – it was strange to be back in a place that held so many memories.

I have heard it said that the full impact of having had cancer hits you after the event. Alone in the hospital room I began to experience deep sadness and shock that I simply didn't feel a year ago. I felt a longing for the life I had before I ever knew about the cancer. I was happy then. Just eight days after finishing the long, hard months of chemo and radiotherapy I was catapulted into traumatic months of betrayal and abandonment. So I never really got the chance to process the emotional impact of having cancer. Suddenly I was reliving it all in full colour. Paper pants and elastic stockings. The walk to the operating theatre. The wait for the lab results. Mr H's serious face as he told me that the cancer was in my lymph node. More surgery. Waking up in ITU. Miranda and Eloise arriving late at night. Friends. Flowers. Morphine. Hospital food. Vegetable juice. The compression bra. Walking to the corner of the street. The desperate search for alternative therapies. The ice hat. Armchairs in the chemo unit. My hair coming out in my hands. Sickness. Lying on the couch with the red tartan rug. Hundreds of pills. Getting a wig. Fatigue. Mouth ulcers. Money anxiety. Crying in the Macmillan Centre. The sleeping cap. Tattoos. Big Bruce.

And Nick.

This time I was glad to leave, although a little hesitant about going home alone. Jamie picked me up from hospital. Ben came over, brought a curry and stayed the night. In the morning I thanked him.

'I didn't do anything, Jessy,' he protested. But his just being there was all I needed.

❖

Text to Iris:

Would you like to see Gainsbourg on Sunday morning at the cinema?

Text from Iris:

God brilliant finally a reason to live

'So how are you feeling?' asks Iris as we take our seats.
'As if I've been trampled by a horse.'

'How big is the scar?'

'About that big,' I say, holding my hands 6 inches apart and then indicating a straight line running down my side under my left arm.

'Like a zipper,' observes Iris.

Iris tells me about her day as a trainee volunteer with the Friends of Highgate Cemetery. She tagged along on all the tours to learn the history of this famous burial ground; resting place of Karl Marx and Malcolm McLaren. 'That must have been interesting,' say I.

'Not half as interesting as the history they *don't* tell you,' says Iris, her eyes ablaze. 'Like for instance it fell into decay in the 1960s and was inhabited by a nasty vampire. By the 1970s its original owners, the London Cemetery Company, abandoned it completely. The dilapidated necropolis became a top spot for Satanic worship and at one point the graves were desecrated. Bones were strewn about all over the place and a woman's corpse was dragged out and staked on the path.'

'Really?' I ask, my eyes wide with horror.

'Really,' says Iris with a sombre nod. 'And they don't say a *thing* about it on the tours.'

The lights go down. The film is stylish and the cast excellent but I'm afraid that I cannot warm to Serge Gainsbourg even though he is a committed smoker and an alcoholic. 'What I've just seen,' I tell Iris afterwards, 'is the story of a charming, self-pitying and sleazy narcissist who, as a small boy, was rejected by a small girl because he was ugly. He spends his whole life trying to get over it by having sex with loads of beautiful women. He then tries to make himself feel like a bigger man by being unkind to them. He is completely self-interested, showing neither love nor empathy for any of his wives, girlfriends or children. Put simply, he is using them to punish and take revenge on all women everywhere.'

'A bit close to the bone for you right now,' says Iris.

❖

This afternoon I went to see Mr Hadjiminas for a check-up following last week's surgery. I've had high hopes that my back will soon be smooth and healed. But it has started to fill up with fluid again. First Mr H removes all the sticky dressings as carefully as he can. It is just not possible to get those buggers off without a certain amount of theatrical wincing and ouching. He then drains the fluid with a big needle. That really does hurt.

'I'm trying not to be despondent,' I say with a despondent sigh.

'Good. It's early days yet,' says Mr H. He wraps my torso in a gauze bandage. Although I can hardly breathe there's something comforting about being all wrapped up like a baby in swaddling. But it seems that I won't be able to wash without removing it.

'Do you have anyone at home who can help you to put it on again nice and tight?' *No, I don't.* Suddenly I get quite upset.

I just want all this to be over and it's not. I don't want a visible reminder that I've had breast cancer. I don't want to live with this constant level of pain and discomfort. I don't want to struggle on my own and not be able to wash because there's nobody to help me put my bandages on. I hate Nick for leaving me alone. I'm so disappointed that I allowed him to take the place in my heart and in my life that should have been reserved for someone decent who might have loved and cherished me. And I really hate the fact that I keep thinking this way.

Why am I still so angry with Nick? During our break-up my emotional resilience was destroyed. With that I felt that I would be unable to recover my physical health, I would relapse, my life would become an endless cycle of suffering, friends would find it too difficult to stay and so would slowly turn their backs on me, just as Nick had. Ultimately I would die alone.

It is so easy to catastrophise because, whichever way you look at it, cancer is something of a catastrophe. And it brings a particularly insidious fear: 'I might return,' it whispers, 'and you can never know why or when.'

❖

The next day I'm back at the Harley Street Clinic, again.

Nurse Honoria has returned! Whilst I was away she gave birth to a baby boy. He is six months old already. Honoria's face lights up when she sees me. I feel the same way. 'Did you have a lovely holiday in Australia?' she asks. I open my mouth but then think better of it. I really must learn that some questions are meant to be rhetorical.

Mr H cuts me out of yesterday's bandages. I'm free – but not for long. He produces a strip of elasticated fabric about 30 centimetres wide. It has Velcro fastenings on each end.

'What's that?' I ask.

'You know when people have abdominal surgery?' says Mr Hadjiminas. I nod. 'When it bursts, this is what we use.' Having planted that hideous image in my mind, he then gets a giant needle and injects some kind of steroid into my back. Mr H and Honoria each take an end of the big pink binding.

'I don't think we're going to get her into it,' says Honoria.

'Oh, yes we will,' cries Mr H. They pull and stretch it tightly around my entire upper torso. My breasts are squashed flat and, if that wasn't bad enough, my stomach is forced downwards, creating a wobbly muffin top. Chemo Chic this thing definitely is not.

'We may have to do another steroid injection, but keep this on for a week and see how it goes.'

Back at home it's already beginning to irritate. Ben has come around for dinner.

'Can you just unzip my dress and try to pull the Velcro so that it's not rubbing on my skin?'

Ben obliges. He is like my brother but I can't be pestering every passer-by to adjust my surgical appliances. And I still haven't solved the problem of how to have a shower.

❖

Three a.m. I'm hot. I'm sweaty. I'm itchy. I'm uncomfortable.

Damn it, I'm wide awake. *Aargh.* I rip the elasticated pink sausage skin from my body.

Whoever knew that lying naked in a cool cotton sheet could be the zenith of bliss?

I wake up rested, *sans* elastic bandage. Oh dear. What have I done? How am I going to get the thing back on again?

With relief I remember that Nana is coming to clean the flat this morning. I will ask her to help me. In the meantime I'm going to have a long, long, hot, hot shower and wash my hair.

After my shower and Nana's visit I return to my bed and sleep until dusk. I'm still bumbling about in my pyjamas when there is a knock-knock at the door. It's Sheldon.

'How are you, Jess?' he asks.

'I'm fine,' I say and then burst into tears. 'I'm sorry, Sheldon,' I say between sobs. 'I don't know what's wrong with me. I keep getting like this. I should be better by now.'

'"Should",' says Sheldon, 'is perfectionism in a single word. Jess, imagine that you hadn't seen me for a year or so and then we met and you said, "Hey, Sheldon, what's been happening?" And I told you that I'd had cancer and chemotherapy and then I'd gone out to Australia and when I got there I found out that my girlfriend had been cheating on me and she left me and I'd had a mental breakdown and wound up in a rehab, then I'd come back to London and gone back into hospital again for more surgery. How do you think I would be feeling about now?'

I look at him. 'Quite devastated,' I reply.

To cheer me up, Sheldon takes me out to see The Jolly Boys. This Jamaican Mento band has been going for over fifty years and have only recently found acclaim. Most of them are in their seventies and eighties. World changing music it ain't, but their current success is testament to Jessy's first principle of living well: *Never give up. Follow your dreams until you die.*

❖

Night after sleepless night I wriggle and scratch inside my Velcro-and-elastic sarcophagus.

Four a.m. I'm in the bathroom, wide awake. I rip off the stretchy bandage. Horrors! My new breast is flattened. There's a big indentation above my nipple. I try pushing it back into shape with the palms of my hands.

Five-forty a.m. I haven't slept all night. I switch on the radio.

'In the news today in 1962, actress Marilyn Monroe was found dead with a bottle of sleeping pills by her side.' Cut to an interview with director John Huston: 'Nobody was surprised . . . One of her main enemies was sleeplessness.'

❖

Next day, at the hospital – curtain up.

Nurse Diana is on duty. She greets me with a big kiss on each cheek. Mr Hadjiminas extends his hand.

'I can explain,' I blurt, pulling the stretchy bandage from my handbag and waving it at him. 'I took it off. It was squashing my breast. I was worried that it might become permanently deformed.' Mr H looks aghast. 'I'm wearing the compression bra,' I add, as if in mitigation.

'Let's have a look at you,' says Mr H. I strip to the waist and he prods my back. 'Much better . . .' Rather than admonish me for being neurotic, Mr H takes a conciliatory approach.

'Maybe the compression bra will be okay for now. Let's see how it goes.' He sits down behind me. The couch tips precariously in his direction.

'Don't get up!' shouts Diana. 'Jessica will go flying into the wall.'

'Steroid,' says Mr H.

Nurse Diana holds up an ampoule and a syringe. 'Expiry 2014,' she reads from the label.

'What, so we're using unexpired stuff these days?' comments Mr H. As he inserts the needle into my back I try to hold still but I can't. My body is shaking with laughter.

'This is looking a lot better,' says Mr Hadjiminas, examining my back.

'Fantastic!' I exclaim. 'So can I stop wearing *that*?' I jab a finger at the compression bra that is lying innocently across the back of a chair.

'What, and throw it all away just when we're winning?' says Mr H. My face falls. 'We could always put you back in the elastic bandage,' he cajoles. I shoot him a sour look.

'I'm going on holiday for three weeks. If it gets worse again, come back and see me then.'

'And if it doesn't get worse?'

'Come back and see me in three months.'

'So, do I have to wear the compression bra for another *three months*?'

'Oh no, three more weeks should do it.'

'Oh, thanks. Enjoy your holiday.'

Exeunt.

❖

Today I'm seeing Suzy Cleator. Remember her? My first oncologist. She went off to have a baby. Well, she had a little girl and now she's back.

In the waiting room is a woman who is obviously having chemotherapy. She's wearing a wig and her eyebrows are pencilled on. Her partner is with her – husband, boyfriend, whatever. I can't tell if they are married or not but what I can see is that he is being so tender and kind to her. I start to cry. I dash to the loo and splash water on my face but I can't stop. When Suzy calls my name the tears are still coursing down my face.

How or when will I ever cross this ocean of grief? It seems I've been adrift here for so long.

Days slide by. I don't really have a plan. The difficulty I have been having is getting out of bed in the mornings. Left to my own devices I can sleep until lunchtime. I dread waking up and coming back to reality. My first waking thought is *How has my life gone so wrong?* followed closely by *What will go wrong next?*

Getting to sleep is equally problematic. Here is how it often goes: *right, go to sleep now.* **Jessy I have never loved you. Nick, I** *don't need you, go away.* **Nobody will ever love you Jessy.** *Nonsense, you're just traumatised by Nick.* **What about that book that you read that said that people who suffer traumas are less likely to recover from cancer?** *For god's sake, forget about that book! These morbid obsessions are a sign of depression.* **That's right, I'm depressed. And I read that depression can trigger a relapse . . .**

Sheldon phones me at nine a.m. every morning. 'Jess, are you out of bed?' he says. It's a great help, not only because I sometimes actually get up but also because a quick conversation with a friend derails my negative train of thought.

❖

Ring. 'Jessy? It's Wanda. I've bought you some of that jasmine tea that you love, as a present. But you can only have it if you get out of bed before ten o'clock.'

❖

Sheldon has gone to the country – well, Essex – for a few weeks. It is so remote down there that they don't have mobile phone reception. No more nine a.m. wake-up calls for Jessy. Meanwhile, Wanda and Mr W have gone on holiday to Tanzania. How exotic.

My knowledge of Tanzania is limited but I imagine that it must be stuffed with zebras, hippopotami, alligators and lions. I'm thrilled when my phone ting-a-lings. It's a text from Wanda. I pop it open in full expectation of seeing an exciting photo of Wanda cuddling a tiger cub or Mr W saving her from the jaws of a rhino.

Text from Wanda:

Jessica, get out of bed. Your life is waiting. Love from Wx in Tanzania.

❖

I've heard depression described as sadness and grief that goes on for a *long time*. If that is the case then I am experiencing depression. The headshrinkers call it 'reactive' rather than 'clinical', but I wonder if the risks are the same?

You may recall that for the first half of this year my psychiatrist in Sydney did not want me to take anti-depressants.

'You need to feel your grief,' he said. But, further down the road now, I receive a revised analysis from a psychiatrist in London: when grief and depression go on for a long time, your brain chemistry can be altered. At that point, no matter how much psychotherapy, hypnotherapy or manicure therapy you have, you cannot climb out of the hole you are in until your serotonin levels increase.

Signs of depression include:

> losing interest in life
>
> finding it harder to make decisions
>
> not coping with things that used to be manageable
>
> exhaustion
>
> feeling restless and agitated
>
> loss of appetite and weight
>
> difficulties getting to sleep

Tick, tick, tick, tick, tick, tick and tick.

The psychiatrist writes out a prescription and hands it to me. It is time to give the anti-depressants a go.

❖

A few days ago I noticed a pinky-purple blotchiness on one side of my left breast. This morning it has spread to cover my whole breast.

'Good morning, Mr Hadjiminas's office, Sue speaking.'

'Good morning, Sue, this is Jessica Jones.'

'Oh, hello, Jessica. How are you?'

'I'm very well. No, I'm not. I'm very worried . . .' I sketch a livid picture of the situation.

'Oh my goodness,' says Sue. 'I will speak to Mr Hadjiminas immediately.'

Fifteen minutes later Sue calls me back. 'Mr H says to take your temperature and come to see him at one o'clock.'

I put the phone down. Now I have two and a half hours to imagine the worst. To counter visions of having my breast and probably my whole left arm amputated, I decide it might be helpful to do some Googling. With a thermometer clamped in my mouth I type in 'muscle death after surgery'. Quick as a flash Wikipedia presents me with a page describing something called 'compartment syndrome' along with a picture of a grossly enlarged foot. The symptoms are as follows: pain; paraesthesia (pins and needles); pallor; paralysis and pulselessness. I can't honestly say that I'm experiencing any of those and there is no mention of a rash either but, still, I could be coming down with a rare, hitherto undescribed form of compartment syndrome.

Or maybe it is something worse. I type in 'necrotising fasciitis', a horror I learned about on *Casualty*. Back at Wikipedia I try to avert my eyes from the revolting photographs of this flesh-eating disease. I learn that King Herod the Great may have suffered from Fournier gangrene, a necrotising fasciitis of the groin and genitals (no pictures on Wikipedia, thanks be). For a moment I wonder if Iris might know a spell for plaguing ex-boyfriends with Fournier gangrene – temporarily, of course. Symptoms of necrotising fasciitis: intense pain; swelling; diarrhoea and vomiting. I tick one out of four, although to be fair the swelling is in my back, not my breast, and it predates the rash. Weighing it up I decide, with relief, that I have not developed necrotising fasciitis.

Then, at the bottom of the page there is a link – *See also: cellulitis*. I'm sure it's not that. My breast is as smooth as a plum. I click on it anyway. Oh my Lord – this could be the one. Cellulitis, it turns out, is not the dreaded orange-peel skin – that's *cellulite*.

Rather it is a 'a diffuse inflammation of connective tissue with severe inflammation of dermal and subcutaneous layers of the skin.' Amongst the predisposing conditions, recent surgery is listed. It is most common on the face or lower legs *but may occur anywhere on the body*. Wikipedia is not that clear on how to tell if one definitely has cellulitis. Apparently you have to see a doctor. Which, thank goodness, I am just about to do.

Behind the screen at the Harley Street Clinic, Nurse Honoria helps me to pull my clothes off. I look down at my chest in order to point out the scary discolouration. 'It's gone,' I exclaim.

Mr H pops his head round the screen. 'It's gone,' I repeat lamely, 'but you should have seen it this morning. It was bright pink.'

'Actually,' says Honoria, 'I can see faintly where it was.' I shoot her a look of gratitude.

Mr H gives it a poke with his finger. 'It doesn't change colour when I poke it,' he declares. That, it seems, is a good thing. 'There is an unexplained rash that people get after they've had their lymph nodes removed,' Mr H continues. 'Nothing to worry about.'

Now he tells me.

❖

I'm having tea at May's flat. I have come to collect the eagle's feather.

'Thank you so much for letting me look after it,' says May, holding out the feather, wrapped in a silk scarf.

'Maybe I should get rid of this?' I say 'It's just another reminder of things I want to forget.'

May looks hopeful for a moment: 'Maybe . . . No Jessy, this feather came to you. You should keep it. It is *yours*.'

'You know something, Jessy?' says May, 'I still can't get over Nick – how he wasn't what he appeared to be. I remember meeting him and thinking: "You two have a really good energy together, I'm so glad that Jessy has found a lovely partner." Do you ever wonder if things would have worked out differently if you hadn't got cancer?'

'Honestly May? I have spent a lot of time thinking about that. I've gone over and over different scenarios in my head: what if I'd gone to Australia and spent more time with him? Would our bond have grown stronger? But really, if that were the case then I would have become more deeply involved with a man who was just fundamentally dishonest. It always comes back to the same thing: in any relationship there will always be turbulent times. And when those difficulties come, Nick will always run. So in the end, things could never have worked out differently between Nick and me.'

'Jessy, that's really useful information.'

You know what? May is right. It occurs to me that what I've just said marks a fundamental shift in my perspective.

Nothing has changed and yet my world is transformed. The anti-depressants have helped me to take the first step on the road that leads back to the sunny side. I have begun to get out of bed earlier in the day, to look up, to take an interest in a life beyond my own concerns and anxieties. I have even managed to watch television without crying.

I'm glad that I didn't take anti-depressants at the beginning. Grief is not a problem to be solved; it is one of the great and enriching events of our life. Equally, I'm glad that I am taking the anti-depressants now – but I don't regard them as a cure-all. Everything that I have read and experienced has led me to understand that health is a product of balance in my body, my mind and my spirit.

To that end I have developed *Jessy's Personal Stress-Reduction Programme*. Rather than trying to flog it to you on a fifteen-part e-book (with bonus DVD), I have decided to share it freely.

Things I wish I'd known before #7
Jessy's personal stress-reduction programme

Feel your feelings: Spending time in rehabs and on psychotherapists' couches has taught me how to identify my emotions rather than suppress them. This can be tricky. It sometimes involves crying in public places. But that never killed me or anyone else. And it's not just the feelings of sadness, anger and loneliness that I need to experience, but also joy and love. Yeah! Laugh, cry, just get it off your chest. I see a therapist once a week and unburden myself of all my craziest, darkest, most shaming thoughts.

Food: A diet rich in plants and whole grains keeps all my organs in tip-top working order.

Fitness: I try to do gentle exercise every day. This could be a walk, a yoga class, a swim or just some stretches and sit-ups on the floor at home. Singing and dancing are also wonderfully enlivening.

Flaking: If I feel I need an afternoon nap, I have one. I've been ill and my body needs lots of rest to heal itself.

Future: The further away I get from cancer and heartbreak, the more I dare to dream again. I have started a 'vision book' in which I stick pictures and write about how I truly want to live.

Fun: Whatever floats your boat. I don't care what anyone else thinks; watching test match cricket on TV is *my* idea of fun.

Friends: I speak to at least one friend every day of my life. I allow myself to really love my friends and my family, my neighbours and people on the bus. That sounds simple but it takes courage. After all, if I love people they might reject me or let me down.

That's enough things starting with 'F'.

Creativity: Writing every day – whether it be a book, a blog post; a poem or just a loony stream of consciousness – gets some of my obsessive thoughts out of my head. Let the hard drive carry it all around. My brain needs the space. If writing isn't your thing try photography, painting, pottery, cooking or gardening.

Perspective: A quick reality check can go a long way to reminding me that my life is not the disaster that I often think it is. I use several methods: A gratitude list; a list of 'things I got for free today' or noting down my daily actions under the headings of 'love and 'fear'. See the world from a different angle – stand on your head.

Prayer and meditation: Just ten minutes or so each day.

Do I do all these things perfectly all the time? Not even remotely. And it can all feel a bit false at times, but this is the only way that I know how to keep going. I have to convince myself every day that my darkest fears are not inevitable. Yes, the treatments have been ghastly. Yes, Nick has been unspeakably cruel. Yes, I feel lonely and afraid at times. But what have I gained from having cancer? I have been shown a great deal of love. The truth is that none of us knows how long we have to live on our beautiful planet. Sometimes I love this world so much that I never want to leave it. The only certainty is that, one day, I will. But I now have the courage to live as I want to live. When I think about it, it isn't the fear of death that has made me feel so utterly bleak. It is the fear of not living.

❖

It's Friday and I'm on my way back to the Harley Street Clinic, my home-away-from-home. At the Highlever Road roundabout I swerve sharply to avoid running over the head of a man who is lying spread-eagled in the middle of the road, smoking a cigarette.

Buddy, I know how you feel.

In the consulting room I strip off and, before Mr Hadjiminas can say anything, I tackle the obvious controversy head on.

'I'm not wearing the compression bra today. I'm fed up with it. But I've brought this,' I add, brandishing the big stretchy bandage. 'I thought maybe we can cut it in half and I can wear it just below my breasts.'

I'm not asking.

'No, that won't work,' says Mr H. 'The best thing would be to cut two holes in it for your breasts to poke through.'

'What,' says Honoria, 'like something you'd get in a sex shop in Soho?'

'No. Well. Hmmm . . .' says Mr H. 'Bring us some photos when you've done it.' He jabs a syringe full of steroid into my back.

Re-dressed, I join the medics on the other side of the screen. 'So, what's next?' I ask.

'Come back and see me in three or four weeks,' says Mr H.

'Then I'm due back in November for another mammogram and stuff,' I say.

'Yes, that's right,' he says.

'*Phhhht*,' say I, expelling air through pursed lips. Then I feel bad. 'It's not that I don't love you,' I hasten to explain.

'I know,' says Mr H.

As I'm walking out the door Mr Hadjiminas calls me back. 'Jessica, if you need another one of those bandages, let me know and I will get you one.'

'What, do you think I'm going to bugger it all up with the scissors? I did go to fashion college you know.'

His face is impassive in response.

❖

Tessa called me yesterday. 'Tess, I'm at the checkout in Sainsbury's,' I said. 'Can I call you back in five minutes?' And then I didn't remember to call her until today. This is not an isolated incident. I wander into rooms and wonder what I'm doing there. I find laundry in the washing machine that has been mouldering for three days. Recently I discovered some money in a savings account that I had completely forgotten about. I have missed medical appointments, too, which has proved costly.

I take some comfort from a study that was publicised on the BBC last year. One of the findings was that 'those with cancer at the study's start were 43 per cent less likely to develop Alzheimer's than the cancer free'.

It seems to me that my forgetfulness could be attributed to a condition known as 'chemo brain'. My friend Dawn has had chemotherapy too. As if to confirm my suspicion, she rings and tells me at length about how it takes her an age to get out of her house because of forgetting this and that. She also describes becoming overwhelmed by simple tasks and daily events. I can relate.

Forgetfulness and a feeling of being swamped can also be symptoms of depression, so who's to say? Whatever is causing our brain fog, one thing is for sure: it's real. The good news is that both chemo brain and reactive depression are temporary states of affairs.

Since nobody knows what causes chemo brain, nobody knows how to cure it. Common sense tells me to take a fish oil supplement. I recall that Bertie Wooster would always command Jeeves to eat a can of sardines whenever they were faced with a particularly thorny dilemma.

❖

Anxiety has been building for the last couple of weeks. *Don't think about it. Don't think about it.* This morning I woke up with an imaginary tiger clawing at my chest. *Don't think about it.* I've meditated. I've been for walks. I've watched countless old episodes of *CSI*. But the more I try to distract myself, the more I think about it: today I'm having my second follow-up mammogram and ultrasound scans.

Since I have been practising *Jessy's Stress-Reduction Programme*, my outlook has begun to change. I no longer feel hopeless and helpless. Weeks go by when I do not think about Nick. I've begun to work a bit and accept social invitations here and there. I am starting to dare to imagine that maybe I will not inevitably be doomed to an early death by breast cancer.

Best not to get your hopes up just yet, Jess.

As I'm meditating away – *breathe, one, breathe, two, breathe, three* – the phone rings. I forgot to switch it off. *Don't answer it. Breathe, four . . .* Ring! *Breathe, five . . .* Ring! It's May. May is coming to the hospital with me. One of the life skills that I've learned in the past fourteen months and twenty-two days is how to ask for help. The old Jess would have just toughed it out and gone to the hospital alone. That is what I did on the day I was diagnosed. I remember my feelings of bafflement as the ultrasound doctor said, 'There is a tumour here and in my opinion it could be malignant. I'm sorry . . .' and my confusion as I stumbled from the room, alone. I sat on a plastic chair in the empty corridor, tears sprouting from my eyes. I desperately wanted a hand to hold.

If I think about it, I might have had some kind of unacknowledged notion that enduring the hard moments alone was somehow courageous. I now regard such bravado as foolish.

So I asked Iris and Flossie and Tessa and Wanda and May to come with me. I wasn't discouraged when any of them said they couldn't make it. I didn't assume that nobody loves me. My friends have lives and commitments. *I* have a life. *I* have commitments. I knew somebody would say 'yes'. That somebody was May. And what woman wouldn't want a talented artist and trainee shaman like May by her side when visiting the breast clinic?

I leave May in charge of the car for a few minutes. 'I'm just going to zip into Pret A Manger and get us some coffees. Here's the key, in case a parking warden comes.'

'Is it difficult to drive?'

'No, it's an automatic.'

As I'm standing in the queue at Pret my phone rings. 'How do you get the car out of park?'

At the clinic May and I are shown into a minuscule waiting room. There are two other women sitting on a sofa about half a metre away. We conduct our conversations in low tones, as do they, all trying to pretend that we can't overhear everything that the other pair is saying.

A nurse comes in. 'Please complete this form,' she says. It's the usual *you agree to exonerate the clinic of any responsibility for everything and pay through the nose should your insurance company fail to cough up* contract. I notice that the insurance pre-authorisation number is missing from the form. I fish out my mobile phone and call my health insurance company.

'Hello, I'm just about to have my follow-up mammogram and ultrasound but the hospital don't seem to have a note of the pre-authorisation number. Could you check it for me?'

'Have you been seen by our medical assessment team?'

'Eh? No. What are you talking about?'

'Please hold the line.'

I spend an uneventful five minutes listening to the annoying phone music.

Radiographer Jane comes in. 'We're ready for you, Miss Jones.'

'Won't be a minute,' I mouth and point to the phone. Another five minutes passes. I feel my shoulders rising ever so slightly.

'Miss Jones, when were you diagnosed with breast cancer?'

'Fourteen months ago.'

'You only joined Bupa in May this year so this is a pre-existing condition. I can't authorise treatment at this time.'

In an exasperated voice I tell Valerie – that is her name – that I temporarily transferred my policy to Australia and then transferred it back on my return to the UK. I explain, through gritted teeth, that although Bupa guaranteed that my cover would be continuous there have been several hiccups of this nature in the last few months and that on each occasion I have been assured that the problem would be fixed.

'Well, you should have called us earlier for authorisation.'

'Valerie, I did. I called you fourteen months ago and was given authorisation. I'm just calling you now to check the number.'

'I cannot authorise treatment at this time.'

Suddenly I am in meltdown: 'Listen, Valerie, do you appreciate that I am at this moment *in* the hospital? Now you're telling me that the treatment that was authorised last year is no longer authorised because Bupa, despite repeated requests, has failed to correct a mistake on my computer record. Whilst you have put me on hold for ten minutes you're not only keeping me waiting but also the radiographer and my friend May and all the other patients. And what we are all waiting to find out is *whether or not I have breast cancer.* Do you have any idea HOW STRESSFUL THIS SITUATION IS?'

The two women sitting on the sofa look totally absorbed in their magazines.

'I'm sorry, I don't like your tone of voice. I may have to terminate this call.'

I terminate the call.

Maybe you're thinking that I could have handled that conversation with a touch more equanimity? On the other hand I suspect that, on some occasion, you too have felt like taking a chainsaw to the computer system of a faceless bureaucracy that has stymied your life with its inane and inflexible rules. Enough said.

I stand before the mammogram machine, uncovered in more ways than one. No clothes. No medical insurance.

Jane inspects my breast. 'Wow,' she says, 'where's the scar? Who was your surgeon? You must be very pleased with it.'

Squash. 'Ow!'

'Don't breathe.' Zap. Repeat . . .

I rejoin May in the waiting room clutching my very own CD of my very own mammograms. The CD has a big fancy 'H' on the front of it, along with my name and hospital number. I wave it in front of May's face: 'Jessy's greatest tits.'

Next up is the ultrasound. By comparison it's positively relaxing.

Back in the waiting room, Mr Hadjiminas appears. 'Come along, Jessica.' May and I grab our coats, bags and empty coffee cups and follow in Mr H's wake to his consulting room. Pictures of my breasts are already plastered all over his light box.

Without any messing about, he gets straight to the point. 'Everything is fine.'

I'm not really taking it in.

Next he examines my back. 'That's settled down well,' he says. Since the last steroid injection a month ago the swelling has not returned. All of my crossing of fingers and knocking on wood seems to have done the trick.

'So, come back and see Suzy Cleator in three months. We will do another ultrasound in six months and your next mammogram will be a year from now.'

Before I know what's happened I've shaken hands with Mr H and kissed Nurse Diane goodbye, and May and I are out the door. I stare about me at the elegant townhouses on Harley Street. My body begins to tremble. I start to laugh. Then to cry.

'How do you feel?' asks May.

'I kind of want to lie down here on the pavement,' I reply.

'Jessy, I think you're in shock.'

I text everyone I've ever known:

All clear!

May and I are recovering with cups of tea and tomatoes on toast at Lowry & Baker, my local cosy café. 'You should mark this day, Jessy,' says May. 'Go out onto your balcony tonight and light a fire in a saucepan. Write down all the things you are now leaving behind and burn them. Then get three sticks to represent what you want for the future and put those on the fire too.'

'I will do that, May.' As I speak I upend my plate, spraying olive oil and sliced tomatoes all over my famous breasts. 'How big do the sticks need to be?' I ask, indicating sizes with my fingers. I lower my hands and they crash hard onto the table, upsetting the teacups. It seems that in the shock and relief of learning that I'm not going to die, I have lost the comprehension of where my body is in space.

'Actually, Jess, I think maybe you should forget about the fire.

You might burn your flat down.'

❖

Standing in the kitchen, staring at the dishes in the sink, I am overwhelmed by a novel feeling.

I'm free! Free of cancer. Free to live. Free to travel. Free to fall in love. Free to do whatever I want.

For the whole of this year I have lived constantly with a barely submerged dread that the cancer may return. On the one hand, I have been cancer free since the day I had the surgery, fourteen months and twenty-three days ago. On the other hand, the doctors won't give me the official 'all clear' until five years have passed. In reality, nothing has changed since the day before yesterday. But somehow in my mind this feels like a major turning point in my recovery.

Today's outing to Harley Street is to see my psychiatrist. 'Fill this in,' he says, handing me the standard depression multiple-choice questionnaire.

'This is remarkable,' he says after reading through my answers. 'Last time you scored 31. Now it's 17. You've gone from severely depressed to only mildly depressed in a month.'

I beam at him.

'Whatever you're doing, keep doing it. I don't think I will need to see you again. Stay on the anti-depressants for another eight months. I will write to your GP.'

❖

It's Iris's birthday. Naturally, the celebrations are taking place at Mayhem Mansions.

Jamie has been away for three months, making a soap opera in Ireland. He's radiating a devilish handsomeness that owes more to an inner confidence born of success than to Botox.

Muttiah is smiling, his face aglow. 'One month off the booze, darling,' he confides. 'Booze. Weed. Everything!' Ted is putting the finishing touches to two cakes: a flourless dark chocolate slab for Iris and a fluffy white raspberry and butter cream sponge for Valentina. I completely forgot – it is her birthday too.

After noshing through a hill of salads, falafels, hummus and cake, we get to disco dancing. Bums are shaking and hair is flying about all over the place, including, I am proud to note, my own. I mean, some of us are nearly f***y years old for f**k's sake but we just don't care.

A shout goes up as wedding bells toll and the voice of Yvonne Fair belts out from the speakers: 'It Should Have Been Me'. Hoarse and perspiring, I fall backwards in a heap onto one of the big sofas and lie there, surveying the room. Sheldon, Flossie and Bert are deep in conversation, with Bert gesticulating wildly. Lydia, Sandi and Geraldine are singing and dancing. Muttiah is smoking on the balcony with a few fellow addicts. Ted is heading for bed.

No amount of money could buy this. No marriage or romantic liaison could provide this amount of love. No job could give me such a feeling of deep satisfaction.

My friends don't feel the need to compete or put each other down. They are perfectly at ease and safe in their own integrity. And so, hallelujah, am I.

Jamie approaches. 'Jess,' he says, 'it's so wonderful to see you yourself again – the friend I used to have is back.' I smile and realise that I have indeed been away; far away from my own heart. And I can't quite put my finger on when I returned.

In my mind I return to the morning of my departure from Sydney airport. The dawn drive from Watsons Bay was poignant: saying goodbye to Samantha and the girls; reading Lily's poem in the car and, as the darkened streets slid by, knowing that I would soon be closing the door on Nick. Checking in was the usual bustle. Nick and I had a final coffee. I smoked a last cigarette outside and then it was time. Unexpectedly, Nick grabbed my hand and held it. And I felt relaxed, walking across the concourse hand in hand with Nick, the man I had hated.

At the security gate I turned. 'Well, goodbye . . .' I started. Then stopped: Nick was crying. And in that moment all my pain, anger and hurt of the last months evaporated. Standing before me I saw the real Nick, who I had loved so much. Throughout the pain and turmoil of the preceding months that flash of honesty was all that I had been desperately searching for. I held him in my arms and he wept.

Nothing lasts forever, not even life. Love always holds within itself the twin possibilities of triumph and complete disintegration. Whichever way it goes love's true value is that it demands integrity. It is an experience of the soul.

That moment did not bring about reconciliation between Nick and me but, looking back, I can see that it marked the beginning of my road to acceptance – my journey back to right now.

Valentina enters the room holding a lit candle. 'Since it is Iris and my byirthdays we are all going to hold hyands around a cyandel.' After much explaining to Sheldon and Bert and shouting at Lydia to turn the disco off, everyone joins a circle around the flickering flame.

'Thank you all for coming,' says Iris. We stand in silence for a couple of beats.

'And eyvrybody remember the poor people in Ayfrrika,' adds Valentina.

It feels good to be home, Jamie.

Two years ago my cousin Gaby died of cancer. Gaby faced her illness with courage. That is not to say that she did not cry. In the three months between her diagnosis and her death she endured a great deal of pain and fear – many times she became depressed, agitated and despairing. That is the nature of fear. That is the nature of cancer. But Gaby always maintained her essential self. She voiced her opinions. She expressed her concern and love for the people around her. She joked. She sat in the sunshine and bathed in the beauty of the world as only the dying can. Gaby fought with every fibre of her being to get well but the cancer overwhelmed her. She was a vivacious woman and a joy to be with. I miss her every day.

I was in Ireland with Sheldon and Doug when I got the call telling me that Gaby had died. We went to the nearest church, lit candles and prayed for Gabs. Sheldon gave me a big hug. Then we went for a walk on a rain-washed Kerry beach.

That was before I met Nick. Before I was diagnosed with breast cancer. Before I fell in love. Before I knew what it was to have my veins pumped full of poison. It was before I had to learn how to cling on to who I am when I didn't even recognise myself in the mirror. Before I understood the anxiety of knowing that there was a malignant force lurking inside my own body. Before

I knew how frightening it is to let go and trust another person absolutely. Before I ever experienced the devastating betrayal of that trust.

Can it really only be two years?

Two years ago I was afraid of cancer. I had seen what it could do and knew for sure that I didn't want it. We don't always get what we want. But how do we learn to want what we get? In my experience it is by understanding the only purpose of life: that it is to be lived in every moment, no matter what.

It is easy to take refuge in the belief that life is only a quality item when it is filled with fun, thrills, sex, holidays, clothes and electronic gadgets. A few of my friends have been unwilling to stay with me on my cancer journey; they have simply disappeared. It has been too frightening, maybe threatening – too *real* for them. I've shed many tears over the loss of those people. If you are going through cancer then you too will be finding out who the hundred-per-centers are in your life. No doubt you will be bitterly disappointed by some people, but try not to dwell too long on such regrets. Those with big hearts and souls will step up – and there will be plenty of them. This is real life. Forget about the people who won't participate in it fully. Our darkest times show us the exhilarating truth of what it is to be human.

Time passes; all things change. The further away I get from cancer and heartbreak, the more I dare to hope again.

I don't believe that there is much value in pretending things away, in saying 'I'm fine' when I have cancer, in saying 'I don't care' when my heart is breaking or in saying 'I forgive you' when I am tortured by resentment. But that doesn't mean that I don't cherish being once again healthy, carefree and generous.

Approaching each progressive set of scans and check-ups I feel a little less afraid, a little more optimistic. After my recent all-clear Mr Hadjiminas said, 'The longer this goes on, the better it gets.' Nevertheless I am aware that a residual dread of the cancer returning may never leave me entirely. In the two weeks prior to each check-up I find myself considering, once again, the possibility of hearing the words *There is a tumour here . . .*

I'm still aware that I may die. Won't we all? And isn't it the ultimate truth that today is all we have? But if one day I find myself facing a terminal prognosis, would I forgive Nick? Of course I would. So why not do it now, on the only day of my life?

Nick, I forgive you.

I would not have chosen cancer but it chose me. I also accept that it may well kill me in the end. But now I can honestly say that cancer has enriched my life. It has brought me closer to my family, to many of my friends and most of all to myself. Simply, I feel more *connected*.

So take a tip from Jessy: don't wait for cancer or a stroke or heart attack to plug you in. Try doing everything you do today with integrity, with honesty, with compassion and, most of all, with love. It's just not worth living any other way.

I love you, Gaby.

ACKNOWLEDGEMENTS

It is a fundamental tenet of many twelve-step programmes that 'We only keep what we have by giving it away.' What I have gained from my experience of breast cancer has been love, the ability to connect with friends and strangers, courage and a stronger sense of who I am. If this book helps you in any way then it will have gone some way towards repaying my debt of gratitude to the countless people who have helped me. You may not know how you have helped. But, trust me, you have.

Adela Campbell; Alice Temple; Amanda Barlow; Amelia Cook; Andy Carroll; Anna Hall; Anne de Charmant; Anton Mossa; Ashleigh Sellors; Astrid Parker; Barry Adamson; Bella Freud; Beverly Marsland; Bob Morgen; Dr Brian Gutkin; Dr Camilla Ducker; Dr Carmel Coulter; Caroline Andrew; Cathy Kasterine; Chris Gration; Chris Herd; Chris Mordue; Claire Gordon; Claire Sullivan; Claudie Layton; David Kaplin; David Remfry; Mr Dmitri Hadjiminas; Emma Howarth; Emma Lyttelton; Dr Erika Chess; Eve Howard; Graeme Hill; Herman Stephens; Imelda Burke; India-Fire Mehta-Cole; Jacqueline Skott; James Ohene-Djan; JD Kelleher; Jennifer Nadel; Jenny Demetri; Jessy Herbert; Jinny Johnson; John (JJ) Connolly; Johnny Rozsa; Jonathan Prime; Josie Pearse; Julia Herbert; Kate Herbert; Kell Skott; Kumari Salgado; Lisa Ward; Lizzie Fleetwood Hartnoll;

Lulu Ainsworth; Lynn Miller; Maria; Marisa; Mark Thomas; Mary Parkinson; Matthew Burton; Melanie Metcalfe; Michele McQuillan; Milly St Aubyn; Mike Cole; Mitsu Sousa; Naomi Howard; Nancy; Natalie MacKenzie; Dr Neil Brener; Nic Flynn; Patricia Peat; Paul Gills; Phillip Donoghue; Rachel Aubyn; Dr Rachel Garner; Radcliffe Royds; Rebecca Edwards; Ree Van Galen; Ros Tonello; Rosie Boycott; Ross Grayson-Bell; Rowan Ainsworth; Ruth Howard; Sally Curry; Sam McEwen; Sarah Sarhandi; Sarah Stanton; Sharif Oussa; Simon Crane; Simon Drake; Sophie Lippell; Sophie Molins; Steven Back; Susie Porter; Dr Suzy Cleator; Tanya Sarne; Tim Cole; Tim Littlemore; Tobias Eaton; Tracey White; Tricia Heyland; Trinny Woodall; Vonni Littlemore; Wendy Bain.

Joss, Lindy, Tash; Carol; Rosa; Sharon; Milly; Kim; Anne and all the nurses and staff at the Harley Street Clinic.

I would also like to thank the institutions, organisations and charities that have been instrumental in my recovery and continued survival: Breast Cancer Care; Bupa; Cancer Options; Content Beauty & Wellbeing; The Department of Work and Pensions; Eco Haven; Environmental Working Group; The Harley Street Clinic; The Harley Street Breast Clinic; The Haven; HM Revenue & Customs; The LOC; Macmillan; Notting Hill Medical Centre; The Organic Pharmacy; Portobello Wholefoods; St Mary's Hospital; St Vincent's Clinic; South Pacific Private; Yes to Life.

And thanks to my publishers, Vanessa Radnidge and John Mitchinson, and to my agent, Sophie Hamley, for believing in this book.

Clearly I could not do any of this on my own.

FURTHER INFORMATION AND READING

WEBSITES

Breakthrough Breast Cancer

A charity dedicated to finding the causes of breast cancer and improving detection, diagnosis, treatment and services.
breakthrough.org.uk

Breast Cancer Action

USA based Breast Cancer Action is a grassroots, feminist education and advocacy organization working to end the breast cancer epidemic.
bcaction.org

Breast Cancer Care

Provides wide-ranging Information and support for anyone affected by breast cancer. They produce a large range of information pamphlets, many of which are downloadable as eBooks.
breastcancercare.org.uk

Breast Cancer Fund

USA organisation campaigning to eliminate the environmental causes of breast cancer.
breastcancerfund.org

Breast Cancer UK

A charity dedicated to preventing breast cancer by campaigning to reduce our exposure to the carcinogens and hazardous chemicals in our environment and everyday products.
breastcanceruk.org.uk

Cancer Hair Care

Filled with insight and advice for dealing with losing your hair.
cancerhaircare.com

Cancer Options

Cancer nurse Patricia Peat provides personalised advice on integrative cancer care. Covering both conventional and complementary therapies she helps you to make informed decisions about your own treatment path.
canceroptions.co.uk

Cancer Research UK

This is the leading UK charity involved in funding cancer research. The website includes a vast range of downloadable information sheets.
cancerresearchuk.org

The Chemo Chic Project

The Chemo Chic Project is a place to tell your story if you, or someone you love, has been affected by cancer, now or in the past.
chemochic.org

Cosmetics Database

Everything you never wanted to know about toxics in cosmetics.
cosmeticdatabase.com

Crazy, Sexy Life

Kris Carr's blog focuses on vegetables, healthy living and all things alternative.
crazysexylife.com

Depression Alliance

Provides information and support for when we're going through depression. A highly informative website that includes a directory of self-help groups.
depressionalliance.org

Environmental Working Group

USA website stuffed with information about environmental toxins.
ewg.org

The Good Glamour Guide

My own website about non-toxic beauty, life and a bunch of my
friends.
goodglamourguide.com

The Haven

This breast cancer charity website is filled with helpful information,
films, podcasts and downloadable advice sheets on subjects such as
nutrition or tai chi, plus information about complementary therapies.
The also run wonderful workshops and provide holistic therapies at
their centres in London, Hereford and Leeds.
thehaven.org.uk

Headspace

An easy-to-do meditation programme. The Headspace app makes
meditation accessible at all times of the day.
getsomeheadspace.com

Herb Research

All about medicinal herbs.
herbresearch.de

Macmillan Cancer Support

This brilliant charity supports people with cancer and campaigns
about issues that affect us. The have a really helpful benefits advice
line and also provide cash grants for those in financial difficulties. If
you have any questions at all about coping with cancer you can talk to
Macmillan.
0808 808 00 00
macmillan.org.uk

Maggies Centres

Maggie's provides welcoming, reassuring drop-in centres. Here
you can have a cup of tea and a chat, get information and advice
(including benefits advice) or attend a course on, for instance,
relaxation and stress management; tai-chi or healthy eating.
maggiescentres.org

Mind

Call Mind for advice if you think you may be depressed or have a mental health problem of any description.
0300 123 3393
mind.org.uk

The Samaritans

If you ever need someone to talk to, the Samaritans are there to listen.
08457 90 90 90
samaritans.org

Sane

Sane runs a helpline and online support forums for anyone affected by mental illness.
0845 767 8000
sane.org.uk

Sex and Love Addicts Anonymous

Sex and Love Addicts Anonymous is a Twelve Step fellowship based on the model pioneered by Alcoholics Anonymous. The S.L.A.A. programme works to counter the destructive consequences of sex and love addiction.
slaauk.org

Time to Change

Campaigning to de-stigmatise and increase awareness of mental illness.
time-to-change.org.uk

Wig Bank

A network of Wig Banks has been set up throughout the UK. People donate their no longer needed wigs. Wigbank wash, condition, disinfect and sell them for between £10 and £20, donating £5 from each sale to charities.
wigbank.com

Yes to Life

This charity supports an integrative approach to cancer care. They run workshops, have a help centre and provide mentors to support, guide and encourage you through your treatment and recovery.
yestolife.org.uk

BOOKS

Anticancer: A New Way of Life by Dr David Servan-Schreiber
(Michael Joseph/Penguin
A sensible, achievable, and thoroughly researched approach to
preventing cancer through diet and lifestyle changes.

Breast Cancer: Taking Control by Professor John Boyages (Boycare
Publishing)
A thorough guide to what to expect following a diagnosis with breast
cancer.

*Dark Nights of the Soul: A Guide to Finding Your Way Through Life's
Ordeals* by Thomas Moore (Piatkus)
Psychologist and theologian Moore explains how our bleakest
moments can bring us to a deeper understanding of life and
humanity.

*Facing Love Addiction: Giving Yourself the Power to Change the Way
You Love* by Pia Mellody with Andrea Wells Miller and J. Keith Miller
(HarperOne)
This is pretty much THE textbook on love addiction and avoidance.

*Daring Greatly: How the Courage to be Vulnerable Transforms the way
we Live, Love, Parent, and Lead* by Brené Brown (Gotham Books/
Penguin USA)
Dr Brown discusses the destructive nature of shame – and how to be
free of it.

No More Dirty Looks by Siobhan O'Connor and Alexandra Spunt (Da
Capo/Lifelong Books)
A nifty guide to non-toxic beauty, including some great DIY cosmetics
recipes. The brands covered are mostly American but this book is still
a useful primer.

Relationships: From Addiction to Authenticity by Claudine Pletcher
and Sally Bartolameolli (Health Communications Inc)
An insightful book about exactly what the title suggests.

A Return to Love: Reflections on the Principles of a Course in Miracles by Marianne Williamson (Thorsons)
A wonderful book for regaining hope and allowing love into your life.

The Toxic Consumer: How to Reduce Your Exposure to Everyday Toxic Chemicals by Karen Ashton and Elizabeth Salter Green (Impact)
An accessible guide to the common toxic chemicals that we encounter in daily life – and how to reduce our exposure to them.

Toxic Beauty: How Hidden Chemicals in Cosmetics Harm You by Dawn Mellowship (Gaia Thinking/Octopus)
A clear and informative guide to what substances to avoid in cosmetics – and why.

Unexpected Recoveries: Seven Steps to Healing Body, Mind, and Soul when Serious Illness Strikes by Tom Monte (St Martins Griffin)
Tom Monte guides us through his 'seven steps to healing body, mind and soul when serious illness strikes'. He also addresses spiritual preparation for death. Includes some good macrobiotic recipes.

Your Life in Your Hands: Understand, Prevent and overcome Breast Cancer and Ovarian Cancer by Professor Jane Plant (Virgin Books)
Breast cancer survivor Professor Plant examines a great deal of research and comes up with various factors that, in her opinion, help to promote breast tumours. She then gives advice as to how to minimise or avoid these factors.

Discover more about Jessica and find out more about the book at:

www.facebook.com/theelegantartoffallingapart
www.twitter.com/itsjessyjones
www.chemochic.org

Gail Affleck Ward
Jessica Ainsworth
Wyndham Albery
José Ignacio Alcántara
Lucinda Alford
Dawn Allen
Simon Amos
Gilly Arbuckle
Sophie Arditti
Ben Arogundade
Penny Arrowood
Rhonaliza Atkin
Olivia Aubry

Jo Ayshford-Scott
Jonathan Ball
Adela and David Bamber-
   Johnson
Diane Banks
Helen Bates
Alexander Baxter
Penny Beale
Rachel Bell
Ross Bell
Luigi Belmonte
Andy Bentley
Peter Bizlou

Joshua Bowler

Edward Bowyer

Mairead Broadley

Louise Brooker

Neal Brown

Geoff Bullock

Nicola Burden

Oloff Burger

Imelda Burke

Serena Bute

Xander Cansell

Viv Carbines

Bernise Carolino

Andrew Carroll

Ben Cearns

Sharon Chan

Jane Chetcuti

Isobel Child

Sarah Churchwell

Jessica Civiero

Lisa Climie-Somers

Tim Cole

Catherine Colley

Michael Collins

JJ Connolly

Michele Connolly

Sally Curry

Jennifer Curtis

Sophie Dahl

Devika Dass

Linda Davies

Melody Davis

Hannah Deller

Jenny Demetri

Charlotte Devereux

Josh Dickson

Christine Donald

Jeanie Donovan

Peter Dowling

Lawrence T Doyle

Colin Edgar

Caroline Edmonds

Susanne Elbeshausen

Derek Erb

Helen Fawkes

Esther Fearnhill

Merrick Fenton

Charles Fernyhough

Ilana Fox

James Fox

Melissa Freedman

Bella Freud

Antony Genn

Zoë Gersbach-Smith

Paul Gills

Jonathan Glenister

Laura Goddard

Sophie Goldsworthy

Catherine Gosling Fuller

Voula Grand

Mike Graves

Helen Gregory

Jasmin Julia Gupta, Founder,
    Charity Cancer Hair Care

Anna Hall

Stacy Harrison

Matthew Hart

Caitlin Harvey

Kevin Healy
Christoph Henkel
Johannes Henkel
Katrin Henkel
Paul Henkel
Hydrox Holroyd
Nicola Horlick
Eve Howard
Cathy Hurren
Louise Jack
Lynda Jenking
Gail Jones
Jennifer Jones
Peter Jukes
Susanne Kahle
Christine Kenny
Janie Kidston
Dan Kieran
Max Kirsten
Katie Knight
Lynsay Kobelis
Lou Kramers
Isabelle Laurent
Alex Lee
Stevie Lee
Arabella Lindsay
Alison Lowe
Sophie Macdonald
Kayla McClendon
Rebecca McColl
Jill McComish
Aideen McConnell
Sam McEwen
Fiona McKnight

Charlotte Macmillan
Emma Marinos
Tolis Marinos
Clare Marsh
Beverley Marsland
Sarah Martin
Sacha Mavroleon
Coral Mazlin-Hill
Rev. Dave Meaker
Sue Mercer
Julianne Miller
Sophie Molins
Kate Monro
Juliet Morcas
Bob Morgen
Rebecca Muddeman
Mandy Murnane
Carmel Murphy
Murugeson
Michelle Myers
Jennifer Nadel
Julia Noakes
Laura Norton
Annie O'Connor
Sally O'Sullivan
Andrew Palmer
Louise Parker
Zara Parness
Josie Pearse
Nicolas Pejacsevich
Christina Pierce
Helen Pilkington
Vince Pitt
Justin Pollard

Lindsey Pond-Jones
Jonathan Prime
Anita Prosser
Brady Rafuse
Mariano Raigón
Mark Richards
Stuart Robertson
Kristyan Robinson
Barbara Roddam
Brer Ruthven
Sarah Sarhandi
David Scally
Hazel Scott
Rebecca Seeley Harris
Frances Shelley
Georgina Shipsey
Monique Simon
Claire Slade
Abi Smith
Antony Phillip Smith
Jennifer Nina Smith
Sarah Stanton
Sophie de Stempel
Edmund Sumbar
Mark Sutton

Annie Swain
Katie Terry
Maya Thirkell
Tokkelossi
Matthew Tomich
Helen Treverton
Laura Tryphonopoulos
Jane Turner
Karen Twible
Georganne Uxbridge
Nick Verden
Clive Walker
Kim Wallace-Croasdell
Diana Waters
Chris Webber
Adam White
Tracey White
Rachel Willmer
Theo Wilson
Dudley Winterbottom
Anne Wolff
Steve Woodward
Rachel Wright
Anni Zambiasi

The body text of the book is set in Minion, a typeface designed in 1990 by Robert Slimbach and inspired by the classical elegance of the old-style fonts of the Renaissance. It is extremely clean, elegant and legible and has a much greater range of characters (known as 'glyphs') than most serifed typefaces, making it extremely flexible. If any greater endorsement were needed, it was also used as the body text font for Robert Bringhurst's *The Elements of Typographic Style* (1992), widely referred to as the 'typographer's bible'.

The displayed text is set in Futura, a typeface designed by German typographer Paul Renner in 1927 and inspired by the clean, functional Modernist Bauhaus design aesthetic. When the Nazis swept to power in 1933, Renner and his friend and fellow typographer Jan Tschichold were denounced as 'cultural Bolsheviks' and forced into exile. Nevertheless, Futura was commercially released in 1936 and has remained popular ever since. It is a 'geometric' sans serif typeface, basing its letterforms on near-perfect circles, triangles and squares. This gives the font a modern feel, which makes it perfect for headlines and signage, but less useful for body text.

The ornaments marking section breaks belong to the Golden Cockerel typeface, designed by the great Eric Gill in 1929.